The White Letter

The Continuum, The

Table of Contents

§1. Footnotes to Plato's Philebus

It is our considered opinion that any theology, including one that only wants to discuss the nature of a sacred text, must begin with the absolute, that is, God. If we want to understand what makes a text scared and how a sacred text is composed, then one needs to find a key for opening up the relation between the text and the absolute whether that means the text is inspired by the absolute, is composed of it, refers to it, or is otherwise in relation to it. The absolute is known from a Pythagorean or Kabalistic perspectives as the *apeiron* and *eyn sof* respectively. The absolute is from this point of view boundless and unlimited and only takes form or creates a world through limitation and binding. The absolute could of course not avoid having these traits. This teaching reveals to us that limited instances of the formless cannot occur without accepting the reality of the void itself. The real entity of the world, numbers, are composed of and distinguished by the void. The entirety of creation is thus a field of limited and unlimited, absolute and finite, void and non-void.

The Pythagoreans of course added the idea that the limitations of the absolute occur in a harmonious way such that world itself expresses itself musically. The very cosmos and every single thing within it is a composition of the unlimited with the limited. Anything that exists somehow entails a relation between the boundless and the bounded,--a binding of the unbounded. At the same time, this limitation is necessarily bound up with the real continuum of numbers. All things are, as is well known, for Pythagoreans, built up from numbers. From the Jewish tradition we learn further that the Absolute itself appeared at Sinai and left behind a text containing a large, but finite number of letters. Given what has already been said, that should not be overwhelmingly surprising since letters are fundamentally related to numbers. It is then only by examining that set of letters in relation to the absolute that we will be also to see how the sacred text itself works and is constituted.

We should also not be surprised that this revelation takes place via a voice, via sound, for it is the musical continuum, the unlimited scale of sound itself, which makes up the absolute. Individuated sounds always take for granted the boundless sound spectrum out of which they emerge. A musical score is of course text, but for it to make music one cannot choose sounds randomly. Rather, the sounds themselves must be differentially related. Even if the continuum offers one an unlimited number of choices, for the music to be audible it must exude order and thus have a scale and proportionality. The Pythagoreans of course busied themselves endlessly trying to find the perfect pitches and ratios. They wanted to know the right proportions between sounds for the maximum effect. But for the Kabbalist, the voice of God, the absolute, does not lead to music, but rather to a text composed of letters. However, the text itself insofar as it is composed of letters is involved with the same issues—a selection and determination of the absolute from which it arises, a relation to the pure continuum of phonemes and possible wordings, etc.

Finally, the Pythagorean and Kabalistic view coincide insofar as both see the absolute has contacted into a single name. For the Pythagoreans, the divine, the absolute, is contacted into the primordial unit that stands alone—the monad. For them, the monad is both somehow the entirety of all possible entities and also the first of such entities. The monad is the origin. It is indivisible. In this way, the absolute as pure continuum contacts into an indivisible point that is also the source for all. The Kabbalists on the other hand said that the absolute itself withdraws into a single point that is both nothing and a name. In this way, the universe is necessarily a text. It is our contention that there is also a discourse, a mathematical one not surprisingly, that today attempts to give yet another formulation of these Kabbalistic and Pythagorean ideas. That discourse is of course Cantorian set theory.

As both Kai Hauser and Christopher Menzel emphasize, Georg Cantor himself at at least one point consciously related in a footnote in his *Grundlagen* his own set theory with Plato's *Philebus* (which is of course the dialogue in which Plato directly connects his own theory to Pythagoreanism):

An important clue for understanding Cantor aright has been hitherto overlooked. In a significant footnote to the *Grundlagen* Cantor defines a set (*Menge*) as 'any plurality that can be thought of as a unity (*jedes Viele, welches sich als Eines denken lasst*).' He then adds the following: 'I believe that what I've defined here is related to the Platonic *eidos* or idea, as well as to what Plato calls *mikton* in his dialogue Philebus. He contrasts this with the *apeiron*, i.e., the unlimited (*Unbegrenzten*), the indeterminate (*Unbestimmten*), which I call the nongenuine infinite, and also with the *peras*, i.e., the limit, and explains it as an ordered "mixture" of the two."1

What Menzel highlights here is that Cantor's notion of the set is in some sense a restatement of the Platonic idea. At the same time, a set is a limited determination of the unlimited. A set even if transfinite is thus a limitation of the true infinite, the apeiron, while at the same time somehow being related to it by mixing together the limited and the unlimited. Kai Hauser working with the same note in Cantor's text emphasizes that like the Platonic eidos any set is a "one over many" and an "autonomous entity" "distinct from the multiplicity of its elements".2 In other words, any set is a unity that can be distinguished from what it contains. It collects together many under one rubric. Sets are thus "particulars rather than universals" for Cantor— particular things in themselves.3 One indication of this is that each set can however be a member of another set.4 Of course, Platonic ideas are also in some sense individual beings. But each is also a specific determination of the unlimited, the unconditioned, per the *Philebus*. In determining the unlimited apeiron is not simply excluded, but rather mixes with the limited.

What is interesting is that Plato argues in his *Philebus* that various qualities are themselves "indefinite" and "indeterminate" such as the "hotter" since there is always hotter experience to be had.5 Our experience of heat admits of degrees, but for Plato there is only a pure endless spectrum of possible experiences and intensities. The experience can increase or decrease anywhere along that scale. For this reason, Plato classifies such qualities as aperia, the unlimited. There is no greatest sound or temperature for Plato. Also, "no specific thing is picked out" when one experiences heat.6 There is no determinate object of heat. By contrast, Plato here calls "perata" things that can be experienced only in a specific way and do not have a range of values and degrees, but are rather specific proportions and measures such as ratios.7 As Menzel notes here, Plato has in mind here that which can be expressed as rational numbers. Such qualities are either equal (one thing proportional to another) or unequal, can be increased in multiples. In this way, there is a determinacy here by way of a ratio and relationship. Rational numbers are not like the irrationals associated with intensive experiences.

Plato finally discusses a third class, the "meikta" which involve a mixture of the two earlier classes.8 While "pitch" can be "characterized by a continuum of tones" such as the spectrum of human hearing, in the musical scale we use there are twelve specific tones in any octave which are ratios and proportions of notes.9 If one determines one note on the spectrum, then the other eleven are determined by relation and proportion. Any arbitrary point one would pick on the continuum of sound then leads to a specification of the other tones in the musical scale. The music we hear is thus a twelve-tone scale wherein the pure spectrum of hearing is related to specific tones. It is the musical scale itself which is meikta, well-ordered and balanced, that can result in the composition of a piece of music wherein those twelve tones are combined and ordered. For example, given that one can have a specific tempo "one beat per ½ second" it is then possible to "assign to each of a succession of notes a length of time that determines how long it is to be played or sung before moving to it successor".10 One can then in addition relate the particular particulars intervals to each other and thus have a song composed of pitch and tempo. The art of music thus expresses for Plato the relation between the limited and the unlimited.

It can also be noted at this point given the manner in which the Philebus introduces many of our themes that it is "divine reason" reason itself which ultimately knows how to mix and compose all that is in the cosmos as finite determinations of the unlimited in a harmonious and positive way (*Philebus* 26e-27c, 28a-30e). It is for Plato up to us to find in all things how they consist of "one and many" and express in their nature the limited, the unlimited, and the relations between the two (*Philebus* 16d-e). It is assumed that anything can be described in these terms. Our search here would be the inverse of the actual creation of these limited unities by the absolute. Rather than beginning with the absolute itself, we begin with unities, with bounded determinations, and from them attempt to proceed to understand their relationship to the absolute. However, one cannot go from a unity immediately to the absolute itself, but must move through the "intermediaries" first (*Philebus* 17a).

We can also mention at this point although mostly in anticipation of what will be articulated later that Plato already sees that the absolute expresses itself in this world not simply musically in the form of notes, tones, and tempo, but also textually as letters: "What I mean is clear in the code of letters, and you should take your clue form them, since they were part of your own education" (*Philebus* 17b). Letters, which primarily mean individual phonemic sounds for Plato, appear as individual spoken sounds, but are "also unlimited in number" (*Philebus* 17b). That is, each of us can hear an individual sound like 'b' or 'p' which are themselves individual determinations of the sound continuum, but at the same time, the number of possible letters and sounds is endless. We do not really know how many kinds and type of "vocal sounds there are and what their nature is" (*Philebus* 17b), but just as with music we should learn how to compose them and combine them in the proper proportions and order. At the same time, even in understanding such a composition, one is always aware of the absolute itself and in its boundless nature such that the one is related directly to the undetermined (*Philebus* 17e).

Here, Socrates in the dialogue says that only via divine inspiration could one have discovered that sound has this unlimited quality: "When someone, whether god or godlike man,—there is an Egyptian story that his name was Thoth—observed that sound was infinite, he was the first to notice that the vowel sounds in that infinity were not one, but many, and again that there were other elements which were not vowels but did have a sonic quality" (*Philebus* 18b-c). The divine is necessary to experience the infinite nature of sound whether by way of an actual god or simply a man with godlike abilities. The divinely inspired then can discern in the sound continuum individual sounds and many of them. The infinity of sound is not an oneness of random noise, but is itself differentiated into multiple elements of sound. Beyond vowels, the one confronting the sound continuum discovers other letters referring to the consonant and to purely mute letters (*Philebus* 18c). However, in any language there are a determinant number of vowels, consonants, and mutes despite the continuum out of which they emerge.

The godlike man selects the letters out of the continuum and distinguishes each :

> Then he divided the mutes until he distinguished each individual
> one, and he treated the vowels and semivowels in the same way,
> until he knew the number of them and gave to each and all the
> name of letters. Perceiving, however, that none of us could learn
> any one of them alone by itself without learning them all, and
> considering that this was a common bond which made them in a
> way all one (*Philebus* 18c).

Plato's argument here is in part structuralist. All the letters must come at once or not at all. This is in part due to all the letters being linked together. One does not simply select a single vowel, but all the vowels and consonants at once. They form a specific set, the alphabet. For Plato, the science that handles letters is called "grammar" (*Philebus* 18d). It is thus grammar that takes up the set of letters extracted from the continuum.

Even though Plato has here determined many of our future key points, it should not therefore be taken for granted that the Platonic determination of the issue matches our own view. For example, for Plato, the unlimited is often thought of as something purely negative and to be avoided. After all, his *Philebus* is ultimately a moral discourse on how to avoid extremes and to find the right proportion and measure in one one's life. To have a good life is to live always in moderation. There is no unlimited Good in Plato that relates to all. Even the Good of the cave allegory is but the most exemplary unity beyond other unties. Plato as a Greek pagan did not see in the absolute infinite a creator God, but rather the mere indefinite nature of things that occurs when one realizes the unlimited and unrestrained nature of things hiding beneath the ordered. Plato lived in a defined and finite cosmos and not one wherein the actual finite could characterize things directly. Plato saw then in the determination of the infinite an improvement on the unlimited. The absolute in and of itself requires definition to be worthy of praise.

After all, it was the discovery of irrational reals that caused the Pythagoreans a scandal rather than joy at exposing a number closer to the divine. The apeiron is mostly the absence of a limit rather than any sort of perfection or ultimate. It is a question of privation rather than true and holy being itself. It is a disordered chaos out of which the world appears and which the world rejects rather than the very most important property of the divine itself. It is very precisely un-limited rather than the absolute itself.

§2. The Non-All

We have thus attempted to project onto Plato our monotheistic ideas in order to make his *Philebus* signal the topics at hand. Although, for Plato, a divine dialectic is involved in determining the relation between the limited and unlimited, Plato would not see this divine reason as itself some infinite mind as mind in order to be intelligent and expressive of good understanding must be limited. There is no absolute mind that is in and if itself apeiron. Plato in other words had no idea of the monotheistic god who is an infinite actuality. Plato ultimately wants a law that t will show how all things are measured and how to measure them within precisely defined boundaries and by way of easily measured ratios.

Of course, Cantor himself defined the actual infinite arithmetically and thereby seemingly removed it from the divine abode itself. In that way, Cantor would seem to be a post-monotheistic thinker. However, this view is far from the truth. For Cantor, while there are actual transfinite sets, there is only one absolute finite, and this absolute infinite precisely transcends the order of transfinite sets which could only ever be finite determinations of the unlimited. Because the absolute infinite, the divine, is immeasurable, even a transfinite set (like the set of all integers for instance) despite being actually infinite is only a mixture of a limit and the unlimited (hence, the necessary reference to Plato's *Philebus*). All numbers are less than the absolute infinite for Cantor including the transfinite. The transfinite introduces a new order of numbers beyond the finite, but less than the absolute infinite. For this reason, they can be seen still, as can whole numbers, as some sort of determination of the unlimited and absolute. The absolute is not a number and transcends any possible mathematical definition for Cantor. The transfinite is precisely something that can be defined mathematically and one transfinite set can be differentiated from another whereas the absolute infinite is unique in and of itself. All the possible transfinite sets from smallest to largest can stretch on indefinitely without ever reaching the absolute itself. One could not build up the absolute infinite from any series of transfinites. Rather one has the endless, the eternal, on one side, and on the other the division between the finite and the transfinite. One thus has on one side a lack of totality and the other a series of infinite computations.

But the gap between the finite and transfinite does not resemble that between all and the eternal. The latter necessarily transcends the order of the transfinite finally. At the same time, the absolute infinite cannot be a set because it cannot be a unity, a one over many. If it were, it would be de-finite. It has no number and no limit. It is thus beyond our ability to know and comprehend it. Transfinite sets can be known and defined. The set of all integers is an actual infinite that can be properly comprehended. Menzel writes:

> The unordered set is like a jumble of notes waiting to be ordered into a melody. By ordering an infinite set we bring number, peras, to an apeiron, as a musician brings number and order to mere notes. The result is a mikton, a determinate mixture of peras and apeiron, number and the indeterminate infinite.11

If ordered sets are like musical rhythms, then the absolute infinite would be pure noise. It would be the entire sound continuum sounded at once insofar as that would be possible since it would never begin or end sounding given the absolute's lack of unity. It would not be a chaos of sounds, but perhaps a pure silence out of which any sound could arise. The absolute is thus "capable of infinite variation" since it lacks unity and "boundary".12 Cantor calls the absolute often Ω and with this letter attempts to name an inconsistent and absolute infinite multiplicity. It is inconsistent insofar as there is no first and last term to be determined. Cantor believed that any set, including any transfinite set, ultimately could be well-ordered (this is of course part of the famous issue of the Continuum Hypothesis to which we shall return) by at the very least a recursive process in which one determines through a series of choices (even if infinite) an ordinal series of first, second, third, etc. terms. One can with any set determine an ordinal series then by way of a choice function. But with Ω this is not possible as it is not a set to begin with.

An infinity like the set of integers clearly has a first term. But for the absolute infinite one could never find and never determine a first number of the sequence. It is not totality, but rather what Lacan calls the non-all (*pas tout*). The absolute is therefore not a whole, all, or totality. It is a non-all. And the non-all cannot be conceived as a unity or totality without contradiction where as an infinite like the infinity of integers can. The divine itself thoroughly transcends the logic of the finite and suprafinite. Following Alain Badiou, we can say that with the absolute 'the one is not.' Plato of course helped us also understand such an idea, but this time we need to turn to his *Parmenides* rather than to his *Philebus* (it will all be footnotes to Plato in any case) where the implications of the lack of the one (the one is not) are outlined:

> "Let us do so." "Well, the others will not be one?" "Of course not."
> "Nor will they be many for if they were many, one would be
> contained in them. And if none of them is one, they are all nothing,
> so that they cannot be many." "True." "If one is not contained in
> the others, the others are neither many nor one" (*Parmenides*
> 165e).

In the non-all, there is no one and other. There is no possibility of such distinction. There is thus no distinction between one and many. There are no unities and no elements. A multiplicity of things implies that we can distinguish a series of ones in such a multiple. But if there not any single thing, there is no-thing. In this way, and we will need to return to this more than once, the absolute infinite is from our perspective nothing. Because there cannot be any distinction between the one and the many, the non-all is not inconsistent insofar as it is disordered and lacking in order. It has no structure and order, but also lacks randomness. One could very easily have an infinite set that is disordered, but that would not make it inconsistent in the sense of the non-all.

The non-all, the divine, is importantly not increasable where as the transfinite can be increased indefinitely. There is thus implied in the name Ω the name of the greatest possible. There is no way of here avoiding seeing Ω as the absolute maximum from a mathematical perspective as it marks a limit for number itself. It is that which cannot be added to and if subtracted from never diminished. It is not the greatest in the sense of a specific number greater than all others, but shows us that the greatest is nothing as anything that names it, names it as absolute infinite and non-all beyond all. One should not attempt to find the right number for God. He is not the greatest number conceivable. He is the inconceivable beyond number as such. The lack of a number for God does not mean God does not exist, but that there is something that insists divinely beyond number and also haunts all and any number. This is why anxiety is the atheist affect per excellence. They mistake God's absence for his non-being. They do not see the void as a veil obscuring the absolute itself. They are thus left with only the void without relating to the divine itself. They do not know how to connect a pure name with its reference.

It is important here to note that the non-all is not a pantheist notion. It is commonly said that if God is infinite, then everything should be in him. But here we see there can be no everything strictly speaking since everything implies a totality in which all has been counted. The non-all however transcends every thing. It is thereby indistinguishable from the nothing for us. The absolute will not be distinguishable from the nothing for us, but that will not imply atheism. The apeiron and the void will be two names for the same thing. The unnamable and ineffable absolute transcends names as it inconsists. The divine absolute is "unruly, unfinished, indeterminate; in short, apeiron".13 Of course, for us to experience anything there has to be limits. There has to be a boundary for us to say what is just as for there to be a set some line has to be drawn around a collection. One has to put things into a limit. This is why the divine cannot be an object of experience in any directly known sense. It is indiscernible pure and simple. It is neither this nor that.

There is only one unlimited, the absolute, just as there is only one void (one would not be able to distinguish between two). But whereas Badiou for instance clearly admits the unicity of the void, it is not clear he is willing to admit the unicity of the divine non-all. The divine cannot be defined without implying a contradiction and without paradox. The divine is never one complete object and thus never a set. We can thus identify the divine absolute, God, with what Badiou calls following Cantor (although deliberately erasing Cantor's references to the absolute as God) the inconsistent and agree with Badiou that the "phantom" of the non-all "haunts" any possible "situation".14 But if the non-all implies a lack of limits, then we will need to explain how limits can exist within it or with respect to it even if we speak of finite determinations since given its nature it is clear that any such definition would be impossible. It is of course set theory that allows us to do so in part, but also divine creation involves itself in precisely that, the creation of the finite. However, that does not mean that this lack of limitation will not "haunt" (to use again Badiou's term) and shadow any finite creation.

With reference to the non-all, great can become small and the small great (BE 35). In this way, the absolute infinite is not simply without ordinality, but also any clear cardinality. Within the non-all, all things are in touch with the unbounded and limitless. This is of course a situation beyond any human reckoning or imagining. If someone like Quentin Meillassoux wishes to name the non-all 'hyper-chaos', then he is entitled to do so. But that can only mean that he has named the creation of the finite and for how this non-all issues finite and defined entities. Anything can arise out of it. There is no limit to divine power. But that does not mean there is anything chaotic about what it creates. It also does not imply that what is created is contingent beyond the sense of its being capable of having been otherwise. Not everything is contingent as there is no 'everything' here. At the same time, the divine one will have been involved in all relations at all times since all such relations involve determinations of the unlimited itself even if those completed beings will be nothing in comparison to the absolute infinite. The divine is here the real, being beyond any thought or conception or existent entity. And as such the divine ensures that there is no set of all sets. The absolute is perfectly impossible (since only sets are possible here in this world) and open in its being non-all. Precisely because the absolute is not a set, it knows no limits, but also it can transcend any thing it creates since it does not diminish it. The absolute infinite even if one were to subtract something from it by its being is not decreased and thus as beyond number is no way diminished. This is already true of the transfinite (set of infinite integers can lack all the even numbers and still be infinite) and thus one can only wonder at the absolute nature of God separate from the world. The absolute need thus does not fail to include all insofar as it is non-all (nothing could be said to be excluded from it) despite us appearing separated from it.

Badiou of course believe that "God does not exist" since there is no "set of all ordinals" (*BE* 277), but such a view makes the classic mistake of atheism. It confuses God's nothingness, not being anything, with God's lack of being. It believes that because the question of the greatest cannot be answered with a set or number that therefore there is no name for this unavoidable question. It confuses God's transcendence with a total lack of God. It does not see that the void is only a veil separating us from God. God is the incomprehensible context for all thought and existence. Badiou speak as if the inconsistent to which he must make reference to necessarily is purely immanent, but it is necessarily and radically transcendent since it cannot be manifested or part of the material world as such. Badiou can never escape the very theological determination of the thought he borrows from Cantor. Also to say it is immanent implies it is somehow within the boundaries of the world, but it is precisely the name of that which explodes and transcends any such boundaries. Badiou partly admits this when he writes

> Cantor essentially a theologian… ties the absoluteness of being not
> to the (consistent) presentation of the multiple, but to the
> transcendence through which a divine infinity in-consists, as one,
> gathering tougher and numbering any multiple whatsoever (*BE* 4).

At the same time, the non-all is such that one could never find anything missing from it. It therefore is complete. Hence, its inconsistency is implied by its completeness. Anything that can be expressed can be expressed by language for instance even though it is not a totality. When we have a totality, we have an intensional set such that all x's are y. But then, as Lacan taught us, one has a necessary exception that interrupts totality from another end. The impossibility of God in this world implies that God is unavoidable rather than voided in any and all senses. God insists in the most eminent sense as the non-all. The unthinkable itself insists on being thought and having each thought related to it. Thus all names speak of it to some degree. All sets are determinations of the unlimited. All names are thus divine names since all names are related to it, but only some names refer directly tot it such as the ineffable or the inaccessible.

Of course, Parmenides rejected this view in many ways. For him, being is only ever limited and one. It is not open like a continuum. It is purely one without any such thing as quantity or quality. Parmenidean being is thus completely sterile and incapable of giving rise to anything. It is an all that is not a many. Lacan, the inventor of the very term non-all that Badiou essentially expropriates and elaborates on, explains this idea interestingly in his twenty-third seminar thusly:

> We rediscover there, in short, something for which I put forward that concerning what I called by the name of the woman: she is not-all (pas-toute). She is not-all, means that women constitute only one set. In effect, with time, we have come to dissociate the idea of the all from the idea of a set. I mean that we have arrived at the thought of the fact that a certain number of objects can be supported by small letters. And then the idea of the All is dissociated, namely, that the circle that is supposed in a quite fragile representation to gather them together, the circle is outside the objects a, b, c, etc.15

Lacan here notes that the notion of the non-all is not a set, and yet it cannot avoid a reference to completion. This completion is itself expressible by "small letters". We will need to return to these letters later.

Of course, many others attempt to deny the divine from another perspective. They will claim that all that exists are unities. But once they claim there is an infinite regress (and if one posits that there is no ultimate object that the others can be reduced to or some transcendent object out of which all things ends or emanate out of, then one has necessarily posited an infinite regress and open situation) of such unties or no largest object they have necessarily presupposed the non-all. Why? Well, if one posits unities, one posits things that are limited and defined. One thus argues there is a non-all of limited things. But to say there is an infinite regress or no largest unity (no all-encompassing unity), is to precisely posit the unlimited itself. Limited things would never possibly fill the unlimited and never possibly constitute it. If there is no totality, then there is necessarily something unlimited. The limited cannot take priority over the unlimited if one says there is no greatest object encompassing all others or allows for infinite regresses. And that unlimited cannot be by definition of the order of the intuited unities or things. It is not an object. It cannot be any one thing. And thus the non-all insists even when one says all is objects. If not, then all one have is an Aristotelian ontology in the most classical of senses (one posits a set of all sets, a totality). But one can always show that such a set of all sets excludes something larger than it. That a set of all sets is thoroughly paradoxical of course will not bother those who speak of the divine in the way we have. But when we approach the divine we approach that which is greater than any possible thing, a set of all sets if conceived as closed cannot match that and it does not (it becomes one and the same as what we have attempted to speak of here). Thus, one is sent back to the absolute, the non-all.

Of course, such theorist of objects worry that if we posit the non-all, pure multiplicity, then it is only ever some sort of amorphous lump divided up by the human mind. But the non-all itself can only ever be related to the divine itself. It is not the human mind that carves it up except in a secondary manner. Divine creation itself already makes sure the real consist in its own right of counts and the counted. The indeterminate itself ensures in terms of its collapse into a name that the world has order and measure.

§3. Ω= Ø

Let us now turn to this idea of divine contraction and articulate it in some more detail. It is clear that the absolute in itself is pure indifference. It lacks a name and anything that would differentiate it from something else given its pure unicity. For this reason, it is not completely wrong to mistake it for the void. But it is precisely by way of its contraction into itself and its speculative identification with nothing that the absolute creates the world by issuing a pure proper name. The divine creation is thus the very act by which a name emerges out of the non-all as a pure condensation of it. Consistency emerges out of the inconsistent absolute; the finite emerges from the infinite. This name is also a veil behind which the absolute infinite withdraws and hides itself forever. We are with the left with the name. Set theory of course calls this name the mark of the empty set, ∅. We are thus left with the pure formula Ω= ∅.

If we were to write this using a Lacanian matheme, we would write S(A̸) => Φ. This reads the barred Other is the phallus. The non-all is itself not a set of course as it is absolute and not a thing. But that means it is something we can only approach via a name, the most proper one. It collapses itself into a limited thing and that thing is the name itself, the mark of the empty set. This mark is the very ur-element (and the only one) for all of set theory itself. While other versions of set theory can posit an infinity of objects as ur-elements potentially, Zermelo-Fraenkel set theory has only one ur-element. Out of it is built all else. It is via this one element that the absolute allows for the creation of individual things. But it should be clear that this ur-element is not a set. It is a pure name. It is a series of letters which is why what exists is the function of the computation and permutation of the letters themselves by the absolute. We call this series of letters the Name of God. What this mark means is that there is always amongst those things that exist, an ultimate point. The non-all and pure inconsistency comes to an end in the mark itself. It is the primitive atomic point that in its iteration allows for all else. All else will be composed of it. It is one particular thing when before there was the non-all.

This is why the Kabbala teaches that *eyn sof* is itself *ayin* and that *eyn sof* withdraws into itself creating emptiness. This mark forms the center, but it is not located anywhere. It is everywhere distributed and only by seeing all as a conjugation of letters can one see that the center is itself displaced in this way. We could thus say with the Pythagoreans that apeiron is itself the monad. This is why from apeiron we proceed to numbers. It is important to note that this Name of God is a mark of pure exception. It is not yet a signifier, but a transcendental lettering. Of course, this lettering is finite; it is a series of letters. Set theory only chooses one letter, ∅, but that is because it is only interested in sets. But if we are interested in understanding what exists, then we need at least two (01) or four letters (YHVH) to allow for things also to permute into their form.

Lacan himself already hinted at the formula we are laying out here in his famous 'graph sof sexuation' where the side of the non-all (the feminine) is equivalent (A to not not-A) to the side of the exception, the masculine. Of course, this equivalence does not mean complete identification as from an intuitionist perspective we can differentiate the two as distinct, as marking a difference (for Lacan, it was the difference between the masculine and feminine). The non-all is itself exceptional. We also see here that the price of consistency is that it is ultimately only ever grounded on the absolute infinite which is itself indiscernible logically from the void (but discernible via intuition in the same way as A and not not-A are) The absolute is prior to any number and not itself a number, and thus number itself (and by implication all of mathematics) is founded on this basis and thus consistent only by way of this act of creation. The divine contraction is the way in which the true infinite condenses itself into finitude itself. And there are an infinitude of such finite instantiations (hence the split between the transfinite and the finite). It is at this point that the true infinite institutes logic itself. This is where we see the infinite made finite. And the transfinite will itself further this logic and elaborate on it insofar as the transfinite is the infinite made infinite via a series of names and instances. The transfinite will thus be further names of God, but never the name itself—only ever permutations of it. The transfinite is itself limited by nature, a set and thus bound to its name in a way the absolute infinite is not. The absolute infinite can be distinguished from its name as an ontological reference. There is an excess that precedes the name and also is signaled by it. The excess of the divine withdraws into the name, but remains an excess always there hiding and awaiting its chance to proclaim itself again.

We see here also why the absolute being identified with the void signals a problem for Meillassoux. For Meillassoux the non-all as hyper-chaos must exclude the void itself. But we see here that the hyper-chaos is already in its own metaphysical nature the void and logically indiscernible from it. We are thus always dealing with the name of the void and thus always with the consistent mark of the absolute. Anything could form that name, but it necessarily collapses into one specific name. And once it is a name it can word itself on the basis of its pure lettering. Both Badiou who wants only to see the absolute infinite as void and Meillassoux as pure inconsistency (hyper-chaos) attempt to think the implication of Cantor's absolute, but neither see that at stake here is the divine itself and the dive named as God. It is important for the logical indiscernibility here to collapse into a name because via names we can know that A is not not-A. The name itself introduces this order of difference and identity. It is on its basis that we can intuit as different what is at the same time equivalent.

We should also be clear that what we are expressing here is not simply a rehearsal of the opening moments of Hegel's logic. Hegel there noted the speculative identity of pure being and nothingness. But Hegel saw this collapse into a dialectic that only ever fractally repeats itself because he did not see this collapse of being into nothing resulting in a pure name and series of letters composing all that is in its becoming. This is the very difference between us and Hegel. It is one can say the difference between Christianity and Judaism, between a theology of the word and that of the letter. Hegel did not see, as far as I can tell, that the speculative and mystical identity of the absolute infinite and the void issues in a name, a self-indicating one, that is in its purity also a series of letters. The letters themselves do not require a triadic structuring in the same way as the word, the signified, does because the letter itself is indifferent to sense and prior to it. The dialect is itself built on sense (the coincidence of opposites), but this latter signified is itself only made possible by the letter in the same way the morpheme depends on the phoneme. As the Zohar teaches, "When the most mysterious wished to reveal himself, He first produced a single point that was transmuted into a thought, and in this He executed innumerable designs, and engraved innumerable engravings".16 In other words, what is issued here is also thought itself. It is at the same time sets and letters, ideas and computed existence. The only design produced in its magnificence is both a matter of thought and existence and the difference between the two.

§4. Being-Essence-Existence: The ontological, the eidetic, and the existential

Because it is a matter of not just sets but also letters we avoid the problem of the possible being the actual. God does not create necessarily and the pure indifference of the letters shows that. It is not a matter of making all that can be all that can be thought. In addition, to what can be thought there is existence itself. Because all that exists is an elaboration of the name itself in its lettering all that is possible is not actual. But because the name itself is a pure name and mark we have access to all the possible thoughts and essences that can be conceived—sets and letters. We thus have with the empty set all the numbers and names, but also with letters a conjugation and elaboration that takes on a particular holy design. It is a design that is both contingent and particular. Our world is but one design. It is made up sets, letters, and numbers.

For this reason, we need to distinguish metaphysically between three categories at work here: being, essence, and existence. God, the absolute infinite, is pure esse in itself as Aquinas noted. God is pure being itself. This is why, as we shall see, there are ontological proofs for that which thing there can be nothing greater than. On the other hand, sets are essences. They are similar to what Plato called eidos. Badiou claims that set theory articulates being qua being. But here he can only mean (and if we examine the specifics of his discourse he does only mean) being qua eidos/essence. That is, Badiou is interested in what can be thought. It would thus be perhaps more accurate to say he lays out the thinkable qua the thinkable, and this is the task of mathematics in its guise as set theory. It lays out any possible thought, but does not indicate what in fact exists. Badiou writes that he does not believe that "being is mathematical, which is to say composed of mathematical objectivities" (BE 8). In other words, Being is not a Pythagorean for him. He is only interested in stating what can be expressed about being itself. His is a theory of discourse. He is therefore less a ontological realist than many might claim (at least in *Being and Event*).

Set theory is ontology for Badiou, but Badiou does not articulate a specific cosmology. That is, he does not have any way of doing metaphysics. Part of the problem here is precisely because Badiou puts all in his efforts into not accepting the Cantor's absolute as the divine. For Badiou, it is only a necessary reference that set theory makes. Ontology is thus for Badiou about what can possibly be thought and determined by thinking. It is about where thinking itself finds its limits. But these limits are always internal to thought itself. It is about discourse. It may indicate that thinking always is exceeded by the pure multiple, by pure inconsistency, but it does not speak to existence as such. It takes situations as given and only wants to articulate the transcendental categories and framework that would apply to any possible situation. It is thus a transcendentalist discourse through and through reflecting and mirroring the real with the possible (this was already Deleuze and Guattari's criticism in *What is Philosophy?*). It does not, as Deleuze would say, tell us what the conditions for real experience are (for us, the conditions of real existence). It cannot say what things are made of, but only what thought can say about them.

This is why Badiou is more truly Platonist rather than Pythagorean in his approach than we are and, to my knowledge, never engages in any direct way with Plato's *Philebus*, but focuses mostly on dialogues such as Plato's *Parmenides*. How the world itself is actually composed is not of interest as Badiou thinks the task of ontology is only to outline what can be said of the world. This is why he speaks of "presentation" and how thing are presented and represented. The basic structure of this presentation is about being as meaning. His question is: What makes whatever is intelligible rather than how what exists exists as such?

For us on the other hand the very nature of the absolute involves creation and that means existence as such. What exists is a computation of the divine name. In this way, existence is not some situation that merely presents multiples, but is found at the very heart of absolute itself. Badiou thus founds his theory on the abstract as opposed to the concrete since there is no way for him to think the concretely directly in its concrete existence. For Badiou, it is about discerning the logic of the Platonic realm, which is itself separable and distinct from existence. It is separable insofar as it exists in discourse and, as discourse, in thought. This is not to say that physical objects are not comprehended by mathematics, but one can only make good on that claim if one treats them computationally. This is why Badiou has no theory of letters and their permutations. He is only interested in the set, the eidos, as the mode of thought itself. Whatever exists does involve sets, but that is only part of the story. And looking at them as sets will not tell us what exactly is contained in those sets and why. Only by treating existence as the computation of the divine name and as a computer can we do so.

Such a computation means that actual Pythagoreanism must be advocated. Numbers do compose the matter of things. It also shows us why things can be understood thoroughly as bits. God, the absolute, is of course incomprehensible. As Joseph Albo expressed it, 'If I knew Him, I would be Him.' But God's radical transcendence prevents this. Pythagoreanism is a realist ontology. It states that anything short of God, anything that exists, can be known. There is nothing so transcendent about a tomato or tennis shoe or literary character such that these things cannot be computed. That means these things are eminently knowable. The issue of the incomputable itself will lead us as we will see to the issue of the continuum and back to the absolute as such. It will not involve us with anything in the finite world and not even parts of the transfinite dimension.

Badiou's theory is ultimately not a realist ontology because he is interested in the formalized figuration of set theory and only seeing sets as made up of sets rather than ever being composed of letters, functions, etc. Thus, Badiou is only interested in the empty set as a pure proper name and not as a series of letters. Part of the reason for this is that his notion of the non-all is sterile. Since it is not God, it has no ability to create and produce. This is why in Badiou it is a total mystery how and why pure inconsistency, the non-all, is apparently for us counted up in the way it is. What counts it? If the one is not, how did these ones get counted as they are? We do not see every possibility actualized. It is not enough to simply state that being and thought are not identical. There is for Badiou something beyond names such as the unnamable. In this way, Badiou would meet us to this point. But one of the implications of the non-identity of being and thought, the radical excess of the absolute, as we have suggested, is that existence is also not identical with being or thought. Thought touches on what transcends itself, but it is blind as to what actually exists until it accepts the computational nature of existence itself.

Badiou only would see pure being contract into a set and a name, but a name is not simply a set and the full nature of the name is never unraveled by Badiou. The sterility of his atheism leaves it a mystery. But this is because Badiou does not take seriously the manner in which the absolute and the void are not sets. But also that what names them is not a set. That it is not a set means it has a logic other than that of pure sets. It is not simply a matter of belonging and inclusion, but of permutation, differentiation, etc. It is not just that we can think of any possible collection, but that all actual entities are made up of the absolute as well. It is not simply that the reflected thoughts of things are composed of the empty set, but that the absolute is not simply withdrawn into the world of sets, of essences and eidos, but also into the world of existence, of letters.

All of being can be thought by sets, but one has still not thought existence (and I find *Logic of Worlds* does not offer a model that truly captures existence and do not see any evidence that the category theory laid out there can speak to any possible actual entity or that it is model that is essentially tied into set theory itself which still founds Badiou's approach at its most basic level). Part of the problem here is that the non-signifying nature of the mark of the empty set is never truly though through by Badiou. Sets are always signified like Platonic eidos, but letters are not. Badiou wants to see how being achieves meaning and sense, but existence occurs at the level of the senseless which is why one needs a model that can engage with mechanical repetition. This is why Badiou for instance has nothing to say about a snowflake other than it is a set collecting together elements like crystals or atoms. He cannot speak to why one is shaped this way rather than that. He is concerned mainly with human speech acts and how they reflect, involve, and relate to the non-all. All being qua essence is thought by sets, but that does not tell us how any given can be seen as the same thing as a set. To do that we need more than a name for a thing or a way of collecting things and names together. We need the very logic that explains their form and nature.

At the same time, since the absolute as pure being is the non-all we can only ever see the thinkable as a set of pure being. It is never the whole itself. Thought is always lacking in some way. It is always exceeded in both the direction of being and existence. Part of the issue here is that there is a fundamental conceptual difference at work in set theory—the difference between the name and the thing named. There is always a difference between the set (one can take this literally as the brackets themselves) and what it collects. But this is an eidetic difference only insofar as being is taken to be mean essence, eidos, thought, etc. This is why we call it conceptual or eidetic difference rather than ontological difference. It is not the ontological difference that occurs between the absolute, the non-all, the divine, and thought and existence. We can say here that Badiou is a true follower of Heidegger; for Heidegger, the question of being was only ever a question of the meaning of being, of its sense and intelligible structure. Ontological difference is the need to think the fact that A is not not-A, that the absolute is nothingness, etc.

For us then there is ontological, eidetic, and finally existential difference. Existential difference would involve the difference between the algorithmic rule and its articulation. If one looks at a cellular automaton for instance, there is both its articulation and the rule for that articulation. Existential difference then involves the difference and differentiation between the two. Existential difference is thus caught up in the question of complexity. It is a relation between the simple and the complex and how order and pattern seems to emerge for free. It is a question of the irreducibility of the emergent and the rules for its iteration. Existence betrays computational irreducibility as Stephen Wolfram would put it. That irreducibility indicates a necessary existential difference between what can be known from a set of letters alone and what it leads to.

Let us return to being qua essence/eidos. Given the absolute's nature, it cannot be said that God does not think all possible objects. They therefore inhere in the non-all even if they cannot totalize it. But God is not God's thoughts. God withdraws from them too. One should not be worried here about parallels with the existential subject or the transcendental phenomenological ego since those creatures were only ever attempts by human finitude to usurp the place of God rather than recognizing the manner in which we are created in his image. But that all possible objects, all sets and names, are thought by God does mean they have an eternal nature since they are thought, but it does not mean they exist here in this world. They are neutralized essences thought thoroughly by God in their finitude or their transfinitude. However, that does not mean these eternal objects transcend God. They do not necessarily exist and are only instantiated in eternity by God's thought of them. But by being eternal they know not of time. Thus to say they could fail to exist or necessarily exist is rendered meaningless by the eternal nature of the mind within which they occur. Second, they are at the same time only the product of divine contraction. That is, there is no set until the divine contracting. There is no thought in this sense until the divine withdraws. God as pure being transcends thought itself. In this way, any set or essence is itself contingent and the result of a pure and free choice of God to create. It is not something God is somehow forced to do. In this way, no essence has any true necessity to it--just as nothing that exists had to exist. It is only the thrust of the contingent name of existence itself--the arbitrary set of letters that occurred in the divine contraction. God is not constrained by his own thoughts. Eternal objects do not contain God, but rather are freely imagined all at once in the divine intellect.

All of existence involves inconsistency which here means in a primary sense a lack of eternity. Existence might fail to exist and at some point does with any particular existing thing. This is why there needs to be some sufficient reason for what exists. It requires an explanation for why it is this way rather than another. The Name of God and its computation provides jut that reason. Essences find their sufficient reason in the empty set itself. There is ultimately one necessity and that is the absolute itself. All things visible and invisible belong to another category. God's unicity is preserved at every turn precisely by differentiating between being, essence, and existence. Without doing so, essences would disappear. They cannot endure if they are reduced to instances of human conception. They have no sovereignty independently of divine thought. If God did not think the actual infinity of all positive integers, then this set of integers would not persist as a transfinite collection. It is not necessary that every number exists and or that even one does. They are not founded by their very nature.

It is also important to note that even if Cantor found in Plato's *Philebus* a precursor for his notion of set, sets in set theory are pure extensional entities. In this way, they do not match what Plato meant by the ideas per a literal reading of Platonism. It is also for this reason that Badiou rightly highlights that a set theory ontology would have to be what he often calls a 'Platonism of the multiple' or an "extensional Platonism".17 While in this reference, Badiou says there is no such thing as extensional Platonism that is because Plato did not see ideas as aggregates of elements. The beautiful for him is not simply the set that collects together a list of elements. Beauty itself is a one over many things. But each thing is itself beautiful and exhibits that property for Plato. Ideas are thus more so intensional sets for Plato. This is why the ideal realm in which ideas exist is for him thought of as totality. But given Russell's paradox, there can be no such set of all sets. This is why we need an extensional theory of the one over the many. For Plato, ideas are the signified. This is why the beautiful itself is beautiful for him. There is no conceptual difference between the beautiful and what it contains. Rather there is a reflection principle at work in which beautiful things participate in Beauty itself and mirror it. This is why for Plato there is a series of scales in which things more or less mimic and mirror the ideal. This is an ontology of what Lacan calls the imaginary. It is caught up with signified that all things point to and refer to. All beautiful things refer to the beautiful itself. In set theory, a set is not a thing in this sense. The beautiful is not a beautiful thing. It is the ingathering of a series of elements. If one changes any of these elements (adds or subtracts one), then the very set changes. In this way, for Plato, the set of beautiful things includes all possible things that can reflect the beautiful. There is a rule and definition for selecting and noting what can be included.

Sets are not simply Platonic ideas. But they are objects of thought. Insofar as each set is a many thought of as one there is a set that matches the Platonic idea of the beautiful. But first and foremost a set is the name of the many. It is thus that the set of all beautiful things is the beautiful insofar as the 'beautiful' names that set. Sets are thus names in the sense of concepts containing objects. These names do not belong to the things they name. The axiom of foundation excludes that. A set is founded thus in the act of colleting the many and there is thus always at least one element that founds here and is not included in the set--the name of the set. Plato did not think ideas were simply the object of human thought since ideas are something and the thought of some particular referent. If they were just thoughts, they would have no connection to their referent. But for set theory every set is a thought of nothing. The empty set is included in each set and that gives it its substance--it founds its name. Also although sets are something, they contain elements. But that does not mean they reference something outside of themselves. The set of beautiful things only references the multitude it collects and not some definition of beauty. For Plato, the beautiful itself best exemplifies beauty. Ideas are exemplars. They are thus images. This is why Plato is ultimately developing for us a pictography. Despite the discussion of letters in his *Philebus*, his own theory of forms is that of a hieroglyphics where there is an image that resembles a thing.

For Gödel the sets of "transfinite set theory" "were not part of the physical world", and not something empirically experienced, but perceived using an intellectual intuition that shows them to be as real as any perceptual object.18 We can be as certain of sets as we are of any empirical perception since they 'force themselves' on us. For Gödel, sets are. There is as much evidence that they are as there is that atoms and quarks exist since sets have being. A quark is thus in one aspect of it simply a set of measurements. It is the name of that set. But what we grasp in this mathematical intuition is not some perfect exemplar such that what we perceive is imperfect. Rather the set of all trees is what collects together a list as a particular tree is itself a transfinite set as well whether it is the set of all possible perceptions of a specific tree or a finite set of all of a tree's atoms or any other collection. The tree can also of course be for us some sort of series of letters, an algorithm and program ultimately, that shows us how the tree itself elaborates itself into its current form.

For Plato, ideas were isolated and purely exist as things themselves. In this way, relating them was a secondary consideration. Plato of course has a model in which all forms participate in the Good or the One. But that is more so a model that is attempting to explain how each eidos is itself a unity. The good or One here is beyond them in the sense that the sun is beyond the field of vision. It lights up the field of vision, but can itself be looked directly upon if one turns. It is thus a condition that all things participate in. This is difference from all sets including and being founded on the empty set. All things do not participate in the empty set, but rather are composed of it. For set theory, the 'one is not' such that all sets do not reflect a totality. They are totalities despite the non-all in which they take place. Sets are because the One is not. They are thus marked by the absolute in a different way than Platonic ideas. The Platonic ideas were mirrors of the One whereas sets are instances of the non-all. Each set is an aspect of the non-all. We have never seen and will never see the non-all. But we are aware of it and in relation to it.

But in being aspects of the non-all there is no correspondence between a set and the absolute. However, no set can divorce itself fully from its dependence on and relation to the non-all. Each set stands on its own and isolated from any other set in its definition of set. It is also important to note that sets have to have a Platonic aspect in order for them to be transfinite. The transfinite set collects together an actual infinite. But we nowhere encounter such actual infinites in the world of perception for example. The set of all positive integers includes every possible integer. This is why they must exist as Platonic-like entities in the mind of God. Otherwise there would be no transfinite realm. We would be stuck with only a potential infinite and a closed Aristotelian universe of substantial forms. This is why again Cantor's reference to Plato's *Philebus* is not arbitrary. Part of the fundamental definition of sets must be Platonic even if they are now extensional entities first and foremost.

That we know claim that Platonic forms are sets means we can understand how a Platonic idea is number. Each number, each positive integer is a set of empty sets. Things exist by participating in number and being composed o f it by being made up of sets and sets of sets. The Pythagoreans already believed that all things are derived from a single point, the monad. Here, we see that the monad can be nothing other than the empty set. That sets are only what they consist of means that there is constantly change. One name is replaced by another. There is an infinity of names. Each name is able to collect together something else. At any instant, a set is what it consists of. But at the same time, it can include mere possibles and thus have as elements what was and what will be, what has been and what could be. We can think of each set in its aspect as name as a rigid designator. The set is called always by name since the axiom of extensionality means two sets with the same elements are simply the same thing. This is why sets are no simply collections with names. If we subtract an element from a set, it is not the same set, but if two sets have the same elements they are indiscernible. Any set is constituted by its membership. But at the same time, insofar as a set can be transfinite they can retain this possibility of retaining identity since they always already had every possible element of a sequence. My family thus would change if it were a finite list of people and new family members added, but it would not if my family is a transfinite containing any possible family member and thus having a transfinite number of placeholders for each.

Even if we empirically give things a different name, they are but empirical names for the same ultimate name of the set—the bracketing. Since all sets participate in the non-all, we can then say each name is a name of God. But there is a difference between a name that refers to a specific series of elements (the set of all things in this room) and a name that attempts to refer to the non-all itself (the ineffable one). Sets of any type are limitations of the unlimited, but not all are attempts to the name the unlimited itself directly. There is also the one name that makes possible for any set to be and for any existing thing to take on its shape. And that is the exceptional name. This name is an excessive mark that stands outside the list of all names by being included in all names. It is a supernumerary name that relates directly to the non-all even if one can have a single transfinite set of empirical names as one can have of all positive integers. This excessive name is included in all sets. It is the mark of the void, the name of God. It makes possible all names to e as such. In this way, insofar as sets are included in the name of God, one can say that unicorn has being qua essence. It is not included in the existent world that the divine name computes, but it exists independently of that existential world as a pure object of thought. The unicorn at the very least has the being of a name.

Also, alls sets have intrinsically mathematical properties and can express all possible mathematical properties. That is why they cover all of being. But what exists also has such properties insofar as they computed. They can be thus identified with mathematical objects, but at the same time all the possible mathematical objects exceed the number that actually exist. Since any computable object is ultimately a series of zeroes and ones, it can be rendered as a mathematical set. We thus do not exist simply in the Platonic world of essences and ideas. We also exist in the existential world, in the divinely programmed computer.

Our acceptance of the tripartite structure of being-thought-existence (esse-essentia-existentia) which is classical and even Thomistic in nature should not lead one to believe we accept the classical model with all its implications. For example, for Thomists, things are created by existence being added to an essence. Possibles are actualized in their full state from the mind of God. Like Deleuze, we reject this possible/real model for creation, but rather via the notion of the divine contraction all of existence as being a computation of the divine name we see the world as itself computational, as a computer. We avoid also here the Deleuzean virtual/actual distinction which seems only to rename the classical potential/actual distinction by projecting a virtual dimension that is differentiated, but not essentially Platonic in nature and not simply accepted as determining what is thinkable or unable to explain why what is already differentiated and figured into patterns needs to be 'actualized' rather than being already so.

For us rather, the actual is but its being differentiated in its computation. There is thus no need to separate within existence between the virtual and actual. For us the virtual would simply be what is thinkable in its being thinkable, but that is not something that is realized except as thinkable. It is a purely sterile world in itself—a Platonic dimension of the multiple that ultimately consists of divine thoughts.

For us this tripartite structure will also help us to justify the ontological vision being presented insofar as we can know assert differing ontological, eidetic, and existential proofs for terms already noted. Given that set theory holds a central place, some have argued that one should speak here of axioms rather than proofs. For instance, there is the axiom of the empty set. The notion of an axiom suggests philosophically one does not need a proof for the empty set as such, but only to accept it as a guiding principle. The empty set may simply be a useful fiction. The axiomatic perspective thereby implies that ultimately we are only dealing with what is thinkable and not touching necessarily the actual structure of what is in itself or making statements about the world. The axiomatic approach also leads to the belief that an entity like the empty set or God is only brought into being by a performative speech act. This is the impression Badiou often gives with his assertion that ontology is about making groundless, axiomatic decisions about what is and what is not. In this way, if we assert a pure proper and self-indicating name like that of the empty set, we are merely prescribing something into existence. We are not demonstrating its actual existence beyond prescriptive act. There is no a description of what is, but a performative speech act that thought makes itself. It therefore gives the impression that the empty set is something one can simply do without. One has simply and arbitrarily chosen a conceptual model wherein this ur-element is a fictitious entity known as $\emptyset$ functions. The signer $\emptyset$ invents its signified. It brings itself into being.

But we would rather say that the axiom of the empty set involves an existential proof of itself. Like the Cartesian 'cogito' (I think therefore I am) and perhaps ultimately on its basis, the empty set is not a fiction, but something that must exist (rather than just be thought). The very thought of it necessitates its existence. It cannot be denied that it exists the instance that thought turns to it. The void set contains nothing and thus by naming it one recognizes its unavoidable existence. It proves itself in and by its own assertion, but not all things have this nature. There is only one void since something containing nothing cannot be differentiated from another set containing nothing. It is itself the mark of difference and not distinguishable from another as it is included in all. The empty set is unique in this regard. It is the proof of a unique mark that exists. It is not merely an object of thought, but rather the basis of existence itself. It is also important to note here that first and foremost what is asserted here is the mark ∅. It is an ur-element more so than a set. The empty set could only be falsified if it has an element that did not belong to it. But since the empty set has no such elements, it is absurd to argue it does not exist. This is also why the empty set necessarily belongs to any set since its lack of elements means it never lacks any elements that belong to any possible set.

Notice here how the axiom of empty set differs from other axioms like that of the axiom of extensionality. Axioms like the latter involve logical principles for how already existing sets interrelate in terms of their being identical or not. Some believe that axioms should be obvious and self-evident to any rational being. However, it is not simply a question of intellectual intuition, but rather one of proof insofar as they can be given from a metaphysical perspective. They are thus principles of thought alone. They are axioms in the sense of indispensible principles for clarifying how to manipulate and articulate thinking itself. They do not assert the existence of something (we will discuss the axiom of infinity shortly). Axioms such as these clearly can be based on reasoning and form the basis of reasoning. Axioms are simply the most basic principles that cannot be deduced from other basic principles directly. No other single axiom or combination of axioms show in and of themselves that another axiom is required. But that does not mean they are purely groundless 'decisions'. As Gödel would put it, they force themselves up on us via the very reasoning found in them. The empty set is unavoidable and exists unlike the set of all things in this room or set of all unicorns. The name $\emptyset$ is a special excessive name that proves itself the moment it is thought. Part of the reason this existential proof works is because one need not assert anything. One asserts nothing and its mark. But the mere thought of nothingness achieved that. One is her affirming something in particular, by affirming nothing at all. The empty set is self-indicating, but that does not mean it creates itself. It is recognized as created insofar as it is thought. It's no more self-creating than the cogito itself.

There is an existential proof for the empty set, but not for set of all round objects. Why not? One can of course construct a set and determine one for any possible property and quality. One can then assert that set. But clearly there is nothing about the assertion that necessitates the existence of the set of all round things. We can engage in an endless process of construction of all sets of all properties. But that again does not show that any single one of them exists. Maybe there are not in this world for instance any round things whatsoever. If one denies round things, no contradiction occurs. If one denies round things, one is still not a round thing or proposing a round thing (only a set of round things). There is thus a difference between a set of things and the thing of which it is the set in way that does not occur. For this reason, one cannot prove any other set besides the empty set exists.

One can only assert eidetic proofs for sets. One thing a thinker like Meillassoux does not realize is that transfinite induction gets only so far and only in the order of the finite ordinals. To get to the transfinite one needs a leap and that means an eidetic proof, but also the positing of a divine mind where such a transfinite essence can be truly thought. Transfinite recursion is not empirical induction. It is also not random, but shows a marked progression. The set of all round things has being, being qua essence/eidos, regardless of whether or not a single round thing ever obtains in any sense outside the thought of the thing. We can do this for any property and for any idea that is logically conceivable. Those sets then in their being defined occur as thoughts and have thought-being (eidos). God has thought all possibles in this way. We thus can have an eidetic proof of any constructible and logically definable property and set of objects exhibiting that property. One cannot restrict this construction in any way.

Eidetic proof is an endless process. One can constantly posit additional sets. One can continue thinking endlessly. We are forced to be Meinongian here. There is a set of all golden mountains and a set of all square circles. But no individual square circle exists. A set as a thought, as an essence, does not require the existence of any such individual since the ur-element is the empty set and not things.

The axiom of infinity is thus not something established by an existential proof, but rather by an eidetic proof. One can also posit arbitrarily larger and larger entities. This is precisely what one does with the axiom of infinity. One posits an ordinal that is greater than any possible finite ordinal (ω). But that does not mean ω exists. It is a set, an essence. It is eidetically proven through the posting of the ordinal greater than any finite ordinal. Now, ω cannot be deduced from previous axioms. These other axioms only can lead one to generate finite ordinals on the basis of the empty set and its inclusion. The posting of ω is a break with that finite order and the posting of something larger. It posts thus a collection of all possible finite ordinal numbers. That assertion logically proves itself, but not its existence. It does not prove its existence in part because as set theory immediately discovered one can then posit an ordinal greater than ω. ω is not the greatest possible ordinal and not even the greatest possible finite ordinal. It is the first ordinal great than any possible finite one. But given that any ordinal contains all the previous ones per von Neumann (each ordinal is the set of al preceding numbers), ω contains all possible finite ordinals.

The axiom of infinity seems in its formulation to posit the existence of something, but it only posits a set. This set is, but does not exist. We should not confuse this eidetic proof for the axiom of infinity with ontological proofs for God's necessary being (we shall turn to this proof shortly). ω is the ordinal number that occurs once one reaches the last finite number. But of course, one could never in time reach that last finite ordinal. There is thus an unbridgeable chasm between the order of finite ordinals and ω. ω is only the first transfinite ordinal. What exists is only ever made of finite ordinals built up out of the empty set. Only those numbers built out of the empty set exist. ω cannot exist in this world since one would never reach or have reached in a finite amount of time. ω is an eidos. It is not a repetition of the empty set in the way that finite ordinals like 2 or 3 are where they include it. Rather ω is a repetition of the one itself that includes the empty set insofar it is a name. It is a name that essentially defines itself. The numbers 3 or 4 are not proper names, but ω is. ω is also an event because it marks a fundamental discontinuity between the series of finite ordinals and the new transfinite dimension it announces. ω names what cannot be presented and not the void as such. It names a totality.

All Platonic ideas, all essences, are ways of renaming it. They are repetitions by other names. When one speaks of the set of all round things, one speaks of a transfinite set containing all possible round things. This is another way of stating ω. ω of course contains the empty set as any set does. And if we can say that the counting empty set is the brackets of a set, then ω would be the continuum of white space inside that allows for an infinity to fit into any set whether it is the set of round things or set of cars in my garage. ω thus signals that there is something always greater than itself. One cannot construct an infinitude by repetition of the empty set alone. This is why the transfinite needs a new name and new definition. One cannot generate the transfinite from the finite. It is a new definition, but a definition of number and thus a definition of what is, what is thinkable.

There is no single finite number that counts up all the fine ordinals, and ω is the name for that lack. ω takes place thus insofar as it names the set of something, a one over many. Each thing then has a set. There are essential things in themselves, and they are sets. These things are not withdrawn, but rather thoughts that are completed ones. They ultimately are in the mind of God since they do not depend on any particular thought in any particular finite mind. Also a finite mind cannot think a transfinite set as anything more than a name. It cannot see things from the perspective of eternity and see at once all possible numbers counted in one set. There is thus a need for an eternal mind again. Human perception sees the set of all possible round things as exceeding it, but as a set it is completed entity even if transfinite in nature. Transfinite is not then something truly transcendent.

But not every set and what it names exists Only the letters and their computation can determine what does in fact exist. And the letters have determined in their permutations that there (at least not yet) are not any unicorns for instance. ω is what imposes itself given the lack of a greatest possible finite number. But ω is not the apeiron. It is not the unlimited. It is very strictly limited. It is for instance the set of all positive integers, but that is not all that is. One here has conceived of a number, a new type of number. It is a second-order number and one that counts all possible numbers. This is again why Cantor turned to Plato since Platonic ideas are precisely those things that count all possible things of a single type. There is also a transfinitude of any type. The eidos is always a transfinite class of any possible defined term. All terms are transfinite terms then in their being. ω shows that alls sets are Platonic-like entities. It points in this way to the absolute.

All sets are thus ultimately able to be transfinite sets and are marked by the transfinite in the same way they are marked by the empty set insofar as they are completed totalities and determinate collections. In this world, existentially speaking, one may have only ever counted up to and computed numbers in the trillions for example in fact. For even if we conceive of infinitudes, we compute finitude. Computation runs into problems when it approaches infinities. In particular, it runs into problems when it runs into finites of a cardinality greater than that of the set of all positive integers and when it must approach infinities that cannot be understood as being expressed by a clear rule (like pi). But of course thought can at any minute access not only exceedingly larger finite ordinals, but also transfinite ordinals like ω.

ω says it contains all those finite sets succeeding the empty set and this way claims to contain within itself all that exists. ω thus forces all the finite ordinals into a single collectivity in the very act of its naming. All the finite ordinals disappear into the name ω just as the divine disappeared into its pure name at creation. This is why ω is an echo of the divine and a divine name even if one a lower level than Ω or the proper name of the empty set. The name itself captures here all that is hidden in it—a single name for a transfinite collection. But of course, there cannot be a totalized set of all that exists. ω thus names the lack of that total set with a name, a name that it substitutes for that lack and names that incompletion. Incompletion does not simply name that something lacking in existence (the set of all that exist), but also issues in an excessive name, a plus one, that marks the incompletion itself and feigns its totality. The set of all existing things is incomplete and necessarily so.

Many see Cantor as engaging in a free creation of thought in positing ω, but there is an eidetic proof for ω and that proof can be reproduced again and again endlessly to pinpoint all the objects of thought alone, all those essence that occupy the realm of being. There are higher and higher powers like the ever increasing vaults of heaven itself. There are higher powers as the higher and higher thoughts of God including those that are inaccessible to us even by name. ω is not the greatest possible ordinal. This is one reason why it should not be confused with God. God was traditionally defined as infinite, but ω is transfinite precisely because there is something greater than it. But ω also closes certain possible ontological proofs. It closes off for thought for instance traditional cosmological proofs for God. In the past, one would say that if the world was not started at some point, then there would be an infinite regress. But such an infinite regress cannot be traversed such that if there were an infinite regress, we would never arrive at this point now in which we exist. And yet here we are. ω signals that a infinite series of this type can be completed. It can be traversed.

Of course, the completion occurs only in thought itself. It does not happen in existence. And perhaps this is all that Saadya Gaon and those like him who put forth this cosmological proof meant. However, if we are basing things solely on thought itself and what is thinkable and using that as a point of departure, then a priori cosmological proofs are closed off to us. We cannot say that the world in any *a priori* sense has a beginning because the infinity of time cannot be traversed. Saadya only wanted to prove that the world had to have a beginning point because then only God could explain sufficiently that beginning. God introduces the idea that which there can be nothing greater and for this reason there is an ontological proof of God as divine absolute, as pure being rather than an eidetic or existential proof of God.

One of Kant's objections to the ontological proof of God was that we somehow presuppose that God exists when we try to prove God follows from the idea of God. But we only need to presuppose the idea of God has being qua essence. We also do not say that God exists, but that God is pure being. God can be shown to be pure being from ontological proofs. Of course, many also say that the ontological proof first introduced by Anselm presupposes Platonism. We agree and that one cannot have ontological proofs without defining some version of Platonism as we have done here. Many have said if there is a proof of the greatest or most perfect, then there is a proof of the most beautiful and most round. We agree but those things are essences and ideas with eidetic proofs. There are ontological proofs for God ultimately because God exceeds even the greatest possible thoughts we can have about Him. No matter how we try to express God's radical transcendence, we will fall short. God involves not simply something greater than the finite or even the transfinite, but the issue of the greatest possible. This is why God is not a totality or a whole. That which there can be nothing greater than shatters all wholes and all sets.

For any finite or transfinite entity there is always something greater than it. But God marks the point at which there is no greater than. Thought has no maximum. One can construct set after set. But being, pure being, the divine does. Thought always necessary leaves something out and that is the real itself, being, God. God thus from the perspective of thought is the impossible and relates to the very impasses of thinking. God appears as the first pure being, the real, that no concept can cover and comprehend. God is the Other of thought, the impossible Other. Pure being is always another name for the impossible and the eternal. God is an eternal, impossible, and necessary Other. God is thus the Other of any essence or conception. God is thereby related to the order of the letter rather than the signifier. God is other than any essence. God is ultimately unnamable and ineffable. It is God's absence that means only names that refer to absence can speak of the divine. The nameable speaks of something present, something definable and finite. It does not express a missing transfinitude. At most it expresses an open set that has to be filled in full. But it touches on no fundamental negation and in no way suggests the ineffable.

God is the Other of all signifiers and is found via the letter. That lettering is mostly understood as YHVH. Lacan calls it also Φ. But once this name is instantiated other names emerge and evolve around this point, the impossible and differential mark. These names both attempt to rename it, to permute it, to conceptualize and express it further, etc. ω attempts to capture all that exists and thus attempts to restate the name of God in doing so, but finds itself suppressed and surpassed by further names, divine ones, that continue the act of naming the impossible and relating to the divine non-all that touches on all. . That which cannot be named also is unique. For no matter how we were to phrase this concept, it all ends in God. There can be no differentiating between two ideas of which there can be no greater than. From the perspective of thought, the very idea of that which there can be no greater than leads to inconsistency. But this is why the divine is named by the non-all. This is why God is different from all. While there can always be a greater number, there can never be that which is greater than God. This is why God is identified with the absolute infinite. The notion of the greatest cannot be avoided. It insists on being named and approached. We thus cannot avoid God and the divine name no matter how much we may desire to do so.

Frederik Depoortere suggests that "the being of God cannot be demonstrated, but has to be declared" and thus implies that we would need an axiom for God just as we have an axiom of the empty set.19 But God is not a set. God is also far from self-evident. To say we simply declare God makes it appear as though God is at best some sort of pure idea that is invented by its own articulation, but then would leave God as an idea. Any atheist would of course accept God as such a fiction. If we declare God does not exist, there is no contradiction and no necessary thought that has been deceptively avoided. Thus declarations and mere speech acts cannot do the work. Rather, one needs an ontological proof that shows the unavoidability of the question of the greatest as opposed to endless progression. A being greater than the greatest cannot be conceived (if one tried to one would end up back in the same place) and hence thought reaches its limit and touches the real. It is not simply a declaration. To say that one cannot comprehend God, that which there is nothing greater, not to be signals that the real itself has been announced.

There also here can be no objection to the inverse of this argument that establishes the void. The void/nothingness is precisely that which nothing less than it can be conceived. Anselm's point here is also one about the difference between thought and reality. If God only was a concept in the mind, then one can think of something greater than a mere concept. God as pure being is greater than such. The point here is that the concept of a thing is not necessarily (and most often not) the thing it is a concept of. Having a concept of something does not make that thing come into existence. But with God we touch on the real with the very conception. It cannot be denied that we have such a conception.

There is no improvement in God and no increasing the non-all. This is why the non-all is related to the unlimited. If one has a scale, that scale implies a point of which there is no greater than any other point since even if one denied there is such a point, one would affirm there is since the endless greater than would devolve into such an unlimited.

§5. On Divine Names

The ontological proof of God is a proof of *eyn sof*. The existential proof of God related to the holy personal name of God, YHVH. But an eidetic proof of ω showed that any fundamental determination of reality as such forms a divine name because it names a fundamental limitation of the limited. ω does that by forcing together all of existence into one block. It therefore introduces us into a new order of reality and reflects that new order in its logic and essence. It is not the name of a particular thing per se. It is a restatement of the first one, but is a restatement at a new level. However, given that all divine names are inadequate for capturing reality itself (we saw how ω fails ultimately to capture all of reality as it is surpassed by even greater transfinite orders). This is because any attempt at articulating a divine name will ultimately be marked by the supreme unknowability of the absolute infinite itself. It is the very ineffability and inconceivability of the divine absolute (its fundamental namelessness and excess over all names) as well as its non-all status that initiates a proliferation of divine names.

YHVH is the pure proper and personal name of God. But one is forbidden from speaking it out loud in order to emphasize that it itself does not truly name or capture the divine. It is the four-letter name, the tetragrammaton, but given that it ultimately fails as a name it can be permuted into new names. For example, there exists a twelve-letter name of God which is simply YHVH repeated three times. Divine names are in part formed on the basis of other names through their repetition and permutation. The twelve-letter name emphasizes the eternal nature of God and thus how YHVH is related itself to the conjugation of the verb to be. God is, was, and will be at once. As pure being, God is eternal, but this pure being can in part only be expressed by repeating the personal name itself and conjugating it as though it were itself the verb to be as such. Part of the reason Jews are disallowed form attempting to verbalize the letters of God's name is to avoid the idea that God is himself finite. The four-letter or twelve-letter names are themselves each in part a finite set of a limited number of letters. They thus present a limited amount of data and information. But God's pure infinite being both causes to be and is always. That is not something that can be confined fully in a series of letters. While God is found in each instant as the creator of all, even in noting those qualities the depths of the divine have not been fully plumbed. We cannot fully know God as He is in and of Himself. But we can know how God creates and order the divine reality.

Each new revelation of a specific order and dimension of that reality reveals a divine name whether it be ω or the empty set. Divine names are thus always only ever limitations of the ultimately indescribable absolute infinite. Thus no divine name can fully determine its reference and can only ultimately mark out a limitation of the unlimited. The ultimate referent always escapes us. This is also why when we think we are detailing predicates of God we are ultimately listing names. If God is unknowable, then there can be no true expression of God's properties. For this reason, when we attempt to determine a property, we express a name instead. We attempt to express a particular attribute of the absolute infinite; we do not truly know what we are expressing and thus are left with the signifier as name. I cannot speak here in a fully intelligible manner and thus simply note a series of letters, a designator. God presents the paradox of the nameless one who has a long sequence and series of names indeed.

At the same time, God names himself. God even in his inaccessibility does not leave himself unnamed, but rather names himself. This is one of the central divine paradoxes. YHVH is that name, a personal name. Other Gods may have names, but they only have a single one because their name fits them. But because God's name is a series of unpronounceable letters, God is not captured by his name. God only reveals himself as a name. God does not appear in the flesh. When God appears to Moses at the burning bush, the bush is of course not God himself. God here gives his name to Moses. God names himself and presents himself as a name.

Edmond Jabes claims that "God resembles his name to the letter".[20] But God is named by letters because he resembles nothing. God cannot be symbolized by a fire, fish, or sun. God names himself with a string of letters to note the nature of existence rather than what he himself resembles. Also, the senselessness of the letter is required for the act of pure self-nomination the pure mark. Only God can himself reveal his true name. We cannot invent this name. And because the name is a series of letters we cannot invent its meaning, but only ever unveil it further through permutations. It is not a description by the letter and not a signification, but a code. We are forbidden from uttering and do not know how in any case to vocalize it which is why it can only be explored by unraveling its lettering. God himself is singular and unique.

But the name despite its being safeguarded in its silence cannot maintain that singularity. Like any name, it can be repeated and transmuted. No name is in itself absolute. The name exists here and now as series of letters. It thus encodes the secret of God while at the same time disclosing it. Thus again, we move from one name to the any divine names. No name or series of letters can be the absolute itself. Existence is plural by its very nature. But it is the pluralism of the letter itself because it arrives to us from the absence of the absolute. A series of names is created due to the lack of there ever being an absolute name or letter. There are other names, always other, divine names to be found. God is celebrated by a series of names. This is prayer itself at its heart. But only a fundamentally unnamable God can be so sung. God in his pure being, in his eternity, self-sufficiency, and necessity, is nameless in and of himself.

It should be noted that nouns are also names, but they appear to be concepts picking out an object. God is not of course any such object, of perception or thought. If we have a name that indicates something has a property or quality, then we have a general concept rather than a proper name. When we have a concept, we have a term that covers a many. But God is not a many. The non-all is itself a unicity. A proper name is only something unique. A concept can be included in larger ones and shown to be identical with other concepts potentially. This is why proper names are required in His case. If God were only a mere object of thought, we would only need a name as a concept. This is what Plato for instance believed that God is simply being itself without any name (*Phaedrus* 256a-250c). The concept of being thus would cover God. But the many names of God always surround unnameability. It leads to repetition and multiplication. God as pure being remains and persists as real.

The 42-letter name is also not pronounceable. It is derived from the first 42 letters of the Torah itself via the permutation system known as 'atbash'21. Atbash consists of permuting letters by exchanging the first letter of the alphabet with the last, the second with the second to last, etc. The 42-letter thus reveals that the silence of the name in its ineffability is related to a code whereby it can be derived. Of course during the time of the temple in Jerusalem, the high priest knows how to pronounce this name out loud on Yom Kippur ('The Day of Atonement'). Also, it is often suggested, such as by *Sefer HaZohar*, that the 42 letter name is the code for the creation of the world. This would not necessarily contradict our suggest that code is YHVH as one could see YHVH as somehow contained in the 42-letter name or the 42 letter name itself as some permutation on the lettering YHVH. That is, it could be a combination of the two.

While the 42 letter name being found at the beginning of the Torah itself (in English, one would say the first line or two of Genesis) suggests that it might be more so that the 42 letter name is that by which the entirety of existence was created (the code at the beginning for articulating the entire text), YHVH remains as the code for existence as such (including the text). The Torah itself, as Moshe Idel notes, "is often called the 'path of [divine] names'" itself such that the Torah itself will be itself consist of the articulating of new divine names, their multiplication, and their permutation.22

This system of atbash also again forms the 14 letter divine name by reversing the letters of the most central prayer in Judaism, the Shema, wherein God's unicity and infinity are declared. Often a divine name will simply consist of other divine names run together. This is the case of the 33 letter name wherein several names of God, each with its own seeming meaning and purpose, are strung together into a set of letters. In this way, the 33 letter name is itself a text, a continuum of divine names. It also shows that all the seemingly divine names are one name. There is thus a unity that pervades the multiplication of names.

One often hears about the 72 names of God. There are 72 names because the numerical value of YHVH in Hebrew is itself 72. This is actually a 216 letter sequence (72 triads of 3 letters). The triads are selected from the text of the Torah within a specific section (Exodus 14:19-21). Here, we see that due to the divinity of the text itself, one can form divine names simply by grouping together a series of letter. An algorithm itself forms the 72 triads by selecting the letters at a specific sequence and distance from each other in the passage. What we see then is that if one applies an algorithm to the letters alone of the text, a divine name or series of divine names that express something about the nature of reality can be found. Since each divine name is a limited expression of the unlimited, the algorithm selects out of lettering of existence a name. It also suggests to us that one can unearth the nature of reality by organizing and counting the letters into distinct sets and subsets. The letters can be grouped and regrouped and thus reveal new dimensions of reality itself.

It is important to note that these 72 names contain all 22 letters of the Hebrew alphabet. The 22 letters are themselves often taken to be names and thus each letter in the Torah would itself be divine name.23 If the letters are themselves divine names, limitations of the unlimited, then every new word created becomes a divine name. Each new set of letters is itself senselessness and yet give rise to a meaning, a linkage to the rest of the names. In other words, once one combines the letters as names they require interpretation. As letters and sets of letters they are not yet a meaning and reference. Abraham Abulafia argued that one can transform any set of letters into divine names, but only through permutation of those letters and the collection of them into sets. Thus, divine names are hidden and must be reveled. They are encoded in the lettering, but can only emerge through a recombination of those letters.

One here transforms verses and lines of text into divine names of God. But this means it "may be done with any other book".24 Divine names may be a product of any linguistic system and any lettering may become a divine name per this method. This means any text can in principle be permuted. This is another way of restating the idea that every letter in itself is a limitation of the divine and any letter is already a divine name. The absolute infinite can be recognized to be at work in any text and in any letter in any language. But this may be because the divine text and the divine language by themselves include all other texts and all other languages. We will need to return to this point.

One of the key points here is that names differentiate the pure divinity of non-all. They name the void and the absolute and are made of them. The act of naming itself in one form involved the number one (the bracketing of the counting of the empty set) and ω the collecting together of all the finite ordinals. Every multiplicity must belong to a unity to be a multiplicity in this way. And that means any multiplicity can be numbered whether by a finite or transfinite ordinal. Many believed that there could not be infinite numbers since numbers had to have this quality of being a collection, of being a unity measured out. An actual infinite multitude was said to impossible. But the eidetic proof of ω shows that while in the existent world there is no such actuality as this world is itself incomplete by its lettering, there exists an essential notion that comprehends all the finite ordinals. It is a definite intention and thought of God himself. This is a thought we only know as a name. It is a divine thought. Divine thoughts are themselves then divine names. We cannot collect together ourselves all the possible finite ordinals. We can only name the act. We thus refer to a divine thought. A divine name in this case is the divine intention itself and the divine act of thought. God counts all including by counting them up also as transfinite numbers. But ω is only the first of these divine names of divine intentions.

§6. Large Cardinals

We can explore these divine names but examining what is known as "large cardinals." While ω is the first transfinite ordinal, it has a cardinality of aleph-null. Ordinality discusses numbers in their ability to count and order (first, second, third, fourth, etc.) whereas cardinality expresses the aspect of numbers in their measuring of size (one, two, three, etc.). Cardinality is determined by establishing a one-to-one correspondence between two sets. Any set that has the same number elements as the set three is of the same cardinality. One can draw if one wanted a line from each element in one set to the other to show the equivalence in size between the two. As Cantor of course showed, while ω is the first transfinite ordinal, there are many other sets of the same size, aleph–null. The set of all positive even numbers has the same cardinality as the set of all positive odd numbers, but also Cantor showed for instance a one-to-one correspondence between the set of positive integers and the set of all rational numbers (using the first of his diagonalization methods).

At the same time, using the second diagonalization method, Cantor showed that the set of all reals is larger than aleph-null and named it aleph-one. This difference in size was shown by lining up a series of reals to try to show a one –to-one correspondence with the infinity of positive integers. However, if one selects a number from each decimal place in the list of reals, one can construct a new number not appearing on the list of reals (which lined up in a seeming one-to-one correspondence with the list of positive integers) and thus show a lack of one-to-one correspondence. Aleph-one is born here. Aleph one is thus a new set, but an uncountably infinite one.

Cantor himself wanted to identify aleph-one with the power set of aleph-null. We will return to these issues with a discussion of the continuum hypothesis, but at this point one can note that aleph-null appears to be almost nothing despite its infinity in comparison with aleph-one. At the same time one could perform the power set operation on aleph-one and produce a set of larger cardinality named aleph-two. One thus can generate a seemingly endless series of alephs. This is one sense of large cardinals. They are a series then of divine names—one after the other. They are attempts to limit the absolute infinite and provide an outlook on some new dimension of it. But insofar as this progression is orderly and moves from one aleph to the next, we essentially have a redoubling of the series of finite numbers in the transfinite dimension. As we pass from aleph-one to two to three, we are not including the empty set as with finite ordinals to achieve new numbers, but rather have the power set function to generate one and then the next.

In this way, despite the seeming incomprehensibility of these transfinite sets, they fall back into some ordering. They would then seem to themselves repeat, if we were to collect, them what took place at the order of the finite. And set theory precisely does engage in this activity. Set theory does so under the aegis of that which it calls inaccessible cardinals. But the first inaccessible cardinal is essentially ω itself. ω was, as we can recall, a leap to a new level. It could not be built up by adding together all the finite ordinals or by noting their progression alone. Inaccessible cardinals are those cardinals that cannot be built up from whatever they collect together, but rather name a gap or break with those that come before. However, no matter how many transfinite steps one lists one can never breach the chasm between that set or collection and the absolute infinite itself. That is a gulf that cannot be spanned. Even if one steps from one transfinite cardinal to the next, one will note reach the absolute. But even if one tries to collect them together, one will at most achieve a new name for new inaccessible cardinals.

This lack of a 'stairway to heaven' demonstrates itself in part the true finitude of our thought and the infinitude of the divine mind. There is always a new path to follow when it comes to divine names. With these names, we can continue the process of transfinite recursion indefinitely. There are a seemingly unlimited number of divine names. But given that there can only be an aleph-null set of names, at some point we will have to speak of ineffable names, unwritten names, divine names we will never name. These divine names would be totally ineffable cardinals. They are thoughts of God we have no access to whatsoever. The most we can do is name part of their operation of formation and hint at their occurrence in the divine mind. These names are always analogues to aleph-null, ω.

Some would say one should posit new strong axioms of infinity for each of these inaccessible cardinals in a way analogous to the positing of the axiom of infinity for ω. After all, any inaccessible cardinal makes intuitive sense and no given axioms, including the axiom of infinity, can establish them eidetically. One needs a new eidetic proof for each new inaccessible cardinal. However, these inaccessible cardinals are not the unnamable itself since even if we eventually run out of actual empirical names for them, then we still have the process for their naming. The unnamable is what is ultimately nameless. The names we give to the inaccessible cardinals are not proper names in the same sense as the pure and singular name given to the unnamable absolute. As Dionysius the Areopagite said, "The Sacred writers celebrate it by every Name while yet they call it Nameless".25

The inaccessible cardinals are not the absolute, but rather figures for further marking the difference between the absolute and all else. Of course, "it is consistent with ZFC to assume there are no inaccessible ordinals other than ω".26 In other words, we have a fully agreeable theory without positing these analogues of ω, but at the same time the positing of them seems to force itself upon us intuitively given the very nature of set theory and also our desire to search out the non-all. Because these large cardinals cannot be reached form what is below them, because they are leaps beyond what is collected together by whim, each of these cardinals exists on its own. It names its own special area and zone of the non-all as if they were secret chambers of heaven.

At the same time, we have turned from the actual infinite to the potential infinite despite using the very tool that articulated for us the actual finite. That is, with large cardinals we begin counting again as we did with 0/1. The question is whether this new series of number has the same proprieties as ordinal integers such as being prime or odd and even. We could ask: what is the analog of being prime amongst large cardinals if there is one? We are also always tracing transfinite series on the model of finite sets as much as possible even though finite sets are collections where the adding together of the elements leads to the limit and transfinite sets are in need of a break. This is how our own thoughts are like the divine--for even if we cannot think an actual infinite, we can think the act of bridging a gap, the event of the name itself. We can think as the divine does insofar as we can name the leap and recognize it as such a discontinuity. We can recognize that we have to posit a name for what is unreachable. But we would not be able to name a series of unreachables if we were not aware of the divine itself. Otherwise, we would think with the first axiom of infinity we had said it all.

With strong axioms of infinity, we pay homage to the divine itself and its radical transcendence and excess. That is, the absolute inaccessibility of a set of all sets is a basis for naming inaccessible cardinals. The constant positing of such inaccessible cardinals shows that Zermelo-Fraenkel is not a complete theory. One can always add new axioms to it of this type without inconsistency being implied. It is therefore not a total theory. But it must be incomplete insofar as it cannot sum up the absolute infinite that is not a set or element of it but that shadows it at every turn.

But given that we cannot truly think the actual infinite other than as a name, it would be appear we are a discussing a name that is other than the thing named. For us, it is the name of nothing other than a name: "the name will turn out to be the name of a name" (*The Sophist* 244d). In addition to that, given that each inaccessible cardinals is repetition of the one of the 0/1 pair, it is "also the one, being the name of the one, will be the one of the name…. The one is thus the name of the one and the one of the named" (*The Sophist* 244d). However, in adding more and more inaccessible cardinal axioms no true effect or new insights seems forthcoming. It only appears that one shows an ability to redouble what has already been accomplished on higher and higher levels. It is not clear what these new formulas and operations achieve through the positing of inaccessible cardinals.

Clearly Badiou however thinks this ability to posit inaccessible cardinals leads to the richness of what he calls 'the event.' The inaccessible cardinal is itself an event, the name of a gap or discontinuity. Badiou takes this model and applies it to speech act theory and political situations. When we proclaim in a performative speech that the 'Communist revolution was a failure,' we signal an event. Or, when we proclaim to another 'I love you,' we articulate a discontinuity in being. Inaccessible cardinals can therefore tell us something about discontinuity in being itself. Even in seemingly finite situations, there are speech acts that open up gaps that separate between one side and the other just as ω separated between the finite and transfinite and further inaccessible cardinals separate between dimensions of the transfinite. There are then an endless number of events that can be named. Since we only know these inaccessible as names, names of names, it makes sense that they would be a model for performative speech acts where the act brings into existence the thing named (such as the end of the revolution).

The finite is therefore here marked by discontinuity because it can be named in this manner. A the same time, there is something finite about these transfinite sets insofar as they are names of names and insofar as they are repetitions of the one. As Plato anticipated somewhat we can say that the set theory is the course for approaching the inaccessible. But there is also the Torah as itself a series of divine names, of names of names. As Philip J. Davis and Reuben Hersh note, "…one could easily manufacture a hand-held computer with [an aleph-null] button to obey these Cantorian laws. But if [aleph-null] has been encased algorithmically within a finite structure, in what, then, consists its infinity?"27 Cantor showed that mathematical operations on the first transfinite ordinal yield results such as ω plus ω is ω or ω plus 1 is ω. One can have a calculator that permits enacts such operations. This is because the transfinite is ultimately the infinite made infinite. They are ones and sets of the absolute infinite. They open a new order distinct from the finite, but that at the same time repeats and redoubles the finite in that new dimension.

We do not know with our own minds or even with our most powerful computational devices do anything or than compute finitudes whether in the form of aleph-null or rational numbers. It speaks of the ineffable and unnamable one. It contains thereby a code indicating what the unnamable wants to say and can say to us. The two discourses of set theory and Torah codes therefore are fundamentally connected to each other. That is, there is a union to be struck between the analysis of Torah codes and the mathematical discourse of infinity. By Torah, with a capital 'T' we mean the five books of Moses (if we use a lower case 't' then we refer to all of Judaism as such, the Torah, Talmud, Midrash, etc.)

One of the things noted by large cardinals and the operation that posits them would be the same as seen in classical Structuralism. There, Levi-Strauss noted famously that the savage, universal mind which is pinned to language is always able to conjure up new floating, empty signifiers that are not attached to any specific signified. Inaccessible cardinals precisely institute this excess of signifiers over signifieds. Many would note that empty set itself already is what Levi-Strauss meant by the floating signifier, the signifier that can take on any signified (the 'whatchamacallit' that offers an empty place-holder), but the excess of the signifier over the signified itself means here ontologically that there are more names than existing things. That is, if one looks at existing things, then the first inaccessible of course attempts to totalize them. A name then outside of all the names is added on to them introducing a new order. But there is an excess of being over names. That is, the real is always in excess over essences. This surplus is the return of the unlimited itself into the picture. Despite Ω not being a set or an ur-element of set theory, it consistently reasserts itself. This is to say that problem does not relate back to the empty set. Because the empty set is an excessive name at the heart of all names, one will always also have an excess over any collectivity.

§7. The Problem of the Continuum

Some of the issues hinted at here of course play out most directly surrounding the question of the Continuum Hypothesis. For Cantor, the issue of the continuum was most basically question of how many points there are on a straight Euclidean line. Cantor was thus asking an arithmetical question about geometry: Can one determine the number or numerosity of the Euclidean line itself? This question is the same as asking how much and in how many ways a line which appears finite to us can be broken up? Cantor revolutionized the question of the continuum by treating it as purely a problem within arithmetic rather than geometry.

But of course Cantor was not the first to pose the problem of the continuum as it is a question that essentially goes back to Zeno's paradox. Zeno proposed multiple versions of this paradox. But these paradoxes essentially relate to the seemingly infinite divisibility of even a finite stretch of space. For example, if one is to cross from point A to point B, one first has to go half the distance. But to go half the distance, one needs to go half that distance, etc. One thus needs, Zeno claimed, to traverse an infinite space to cross a finite one. Here the unlimited division of space into intervals was an attempt to prove the impossibility of motion itself. The paradox lies in how a seemingly completely finite distance becomes finite and unable to be traversed through simple analysis of its divisions. Since one cannot deny that one goes half the distance in traversing the whole, it is not clear how one can dispute the inherent logic behind the paradox (hence the paradox's fame and seeming intractability over the centuries).

Part of what is fascinating about Zeno's paradox is it claims that the infinite can somehow fit into the finite itself, that the finite contains as it were the infinite. In this case, it would be the transfinite in the sense of cardinality aleph-null seemingly as each division would appear to be in one-to on- correspondence with the infinite sequence of natural numbers. Zeno also proposed a version of this paradox where Achilles chases the tortoise. But Achilles cannot catch the tortoise since he has to go half, etc. at each interval. As Lacan put it, Achilles "cannot catch up with" the tortoise except "at infinity" itself.28 Zeno seemed to say the power of the continuum was aleph-null.

To seemingly solve the paradox one would have to show how an infinity is itself traversed in finite time and space. One has to complete an infinity itself. With the notion of infinitesimals we will in part show the point was to show that completed infinities are more like 0 than anything larger. In the existent world, completed infinities are thus more like a restatement of the void itself. They are a nothing and thus easily overstepped at each instance. But at the same time, if we accept the real nature of Zen's problem, then we will see that something unlimited will be needed to enable every distance no matter how small to be traversed. In other words, one will require God to intervene at every moment and moment to enable my hand to move across the keyboard or the cloud to cross the sky. The more we accept the truth of the continuum problem, the more we will need to accept an occasionalist God that creates everything at all moments. Every day of every hour of every instance this world of existing entities is being informed by the same primordial activity by which it came into existence in the first place. God is involved in all relations at all times. God will be involved in any every issue no matter how great or small since without the unlimited there will be no way to understand why completed infinities can be reduced to nothing in existence.

Of course, many have rejected the reality of the continuum. This rejection started (as with many of the great errors in the history of metaphysics) with Aristotle. Aristotle famously rejected the idea that there is a continuum since this idea presupposes something that can be endlessly divided. In the sixth book of his *Physics*, Aristotle attempts to show that continuity cannot be reduced to anything discrete—whether points on a line or atoms. Aristotle thereby accepts the continuum only as a pure continuity that cannot be made up of indivisible points or smallest possible parts. For Aristotle, if we lined up a series of indivisible points succeeding one another, then they can only be continuous if all the membranes, as it were, of each point touches each other somehow. For continuity, there can be no intermediate space between these points. But if we propose that the continuum is made up of intervals or atoms, then we are precisely saying that there is something in between them. There is then no continuity to speak of. In this way, for Aristotle, all in its true being and reality is not made up of points. The line is continuous and any division of it is a retroactive illusion. Seeing it as made up of parts is to render its basic reality null.

Part of Aristotle's point here is to claim that even if one posited an infinity of indivisible atoms each touching the other, one would not be able to fill up the space or would be simply positing one large atom. In this way, for Aristotle the whole question of 'how many points are on the line?' is an absurd question in and of itself. For Aristotle, discrete elements can never come together to form a continuity. One cannot derive the continuous from the discrete. No true continuum thus can be made up of parts—especially not if those parts are treated as indivisible. There is a succession where there is nothing in between points and things. All is thus truly a flow. Time itself is not a series of intervals known as now's, but a duration or flow. Therefore, for Aristotle, the continuum is undivided in its very nature. To divide it is to miss what it is in itself and deal with an illusion of mind. One can only mentally divide things without limits. There are no indivisible atoms since one cannot divide up the continuum endlessly until one reaches points. One will never reach a smallest part because the continuum is not fundamentally made of parts. The problem is that anything with parts can be divided and anything without parts is itself indivisible. For Aristotle, then the issue of the continuum is that it shows that space or time can potentially be divided endlessly, but that this infinity is only a potential and not actual one. The continuum is divisible without end only in a virtual sense. The continuous must precede the discrete finally for Aristotle. But Aristotle also does not accept that the continuous can itself be the apeiron, the unlimited.

Since Aristotle argues that any infinity is potential in this way, he must also reject the apeiron as an actual infinity or unlimited. For Aristotle, the apeiron only ever exists potentially. In this way, Aristotle by positing the priority of the actual over the potential at the same time as positing the continuous over the discrete ends up with a finite and closed universe. It is a universe that must be closed in on itself like a circle and where all is caught up in the endless cycling of the spheres. But what is hidden in Aristotle's analysis is that the continuum cannot be a unity just as much as it cannot be the addition of unities whether one calls them points or atoms. The continuum necessarily presents one with the problem of the unlimited.

The Aristotelian error is repeated of course by Leibniz in reverse who said that the continuum is not a reality, not real thing, but only something that has an ideal nature. Wholes only exist ideally and precede their parts (presumably these wholes exist in the mind of God), but Leibniz did not see that even if wholes exist ideally, this idea itself will involve the unlimited as such. For Leibniz, what is real is finite and defined. Leibniz thought thus that all of the real is discrete and made up of defined parts. Any whole is then a composition of simpler parts and units. One only thinks there is some sort of continuum because one projects it on to the discrete. Thus, for Leibniz, what is real is the discrete and the continuous itself is ideal or potential. The real does not involve indeterminacy in any way for Leibniz. If one can divide something, then there is an actual division of things down to some indivisible point. This is why infinitesimals are ultimately able to be treated as nothing, as zero. The ideal itself is nothing. Leibniz would build his most developed metaphysics on the basis of indivisible elements—the monads. But he finally there needed the mind of God to think through each monad thoroughly and thus the continuum could not be truly built up from monads, but instead needed the infinite mind of God to complete all.

It is also clear that part of the problem here is that if Leibniz believes that real entities are built up from unities and at most multiplicities of unities, then there is some sort of mereological whole that can be posited. This is again why time must be seen as something as ideal rather than real for him since time can seemingly be endlessly divided. All the possibles exist in an ideal space, in the mind of God. The real and ideal thus mirror each other in reverse for Leibniz. Real things are wholes prior their parts, but in the ideal there are unlimited possibilities. Only the mind breaks up the ideal continuum into parts. At the same time, as has long been recognized, if there are indivisible parts, then there is no endless division. One would stop at the indivisible part, or atom, and thus end the issue. The discrete would then be the fundamental reality and the continuous itself would be made up of out of it or now an illusion of mind.

Many advocated this view because otherwise one seemed to advocate the contradictory idea that any finite extension has within itself an infinity of parts. However, clearly we can conceive of such an infinite division a la Zeno. Part of the issue here is whether or not reality contains essentially some sort of break, discontinuity? But clearly we can conceive of the world in such a way as it appears to be either discrete or finitely divisible. The problem with seeing reality as made up of irreducible wholes is that as we saw earlier one can only maintain that position if one at the same time says that there is an ultimate totality of those wholes making up a single and complete world as Aristotle and Leibniz did. If one admits actual infinites whether in the sense of an infinite regress of unities or a lack of a totality, then one has destroyed that model. In the Aristotelian model, infinite is only potential or only like the very eternity of the world which is again modeled on the circumference of a circle. Such a circumference is endless in the sense that there is no discernible endpoint. Thus, Aristotle said the world even though a totality is an eternal one. It was however despite this eternity not infinite in any actual sense.

The Aristotelian view takes continuity to be an irreducible idea. And a continuous whole only actually has at best finite division or perhaps none in its irreducibility. These wholes and thus space itself have a homogeneous character. This problem of the discrete and the continuum of course took on a new nature in 19th century mathematics with the work of Dedekind, Weierstrauss, and Cantor. In this way, on the basis of their work, there is hope that the relation between the discrete and the continuous can be engaged with anew also metaphysically. The problem of the continuum leads us to pure being in itself for the only true unlimited is the divine absolute, the non-all, God. To solve the tension of the discrete and the continuous one ultimately has to see the very problem as arising due to the fact that existence is itself a result of the contraction of the divine. There is then an infinitely small as well as absolute that meet at one point. All things are connected to the continuum in their essence and existence. While the absolute itself cannot be the result of the aggregation of discrete elements, it is fundamentally connected to the existence of a discrete world. That is, one can see the world as discrete precisely on the basis of the divine absolute itself being withdrawn from this world. Only then can one find infinities completed in the world.

The first point that should be made about the Cantorian engagement with the continuum is that it involves a pure arithmetization of the problem. We can after Cantor ask about the size of the continuum such as whether it can have a measurable size or not. As we will see later, Dedekind cuts offer us a strict way of understanding how the continuum itself can be made up of indivisible parts. The division itself thus stops at a discrete element of a special sort. The infinitely divisible itself will itself find its own limit. At the same time, the adventures of post-Cantorian will show that there is in many senses an actual infinity contained even in the finite.

Cantor tries to relate the set of points that would exit on any Euclidean line with a number domain in order to define the size of the continuum and thus resolve the continuum problem. This means one has to ask about the size of the number of points one can image being contained on a line (say the space on the number line between 0 and 1). Cantor begins here by assuming that one can put that set of points into one-to-one correspondence with aleph-null. That means one has to list all real numbers between 0 and 1 and match them up with the set of positive integers. However, in attempting to do so, one can show using the diagonal method (taking a number from each succeeding decimal form each succeeding real number) and construct a new non-algebraic real that would not be included in the list. This showed that size of the continuum was somehow greater than aleph-null. The continuum problem thus comes with a questions of how much greater it is insofar as that greatness can be determined.

Cantor wanted to identify aleph-one with the power set of aleph-null. That is, there is a progression from one transfinite cardinal to another via the power set axiom. Just as the power set of a set of elements is eight (two cubed) so the power set of aleph-null would be two to the power of aleph –null. The Cantorian formulation of the continuum is then that between aleph–null and aleph-one there are no infinities and that the transfinite of the next size greater than aleph-null is aleph-one. Aleph-one thus has an easily defined size. In Badiou's terms, the excess of the power set over the original set is here confined and measured. It does not cause disorder or unruliness, but rather can be configured as a new well-ordered progression in the same way as was achieved via the inclusion of the empty set amongst finite ordinals.

Part of the issue then is what the true meaning of the power set operation is and whether or not it upsets any possibility of order in the transfinite realm. It is already known that a transfinite set is by definition not necessarily greater than one of its proper subsets. For example, the set of positive integers is the same size as one of its proper subsets (the set of all even numbers for example). But with the transition from aleph-null to aleph-one, one is presented with the idea that the set of all the subsets is greater than the original set. For Cantor to be wrong the size differential will need to be such that one could posit infinities between aleph-null and aleph-one. It is also ultimately a question of whether aleph-one can be ordered as well as aleph-null which for instance is simply the well-ordered set of positive integers (that is, a set with a clear first element and algorithm for producing all succeeding elements).

Cantor's view is of course known as the 'continuum hypothesis' since he argued that all transfinite cardinals are arrangeable into a clear, continuous hierarchy. Also, if Cantor is wrong, there are then essentially differed orders of infinity--perhaps infinite orders of transfinite sets as well as transfinite sets that do not know from order itself. With finite ordinals, it is clear there is a set of some size between a set and its power set. Between the set of three elements and its power set, there are four such sets. Cantor is here essentially deciding that the power set axiom itself functions to determine the order of sets. But it is not clear why that should be the case. Why would there not be a set between aleph-null and its power set if it is so with finite sets? Cantor has already admitted that transfinite sets are different than finite sets. For Galileo, for instance, the very paradox that part of an infinite set can be the same size as the infinite set itself, per our above example, was a clear reason for rejecting the very concept of an infinite set. A finite set can be equal to a subset of itself but only the subset that is itself—not a proper subset. The violation of the part-whole distinction (that all parts are smaller than their whole) was reason enough for rejecting what Cantor simply accepts as a non-paradox or part and parcel of the transfinite. In fact, in some ways the difference between Galileo and Cantor is simply the acceptance of this violation of the typical part-whole relation. It seems that with Cantor having accepted the actual infinite, he wanted to constrain the transfinite in some way in order to make it appear as though it were not purely contradictory or chaotic.

At the same time, Cantor's claim here is that the set of all real numbers including the non-algebraic reals has a certain and clear cardinality and thus size. However, such non-algebraic reals are not only infinite, but also irreducibly complex. That is, while a real like pi is infinite, there is a clear rule for generating its string of numbered decimals places. However, the set of all reals includes numbers with perfectly infinite and random decimals strings. It was this fact that enabled the diagonal proof in the first place. If one had a list of finite ordinals and listed them, even if one diagonalized one would only reach a number already on the list precisely because of the finitude of these ordinals. But all non-algebraic reals are infinite. Also the non-random reals like pi are but an infinitely small fraction of the total set of all possible reals. It seems that while Cantor exploited the infinity of such reals for his diagonal proof, his continuum hypothesis is based on a discounting of the random nature of non-algebraic reals having any fundamental effects.

Also the problem that looms here is the measurability of the continuum itself. When we speak of the continuum as being for instance the real line between 0 and 1, we immediately take it to be something that has a finite quality to it. But the continuum as we saw with Zeno, Aristotle, and Leibniz always touches on the very reality and nature of the unlimited itself. The unlimited of course cannot be given a determinate size. The irreducibility and unavoidability of the question of the continuum in the sense of the apeiron cannot be removed even by way of the Cantorian arithmetization of the issue. If the true continuum itself is the absolute, then Cantor's view will not work. However, at the same time, it seems odd to identify the absolute with a line like that of the line in ideal Euclidean space between 0 and 1.

Recall already that Cantor himself called aleph-one an uncountable transfinite. Since the diagonalization method showed that aleph-one is necessarily greater than aleph-null, it is in itself innumerable. But it can be that multiple innumerables are all ultimately identifiable in the same way that there can only be one void. At the same time, all sets included the empty set, and the empty set can be written as any set in particular. It thus is always open to its own dissemination. The same may be true of the absolute. While there is only one absolute, it is dispersed through all sets. This view would only reinforce the idea that the absolute is contracted and withdrawn. The diagonal proof opens up our recognition of the uncountable as such. The set of all real numbers is not countable. However, the set of reals is also identifiable with the continuum in the sense of the real number line.

This problem is here deepened by the additional proof that all segments of the real line have the same size. That is, the segment between 0 and 1 has the same size as the entire continuum itself for example. This is less than an amazing result despite the fact that there are an uncountable number of transcendental numbers (non-algebraic reals). It is not surprising given the considerations above about the indescribability of immeasurables. If the line between 0 and 1 is itself uncountable, then it is immeasurable, and it makes intuitive sense that one cannot distinguish the size of one immeasurable from another. One can of course perform the power set operation on aleph-one to produce aleph-two, but it is not clear what aleph-two corresponds to other than a new name, the name of a name.

Cantor's diagonal method assumed at first that the set of reals is countable in order to show that by diagonalization one can produce a new number not on the list and thereby show it is uncountable. But the diagonal proof itself assumes that the set of all real numbers can be written even in such a sequence where one lists each real number only once and in order. If it is uncountable, then why should that be the case? Cantor never imagined that the uncountable might mean inconsistency since only the absolute infinite itself was inconsistent for him. Might we have to identify the absolute itself with the set of all reals as a consequence of divine contraction? If all segments of the real line have the same cardinality, then any finite extension has the immeasurable hiding inside of it. That is, just as the empty set is included in all sets, in all sets the divine itself is hiding in wait contracted. Within any number there is a continuum that cannot be specified by any number. Within each name, there is the unnamable. The problem of the absolute here would reassert itself. Not only would God be involved in all relations to complete them as infinite, but all sets would become mirrors of the divine itself a la Leibniz.

If the power of the continuum involves the uncountable and the immeasurable, then it must in some profound way be related to God. It may not be fully identical with God as He is in Himself, but clearly it overlaps in some sense with the God of divine contraction. God is purely beyond number, but makes possible all numbers. God is also beyond the world, but the nature of the continuum will allow Him a way to involve himself with it at all occasion and cause the creation and movement of all things. God is certainly immeasurable and uncountable, but by the very power of the continuum He is involved in all things of all sizes.

Part of the issue here is that each real is a gap in the continuum itself (per Dedekind). The uncountable set of all reals is thus a set of gaps, of discontinuities. These non-algebraic reals are only conceivable as gaps. They are incomprehensible for us insofar as we cannot know all of them or how their decimal string plays out into infinity. Even if we exist for all time, we would never be able to calculate them. These gaps would seem to spell anarchy and disorder, but at the same time the very ability to isolate a gap and name it might itself form order out of chaos.

Badiou takes these question here to involve the issue of whether to not there is a "numerosity" of being qua being (*BE* 265). But this is to restrict the question too much. It is not a question of whether or not all that can be thought can be expressed as having some sort of size. It is the question of whether or not God is reducible to the world or not, to being qua being, and what the effect of God, the absolute infinite, being unquantifiable has not only on being qua being (essence/the thinkable), but also on existence itself. For existence appears to be completely finite and countable. How can something finite, like a finite line in space, always be referred to the absolute and connected to it? In this way, while people often think that Cantor's view of the continuum hypothesis is about measuring numerically and thus unfurling an ordered world, it is a way to truly approach the divine in and of itself for the divine itself requires us to allow for the immeasurable to play an active role at all levels. Otherwise, we restrict our understanding of both the creativity and power of the divine. What would an all-powerful and omnipresent God be if there is numerically measured world without the direct involvement of the unlimited?

It is here that we see how Cantor was still too Aristotelian and still too classically theological. He felt that the radical transcendence of the divine meant it played no role in even the smallest of things. To the refer to the smallest of things means not only to refer to the void, nothingness, and the empty set, but also to infinitesimals. Part of the question of infinitesimals is what is the first one after 0 between 0 and 1 for example? Such a number would be a decimal point with an infinity of 0's with a one at the end intuition tells us except there can be no end to an infinite sequences. We thus model this number on .01 or .00001 but this model fails given the infinity involved. As we see then the question of the smallest is perhaps already a question of the immeasurable and indefinable as such. One cannot get past zero it seems to get to the smallest.

Aleph-null is of course intuitively the smallest possible transfinite given that it is by definition the first ordinal greater than all finite ordinals. But this intuition does not work in reverse when it comes to the smallest, the infinitesimal. It was partly for his reason that Cauchy and Weierstrauss rejected the infinitely small in the previous sense of the term and employed the idea of the limit as a new way to engage with it. Infinitesimals thus become a number as it infinitely approaches zero. We then have an image of an infinite progression to the absolute itself. The absolute is thus situated at both ends of the continuum. In this way, with the notion of the limit, we have the idea of a well-ordered continuum going towards zero which is intuitively the 'starting point' of it all. But in exchange, we may get on the other the hand with infinitely great a new disorder. That is, it might not be the case that the power set axiom can function as well as the notion of limits did at the other end of the scale.

As Hersh and Davis note, infinitesimals violate the Archimedean property by which one can add a number to itself and it will grow in size until it reaches some "arbitrary" size if we add itself to itself "enough times".29 An infinitesimal even if we added it to itself an infinite number of times would remain less than one. The infinitesimal thus cannot grow in the way other numbers can. Even if one keeps adding it to itself, it remains infinitesimal. This shows us the infinitely small is not truly measurable. Or, perhaps better, it shows us that the infinitesimal is at the limit between the limit and the unlimited. It is that limit. It is therefore the point at which the unlimited allows it to contract into the unlimited.

The intuitionists (Brouwer, Heyting, etc.) always believed that the very concept of the continuum was a pure chasm beyond number itself and that no mathematics could ever fully count or account for it. The continuum thus on an intuitionist reading is the apeiron and cannot be filled with individual points or units. They are partly right. But at the same time Dedekind with his cuts is also right. A is not not-A here again as with Lacan on the graphs of sexuation. But to see how that is the case we need to follow the paths of Gödel and P. J. Cohen and show how the continuum hypothesis is ultimately undecidable and how that undecidability confirms what we have said so far as well as opening new avenues for approaching the divine.

§8. *The Axiom of Choice*

The combined work of Gödel and Cohen shows both that it is consistent with the basic axioms of set theory (that is, no contradiction is implied) both to deny Cantor's continuum hypothesis as well as affirm it. What is often not noted is that this affirmation or denial of the continuum hypothesis is coupled with the same affirmation and denial of the axiom of choice. That is, the fate of the continuum hypothesis is directly tied to the fate of this axiom. Any theory that includes acceptance of the continuum hypothesis must also include the axiom of choice since it is only by application of the axiom choice that one can show the desired implication—that every transfinite set has an aleph numbered cardinality and is identifiable by its number with its place in the ordinal progression of the transfinite (aleph–null first, aleph-one second, etc.).

It is also not here simply a choice of whether one accepts or not the axiom of choice, but that it is strictly undecidable whether or not the axiom of choice holds. It can neither be disproven nor proven as holding necessarily to determine what is thinkable (the same goes for the continuum hypothesis). In this way, one has a specific example of an undecidable statement. Whereas Gödel in his early work on 'incompleteness' showed that it was possible to construct undecidable statements (without specifying which—that is, only the possibility was shown) within pure mathematics with the axiom of choice and continuum hypothesis one has a specific and actual example of an undividable ('this statement cannot be proven').

The axiom of choice in most of its formulations expresses the idea that one can form any given collection of non-empty sets a new set composed from selecting exactly one member from each non-empty set in the initial collection. The name 'choice' thus has to do with this act of choosing one member from each set and placing that member in the new set. The question of the axiom of choice is not only about what is involved in the act of choosing itself, but whether or not it is possible to make an infinity of choices. This is especially problematic if no rule is laid out for how to make choices or what particular elements to choose (that is, if one chooses blindly).

With finite sets, the axiom seems obvious and intuitive. If one has a set of three different colored balls, one can then easily list the eight subsets of that original set, its power set. One could then without problem select one ball from each subset and place it in a new collection. All of this can easily imagined and done. Complications arise when one tries to apply the axiom of choice to transfinite sets. The axiom of choice is not universally accepted since it claims one can define a set based on an infinite number of determinate choices to form a new set from a collection of sets. Intuitionists and constructivists do not see how it is possible to ensure such an infinite number of choices. Of course, despite these protests, the axiom of choice at the same time seems necessary in order to produce various required results that are acceptable in mathematics (and cannot be seemingly derived in another way).

Another way to express what is at stake with the axiom of choice is to say that one can always demonstrate that there is a recursive process by which a set can be constructed. With the set of positive integers, this recursive procedure is obvious— one iterates the operation of including the empty set. If a set can yield to such a recursive procedure, then it is obvious how all sets are well-ordered. The idea of an infinite number of specified choices requires also the idea that all sets are well-ordered. Well-ordering says for instance that any set has a least element. It says that any set that has binding principle, has a lowest bound as it were. Constructivists and intuitionists would seemingly allow the axiom of choice if one allows for a clear algorithm for determining the order and members of a set. One may not be able to count into the millions for instance, but once one has the algorithm for the set of positive integers it is easy to determine what number comes after 188,282,888. One can thus designate the element here especially even if there is an infinity of elements.

If every set can be well-ordered, then the algorithm for each set can be discovered. Even if one were to make an arbitrary number of infinite choices, the set one produces would also yield to this principle per the axiom of choice. That is, the axiom of choice is stating one can make finite choices on a finite set randomly or per a rule and produce a well-ordered set (this is clearly demonstrable and taken as intuitive), that one can make an infinite number of choices to produce set using a defined rule/algorithm, and finally one can make infinitely many choices without using any rule and also yield a well-ordered set. The idea here seems to hinge on all sets having the quality of being countable one by one. As Bertrand Russell famously said, it is obvious that if one has an infinite set of pair of shoes (non-empty sets) how to choose all the left shoes in each couple and form an infinite set of left shoes. But if one has an equivalent pair of socks, it is less clear as there are no left or right socks. At the same time, clearly one can choose just one just one sock from each pairing. That is, the axiom of choice asserts there is a choice of set of socks.

Ultimately, however when it comes to the continuum hypothesis, the question will hinge on wither the set of all real numbers including non-algebraic rules can be shown to be well-ordered. Cohen and Gödel, again to anticipate the results, showed that the axiom of choice is independent of the standard list of set theoretic axioms (it can be added or left out without contradiction). Of course, we as finite minds would only ever see a finite part of any set. We only for instance can ever list a finite part of the set of positive integers or the decimal expansion of pi. A choice sequence involves taking that initial segment and explaining what rule would elaborate the rest of the series. The rule itself is only in many cases given in part. One thus has also a free choice here for how to construct the rule as it were. If one is involved in an infinity of choices, then there is some sort of indeterminacy in what the next elements will be. One can thus specify the choice function in such a way that one chooses the actual element that satisfies the rule. Given the infinity, a large number of possibilities will fit the rule and thus there is some free play as to what will come next. One can thus in principle make a choice at each step of the process given the boundaries set by the algorithm. As long as one chooses an element that satisfies the rule, it is up to one to say what element that should be. The subject thus decides him/herself what should be there. It is a restricted, but free choice.

This is of course a highly intuitionist view of the issue following Brouwer. A realist would see the set of elements as fixed by pre-existing domain and not as a matter of choice. But since I as finite cannot see a transfinite domain of elements, I have the freedom to compute within limits what will come next. Since I have limited free choice, I can thus compose different sets using the same rule. The axiom of choice thus opens up the possibility of constructivist and intuitionist elements to enter into pure axiomatic extensional set theory. From this perspective, the continuum is all possible choice sequences including ones consisting of choices I have not made and cannot be aware of having made. In other words, the continuum is always itself incomplete and awaiting me to complete it with my free choices. The continuum does not pre-exist as a domain, but is made out of choices. The continuum is thus unsettled and awaiting free acts.

However this rendering of the axiom of choice in intuitionist and constructivist terms offers it perhaps more freedom than is typical. For the continuum hypothesis as Cantor sees it to hold, the continuum cannot be some indeterminate and open entity made up only of choices. The freedom involved in the axiom of choice needs to be restricted. It says that the sets have a rule and that rule is more deterministic concerning what elements can come next. As we will see, Gödel's notion of constructability does not fit with the freedom of intuitionism and constructivism as previously laid out. The acceptance of the axiom of choice in this sense will involve restricting the power of axiom of choice from having the power itself to make up the continuum. The continuum will itself be shown to resist it. This already hinted in the idea of linear order and having a least element.

Part of the issue here is that if one makes seemingly random choices, then it is not at all clear that list of choices can be expressed by a clear rule. That set might be irreducibly complex as are non-algebraic reals. But is such a set well-ordered? The issue in part would then be if this set has ordinality. That is, can one say that such a complex set comes before one and after another set? At the same time here, because one speaks of an infinity of choices and we are finite, one has to take it on faith as it were that the choice function truly exists for selecting infinitely many times from sets one element. In particular, if the issue is choosing one element form a set of sets of real numbers, then each set is itself infinite and thus it is not clear how one can choose just one element or have a rule for doing so (if all are well-ordered then one could choose the least element, but it is not clear how any other elements could be chosen suing a function).

However, aleph-one was shown to be uncountable. The axiom of choice thus contends that it can bring real order to such uncountable sets. Part of the problem here is that the choice function might itself need to be infinite in nature to make the choice clear. The real line has a lower bound seemingly always at zero. It also seems that between 0 and 1 1 functions somehow as an upper bound. But even if that is the case, as noted already, it is not clear how one determines the first real after 0. Let's be clear that a non-well-ordered set has no first element. Such a set would have no clear beginning in other words. Of course, the absolute infinite does not have such order, but if a set such as aleph-one has such a feature then it would appear to somehow be identical to the absolute infinite.

If a set has a least element, then it has some sort of successor to that first least element. Another way of expressing well-ordering is to say that all sets are well-founded. Any set that is founded on the empty set is ultimately well-founded. Anything and everything is an upper bound for the empty set. Any set with the empty set with that formation can be seen to have all its elements built up from it. One can thus use the axioms of set theory to elaborate on this empty set. It need not be simply the rule producing the positive integers. In any case, within set theory there is a way of saying one element precedes or succeeds the next and why. The elements here are distinct and thus can be distinguished as following in a series. This series itself followed from its least element since the least must have an immediate successor per the axiom. The empty set is the ultimate least element since nothing is smaller than nothing. Whether or not the series goes on indefinitely is not the issue here it would appear as the order can obtain even if there is no greatest element. Finite sets have of course a least element as they are bounded.

One of the reasons the axiom of choice is an unavoidable possible truth of thought is because there is always the empty set to function as an origin. Any set is marked by the empty set and includes it. This is a remarkably finite origin despite the thinkable nature of the transfinite. The empty set is always there to prevent infinite regresses within thought itself or to show how any regress begins from some point. Every set thus has a founding element even if that element is simply the empty set. This element might be included in the set, but is not a member of it. It succeeds and can be distinguished from it. It is ultimately thinkable only as letter and exists as such.

All of the above considerations then have to be applied to the issues of the power set in order to show how the continuum hypothesis holds via the axiom of choice. The issue of course is, as Badiou would put it, whether or not the excess of the power set over its extensional, original set can be constricted and confined by the principles of well-ordering found in the axiom of choice. The axiom of choice assures that the power set even of aleph-null does not exceeded by more than a certain measure. While aleph-one is then uncountable, it is, as it were, countably uncountable. When we take the power set of a set, we obviously with finite sets do not find anything new in the set. We only find the given elements arranged into distinct subsets beyond perhaps the empty set itself. The axiom of choice would thus show us that while the power set of aleph-null might be larger, it also does not include anything more than is already in the original set except a larger way of re-arranging those elements (and the empty set). If that is the case, then the number of ways to arrange the countable infinite is countable as it were as larger.

The axiom of choices introduces ordinality back into set theory in a way no other axiom does (and only perhaps the axioms of the empty set and infinity relate directly to ordinality whereas the rest speak to cardinal relations). The axiom of choice says that the subsets of a set are arrangeable in a way such that one can speak of which element comes first, second, third. That means one can now differentiate sets based on the ordering. The axiom of choice thus introduces in as much as it is possible principles of intensional sets and ordering into extensional set theory. If one can say what elements come first, second, third, etc. then one can determine more precisely how many subsets there are. For example, if one has the set [o, d, g] from an extensional perspective the set [g, o, d] and the set [d, o, g] are the same since extensionally they have the same elements. But from the perspective of ordering and determining what is first, second, third, etc. one can see now a difference in the sets. If one takes into account ordering, then one has a new of seeing the power set of axiom. This axiom as purely extension did not look at differences in order. But now with axiom of choice, we can say that there is something new introduced in the re-arrangement of elements.

Also, we can say that the empty set is no longer a true subset for the axiom of choice. If we take the set [o,d,g] as a set with three elements it has 14 subsets when the ordering is important. This calculation is of course based on the following formulate of course: $N!/(N-R)!$ where N equals the number of elements and R equals the number of elements being selected. For example, if we want to know how many re-ordered subsets of a particular set are possible we take the number of elements as N. In our example of [o,d.g], n=3. To know how many sets of 3 elements are possible then we take $3!/(3-3)!$. We thereby have 6 as a result. The factorial of 0 and 1 are of course importantly the same as both equal 1. We can do the same calculation for how many sets of 2 elements we can get from [o,d,g] and get again 6 and then how many sets of 1 element (2). Thus the total is 14. I know how many set of no elements here would count as nothing. That is, I do not ask how many sets without elements are possible even thought it could be calculated as 1. I do not ask because I am interested because the issue is how many elements can be selected and how many are actually selected. If one had aleph-null elements, this is like saying there are $\omega!/(\omega - \omega-1)!$ plus, etc. But the result of such a computation is ω and nothing greater. Even if I were to count here the empty set, it would not add anything significant or change the countable infinity of subsets. The result is that one is always left with a countable set of subsets.

The power set axiom counted the empty set as a subset. That is, it counts the empty set not as a set but rather a pure proper name since the empty set counted as a set is indistinguishable from the set for one. It was thereby counting it as pure proper name that made it excessive over the original set. But when the empty set is no longer counted as a name or counted as nothing different than 1 itself, then the size of the re-arrangement of sets is limited. This is why 0 and 1 being indistinguishable from the perspective of factorialization is significant. Why is the value of 0! 1? This is itself a convention known as the 'empty product' or 'nullary product.' The empty product occurs when one literally multiplies nothing. Thereby, the issue is that when we deal with combinations and permutations being significant nothing is itself implied as nothing. It is not a pure name but simply a nullity. It is nullity rather than the name of nullity. This is why 0 and 1 are the same since 1 is itself the name of nullity, the counting of nullity in extensional terms. 0 is here indistinguishable from the implication of identity itself, 1. For this reason, the factorial of 0 is like the empty sum where one adds a number to zero and simply receives the number itself back again (3 plus 0 is 3). The empty product make the same difference as the empty sum—no difference. It is equivalent to identity itself. In so many words, extensional sets distinguish between 0 and 1 while here 0 is 1. Mathematics itself at its basis is about whether or not one can distinguish between 0 and 1.

Let us also note here that 0 counting as 1 is necessary for all recursive procedures and definitions. 0 has no numbers in its when one looks at its factorialization. Thus, the product of this lack is itself one. But ultimately mathematics saw that to have results consistent (to have the principle of commutativity hold) with what they do when they take recursive definitions they need the empty product to be zero. Since the axiom of choice is about recursive procedures it is not surprising that the empty product in this fashion plays a role. In other words here, lack can only count as one and not as pure lack.

Ordinality here restricts how large the number of re-arrangeable sets can be. This idea seems intuitive since the power set axiom could never re-arrange things such as to bring out something hidden in the original set other than the empty set itself. If the empty set counts for nothing, then one sees that the only thing that makes the power set larger than the original set is the empty set itself. In this way, aleph-one is only larger than aleph-null via inclusion of the empty set just like a finite ordinal. And thus, the only thing that increases with aleph-null to aleph-one is the revelation of the empty set being included in the set. If all that is included that was not already included is the power set, then each transfinite has an aleph cardinality in a neat progression just as the finite ordinals do.

Here (with the axiom of the power set)rather than including the empty set to perform the progression, the empty set is exposed as included and counted to show the progression. If the empty set were not included, then the power set would be never be larger than ω. No new subsets are thus hiding in the original set even if an infinite one beyond the power set. Otherwise, if one re-arranges elements given ordinal considerations, one has only ever ω. This is why there is no transfinite set between aleph-null and aleph-one. Ironically, a set that with finite sets is larger than the power set is smaller with transfinite sets. For example, the number of sets with ordinal considerations and ordering conditions of a set of three elements is 14 whereas the extensional power set of a set with 3 elements has only 8. But with transfinite sets this size difference is reversed. The set of ordered sets is only ever ω because the empty set is not counted whereas the power set is larger due to the exposed inclusion of the empty set.

The axiom of choice allows one to construct sets, but one does so using a recursive procedure for example. Such a procedure makes ordering of the elements of set in a series significant. Constructive infinite sets are only ones that exhibit something like ω. Choice is limited to well-defined recursive procedures that determine the series of elements. Each possible set and subset has a choice function that expresses the law of the set and restricts freedom. It is a determinist view. One only finds what was already contained in a set in re-arranged patterns. For freedom lack, the subjective agent, must be involved or God himself. That is, in a text generated by a human, the subject is the lack, but in the text that is the world itself, God is the lack at work, the absent cause. The patterns here themselves function per a law. One does not have the freedom to introduce things into an open and unsettled continuum or to extend the scope of the power set by finding within a transfinite set things included beyond the empty set that one never expected and do not consist simply of a re-ordering of the existing elements. That is, one never finds included something that is not simply a set of existing elements.

The axiom of choice thus restricts the gap between set and power set. This introduces as it were some of the aspects of intensional set theory back into the mix. Intensional set theories tried to define sets based on a rule for what could and could not be included in a set. The axiom of choice simply makes it such that what is included can only be a subset consisting of already existing elements. Nothing new can thus be included (outside the empty set). The set of all round things would thus in intensional form pick out from all that is all the round things and include them. But the same end is met with the axiom of choice as it were indirectly. There is a restriction on how the members can be re-ordered and turned into sets and thus there is a restriction on what can truly be included in a set. There is thereby an intensional definition of a set that appears retroactively. What can be said to be included is only re-arrangement of elements.

Intensionally the set of all round things included all things matching that property rather than (as with an extensional set) this set being simply whatever is in the set. The extensional nature of the set seemed to make it completely open. Anything put into the set was in the set. If one collected together six things and called them round things, then that was the set regardless of what properties those six things had. With the axiom of choice, one has now restricted the set itself to those members and thus closed off further belonging. Intensional sets closed off further belonging using a property while the axiom of choice does so by restricting what can be found in the subsets.

Subsets of course state what is included in a set without belonging as an element. The set of all even numbers is included in the set of positive integers, but is not a member of the set as only individual positive integers can be members. Let's be clear. With the axiom of choice, the power set of all things that are blue is not going to include any green things even if there is a transfinite number of blue things. If sets are numbers (they have cardinality and ordinality), then they are either restricted in terms of their meaning. The power set will not be immeasurable. It will be completely restricted as to what can be exposed in it. The axiom of choice on this reading is what constrains the unrestricted construction of sets with arbitrary properties and arbitrary members. We may now form a set of all objects with some given quality and then restrict what is included in that set. Even if a set is simply named and has any members, it is now restricted in terms of what can be deduced from it as being included

The theory of extensional sets was adopted to prevent Russell's paradox. The set of all red things is not itself a red thing. It is only a collecting. One here distinguishes between the frame and the things inside the frame. But that does not mean one cannot still speak of for instance a set of all round things. It just says that that set comes to aggregate that multiplicity. With extensional sets we can make up whatever set we want now, but we are now restricted from another direction by the axiom of choice. The key issue is membership and inclusion rather than fitting a property per se. What we see here is that ordinality can affect cardinality, but that cardinality does not determine or affect ordinality. When ordinal difference is introduced the number of subsets changes, but cardinality only sees sets of the same size that can be put into one-to-one correspondence ('dog' and 'god' are the same for cardinality). The axiom of choice demonstrates this power of ordinality versus cardinality profoundly. In doing so it ensures the continuum hypothesis by making the empty set reasserts itself as the only difference in sets of increasing size.

These sets of increasing size are also precisely the large cardinals discussed earlier. With the excess of the power set literally identified with the empty set (with nothing), the axiom of choice shows how the continuum hypothesis works in a world where the absolute infinite is not found except in extreme transcendence without any immanence. God here does not seem to have a way to intervene in the world or to create. Now, of course many will say we have not adhered to Gödel's actual text in this presentation. We have not spoken of constructible sets, the formula V=L, etc. But this presentation captures the key ideas, and we can see this in a brief reflection on Gödel's work. Gödel's' work on the continuum hypothesis essentially says any set must be constructible in precisely the sense of the axiom of choice, where it can be defined by a recursive procedure. It also states that sets should be defined in terms of properties. Thus, a constructible set is a set like the set of all round things. In the model Gödel constructed to show the continuum hypothesis holds, each set obeys a rule and only the bare minimum of the axioms of set theory are used. Gödel defines sets only in terms of other sets that obey this principle. This means again that there is a limit on what can be said to be included in a set even when the power set axiom is operated on it. Thus, Gödel's method more strongly re-introduces intensional elements back into set theory. Sets have a rule, a predicative function, that makes it clear why a member belongs to it here. To say sets are built up out of preceding steps is another way of stating this recursive model.

The model here of Gödel's (expressed by the formula V=L) is a countable model in the sense of the countable infinite versus the uncountable infinite. The uncountable here is not taken to have inconsistent properties because of the well-ordering principle found in the predicative and constructible nature of sets. Gödel's model makes use minimally of the basic framework of Zermelo-Fraenkel and adds to it the axiom of choice. But rather than truly expanding this theory, the addition of this axiom confines this theory to the order of the continuum hypothesis. The original set defines the nature of the members belong it of (round things, blue things, positive integers, etc.). This restricts again what subsets can appear even as what is included is spelled out in the subsets via the power set axiom. The limiting definition of the original set does not yield anything more than what was already packed in from the beginning. The deck is not only stacked; it is perfectly arranged. There are no cards up anybody's sleeve and none will appear out of nowhere.

Meillassoux of course writes from the perspective of the failure of the continuum hypothesis. Meillassoux thinks there is only hyper-chaos which means order can arise or not. But this actually should be seen as a perspective that takes undecidability seriously. Due to undecidability, one cannot rule out order as much as a lack of it.

§9. Forcing and the Failure of CH

Paul J. Cohen's establishment of the consistency of the negation of the continuum hypothesis and axiom of choice with the basic axioms of set theory also involves the role of the power set axiom and its relation to the original set centrally. As Raymond M. Smullyan and Melvin Fitting comment, the "power set operation turns out to be one of the least understood operations of set theory".30 Cohen shows that the power set axiom exceeds the original set in an immeasurable way such that the continuum can be 'forced' to have any value "at least aleph-3 or aleph-100, or as big as we want".31 The negation of the power set will thus not only lead to the conceivability of the continuum being as big as the non-all itself, but also that one can interpose transfinite cardinality between an original set of aleph-null cardinality and its power set.

From within the model where the continuum hypothesis held, we forget how this very consistent model leaves one thing radically distinct—the absolute infinite itself. All the transfinite cardinals running down the line from one to the next will never in themselves be able to reach the absolute infinite. This universe is thereby fundamentally incomplete and yet related to the radical transcendence of the divine. At the same time, anything short of the divine was said to be supremely computable, that is, it was orderable by the axiom of choice. But, just as Turing did, we can construct an incomputable sequence that is short of the continuum itself in some way. By naming this incomputable sequence, we can note how the continuum hypothesis fails since there will be a name for that which is missing that is itself less than the name of the absolute in some way. There is thus in our estimation a very deep affinity between the work of Turing on the incomputable (and after him Gregory Chaitin) and that of Cohen even though I know of no such dialogue or discussion of it.

Just like Turing, Cohen constructs what he calls a generic subset by using the diagonalization method across all the computable reals. All reals are considered computable by the model upholding the continuum hypothesis by way of the axiom of choice and well-ordering theorem. By producing this incomputable real, what Cohen calls a generic subset, one expands the original model as it is now added to it. We have thus with the notion of the generic subset, the incomputable set (the non-well-ordered), expanding the model. This expansion itself is made possible due to the absolute infinite lurking beyond the horizon. But the generic subset despite its lack of order is not the same as the non-all. That is, it is indiscernible from it and yet named as different. The generic subset is indiscernible from all the computable reals. That is because it contains all the possible information that could be contained in those computable reals. This is similar to the familiar saying that a number like pi contains all possible information.

But this generic subset can be constructed also simply from the list of all possible subsets of a transfinite set. There is thus a difference in size between the size of the generic subset and the power set. The generic subset is both larger than the original transfinite set and smaller than the power set. One way to see this at work is to render any numbers as zeros and ones in binary. One then moves diagonally across these strings of zeros and ones. One also needs to remember here that in the power set of any transfinite set are infinites just as the set of positive integers includes the transfinite set of all odds, evens, etc. The generic set here generated here is as it were only one non-algebraic real and thus cannot be seemingly the continuum itself. The creation of the generic set then creates a new name when it seemed all the names had been exhausted. The whole universe seemed to be exhausted and yet it is now expanded.

This is why Cohen's' method is often explained as moving from one model to another, of moving from one dimension to another, where we can look down at the previous model. But of course within the context of the absolute infinite, there is always a new dimension to jump to. The entire model that upholds the continuum hypothesis appears countable insofar as it poses the transfinite cardinals as being in a measurable procession. But one could as well perform a diagonalization across those transfinite cardinals. But the generic set is not outside. Since it is formed via diagonalization, it is somehow within the set even though it was not included. The generic subset therefore forces one to admit that there was more included than previously imagined or allowed.

The generic set also can be seen as being produced via a random collecting of an element from each subset. The axiom of choice would of course see such a product as already included in the list. But with the denial of the axiom of choice the new random aggregation has no recursive procedure for making it up and is irreducibly and infinitely complex. The set thereby includes more than is already in it other than the empty set itself. It includes the incomputable. The model that affirmed the axiom of choice and the continuum hypothesis argued that all can be ordered. But here the non-ordered has been found hiding within the ordered itself. A new supernumerary name was produced when it was believed that all the names were defined and all rules noted. After all, each set was named (the set of round things, blue things, etc.).

The generic set by being in principle random in its construction takes a little bit of something from all proper subsets. In this way, the generic subset is anonymous because it has no differing rule or algorithm to determine it. It thus introduces the problem of the nameless itself. One can think here of course of Chaitin's constant. The Chaitin set would only have an algorithm that is infinitely long. It would take us forever and a day to list it. And we would need to list each element point by point. This means we cannot say clearly what it is. It is indiscernible for us. It may as well be the eternal set of all things except it does have elements that can be read off one by one and thus on the face of things includes an infinity of elements not thereby listed or listed in a different order.

The generic subset shows that there are always more sequences of zeros and ones to be found in a constructible model or in any transfinite set (the two overlap in most ways). The generic set is an unnamable set somehow less than the continuum. But there are uncountably many such incomputables that could be had. Chaitin's constant is for instance only one example (the only one we know of where we can speak of it with some specificity and with reference to a distinct issue—Turing's halting problem itself). The generic set exceeds all the sets it was constructed out of. It takes a little bit form each one, but it has such complexity that no rule or predicate could ever clearly define it or say how it was constructed. It can only be counted by going through it element by element. No rule will reduce it.

Badiou speaks of this set as being subtracted from the universe. It is as if by its excess something was removed from the world of the computable. It is an unnamable and thus taken out of the rule of named tings. It is not a predicative set like that of round things as it is not clear what it is in it or if it can be named other than as unnamable. It has no clear identity or order. It is directly due to the generic set having these properties that makes it so one cannot say it is in one-to-one correspondence with a countable transfinite set and thus has a different cardinality. Of course, Cantor used diagonalization to prove that aleph-one was larger than aleph-null. But he wanted to identify the power set with aleph-one. He also did not look at diagonalization over the power set itself, but rather over the set of reals and that set was not considered by him as being in part or as a whole included in aleph-null. Cantor also wanted to determine a clear measure of the continuum. But if the continuum is connected essentially with absolute then it cannot have such a clear measure. What Cantor's view really seemed to say was that the endless progression of transfinite cardinals (aleph-null, aleph-one, etc.) was somehow the continuum. But that is no more convincing than saying that finite ordinals somehow fill in the real number line.

The absolute infinite insofar as it is connected with the continuum means the continuum is going to be bigger than any aleph and thus (insofar as uncountable alephs are fundamentally indiscernible from the continuum in one sense) cannot be the same as any scale of any alephs above aleph-null. In the case we have been probing the continuum is simply the power set of aleph null. And thus the empty set that is there included is itself the key again. Here it is as the name of the absolute that which makes the power set immeasurably larger than the original set and in between one has the generic subset. In other words, we simply cannot say what the cardinality of the power set is and thus it could be any range of alephs above aleph null and the generic set. This is for us further proof of one of our leading formulas: $\Omega = \emptyset$. Cohen has shown us with the generic set that contra Gödel and the conductible universe that a set does not have to have a determined algorithm or rule to be a set. In other words, whereas with Gödel ordinality and intensional issues made their way back into consideration, with Cohen and the negation of the axiom of choice set the pure extensionality of set theory reasserts itself.

The generic set is a pure and acceptable set despite its unruliness and infinite irreducible complexity. What is intuitable in the notion of an extensional set proves here refractory to ordering methods. What is also interesting here is that the generic subset is added but also found to be included at the same time. That is, it needs to be constructed in order to be found as if waiting inside. It is important to not forget here that the generic subset must by nature be infinite. It cannot be finite in nature. Once we establish that this generic subset is found in the original set, then there are any uncountable number of others there that could be constructed. This observation only reinforces how the power set must truly be larger than the generic subset and aleph null and immeasurably so. But it is only with first constructing the generic subset that an uncountable number of subsets can be posited.

Now that the generic set has been constructed, one can ask what it contains and attempt to gain knowledge of what seems unknowable in itself. This is similar to asking what bits make up Chaitin's constant (that is, what the decimal expansion of such an infinitely irreducibly complex real is). This is also the context in which the notion of 'forcing' is perhaps most accurately used. The properties of such a generic subset are forced out of it. These properties are found by conducting an examination of the set. If the generic subset were finite, it would be a much simpler matter of learning its composition. It certainly would not be an endless task. If the generic subset were finite, one would have only finite complexity and thus an algorithm (perhaps an extraordinarily long one, but a finite rule for generating the set). But the generic subset itself contains all possible knowledge given its infinite irreducible complexity. It is an encyclopedia of all past, present, and future information. In this way, it is not clear anything is not contained in it and yet one must search it element by element to force out its specific order. Even a random ordering arises in a series. One can thus only test statement by statement or bit by bit about what belongs to the generic subset as its elements. The inscrutability of the generic subset is part of its indiscernibility. I will only ever be able to force a finite amount of the information contained within it.

Part of the problem here is that we need to check all possibles contained in the power set to see if it is in the generic subset since its elements were selected as it were randomly and it has no rule. In other words, if we want to know if a specific element belongs, we need to check that specific element itself and cannot know in advance. We need to do that with all elements. We can only go element by element and check to see if it is included in the generic subset. Gödel said forcing is "a method to make true statements about something of which we know nothing".32 It is the fact that we can only progressively and haltingly unravel the generic set that makes it indiscernible, neither truly knowable nor completely unknown. The generic subset has no known totality. It is not in this way truly a unity at one level. Also, even if one can test one particular element and find it belongs it tells us nothing about the entirety of the generic extension. It only tells about that one element. Even if we garnered a seemingly long list of elements, we would not be able on their basis to project out any further elements. The finite information we have must be seen in comparison to the infinity left unknown.

This is different than for instance learning of the decimal expansion of pi. There, we have a rule as it were for slowly moving from one decimal place to another. Here, we can only test one element and set if it belongs without proceeding in any definable series. The information here is "purely extensional" as Mary Tiles puts it, and the infinity of sets contained in the generic set are "indistinguishable" previous to investigation.33 We thus determine things that are true for the generic subset even if we cannot actually look at all of the generic subset itself. It remains opaque to us.

Since finite information forces the membership of the generic subset, Badiou here again makes use of performative speech acts to show what is going on. If we declare that space aliens should be included as citizens of the state, what we have essentially done is used a fine amount of information to force them as members of the generic subset of the transfinite set of all possible citizens of the state. By this act, we discern what was not before discernible as included in the set of all possible citizens. But as Badiou would say, one has to take this act as it were on faith. Since the generic subset is unknowable at one level, the finite information encoded in it and announced in the speech act describes something that is opaque to us. We thus have to choose whether we accept or not this inclusion. The faithful subject here selects out via the speech act what belongs. Forcing thus appears to make use of rather arbitrary statements and shows those statements to be true. The final determination of the generic subset would take a truly infinite procedure and thus it will never be completed as the infinity here is finally uncountable. We thus provide conditions and a finite number to unearth element by element the generic. We should not be able to truly name these derivations and selections and yet we do because the very power of the uncountable authorizes us. There is no rule here and thus we invent the rule with our performative speech act. We appear to be self-making law-givers.

It is important to remember that the infinite here is always for us incomplete and that forms a basis for this forcing of finite parts of the indiscernible. The indeterminacy which lacks an algorithmic rule thus offers itself to us to be filled in. The propertyless nature from one view of the generic means we can find in it ultimately any property we want. We force the properties of the generic. We should take this as seriously as possible. What we see here is that the generic subset as a name of the nameless cannot help but show how the absolute is itself hiding within any possible transfinite set. This is the divine omnipresence. It means that despite a set seeming on its face to have a definition and restrictive form as per the axiom of choice, the axiom of choice fails, and one can find included in a set anything. After all, nothing is excluded from the non-all and when we construct the generic set we offer a name for the non-all, a name for the unnamable. One can find then included in the set of all round things, square things. Because anything can be included in the generic subset, we can find that anything is there. This pure openness leads us to the absolute itself.

After all, the truly indiscernible is the divine itself, the absolute. Badiou seems to recognize this himself when he notes most would say that God is the truly indiscernible: "For an inhabitant of S, in any case, it seems that God alone can be indiscernible" (*BE* 373). Everything is then potentially in everything else. It is via these considerations that we can confirm Leibniz's insight that all things are mirrors of God and reflect the whole. Here they reflect the non-all because it can be shown via an operation that they have included in them a direct relation to the non-all. We can reach into any essence and get out the world. This is because inside each thing is a name of the nameless one. We construct with the generic subset a name for the non-all itself. The transfinite attempted to put the absolute into a box and make ones out of it. But those boxes turn out to be Pandora-like and if one finds the key to opening them everything comes spilling out.

The key is the construction of the generic subset itself. It leads us back to the limitless, the true infinite. Thus, the apeiron appears again here after its transfinite and eidetic reduction. It appears even more directly and markedly since it connects all together and pierces the veil of distance. We are here discovering both new aspects of creation as well as the workings of the divine mind itself. In the divine mind, all thoughts interpenetrate. But also when we construct new names, we are allowed a glimpse of the divine itself and its omnipresence. We see the creation of things through thought alone. Each set has an endless expanded membership included in it. We can then force out this hidden inclusion and ask that the new set with the same name be formed around it. We are searching out the spaces of the expanded universe, the one expanded to the absolute horizon itself. We are plumbing the depths of the mind of God. We are in a new dimension here and have entered a new level of the non-all. There are lots of new subsets to be found. They were not there in the previous incarnation when the axiom of choice blinded us to them. The violation of the continuum hypothesis does not deny us the divine, but connects us to it its true omnipotence and omnipresence. This seems impossible perhaps, but it is part and parcel of accepting the absolute infinite itself.

Let's take an example. If we had a set of all Americans, then if the continuum hypothesis holds along with axiom of choice there is no way to find anything indiscernible in the set of Americans. What belongs there is what is there. Dogs, cats, etc. who are not members of the original set, would not be found in a spelling out the subsets. But if the axiom of choice is denied and the continuum hypothesis fails, there is no longer simply just a re-ordering of the members of the set when the power set is spelled out. Instead, one can construct a generic subset and ask what is in it. Then, one can force out what one wants and what one will accept as being there. As Cohen noted, we do not yet know what the power set operation was saying. But it is saying that each individual essence expresses the non-all itself. Each divine thought is marked by the divine thinker. It is saying that the larger is contained in the smaller. It means that all permutations exist and that beyond a re-ordering there exists a new generic subset that exceeds those re-orderings. All permutations of a thing are contained it, and further the non-all itself is at work at the heart of an essence and a thought. The thinkable qua thinkable cannot exclude its relation to the non-all and the divine mind.

We can then extract from any essence what can arise both from the permutation of things and what resides in the great continuum for the failure of the continuum hypothesis is actually a moment where the true name of the continuum asserts itself, the apeiron, *eyn sof*. With the absolute infinite all is latently contained, we can then name parts of the nameless. What this is saying is not that the parts of an essence cannot access the thing itself, but that the parts of a thing always exceed the thing itself because the thing itself cannot be truly disconnected from the non-all. Defining a set might involves limiting it and drawing a boundary, but when we search deeply enough into its parts we find that the whole is only one more part and that the parts exceed whole. This is the topsy-turvy nature of the non-all, and it affects all concepts. The set is thus not expressed by its members because the parts always express more and not simply regimented permutations, but ultimately they express the non-all itself. The object here is not reducible to its parts not because it exceeds it, but because it is exceeded by its parts and its relation to the divine.

This is partly true simply because any set is made up of other sets and ultimately the empty set. Anything that is included in it is itself already a set and essence unto itself, a unity. The lack of a set of all sets, of a final totality, means all is subtracted form that totality and thus nothing is excluded from being included in anything else. The non-all is itself ineffable and beyond any possible description. It is the unnamable. But the unnamable is not divorced from every name and hides within them. There is a divine name waiting to be constructed by diagonalization. This is the point where human reality of course breaks down and one can enter into an ineffable contact with the beyond. The untenable makes nameability itself possible, but remains as the impossible limit within it. There is always more being than what is named. The unnamable differs from every name we can name. But what is named is ultimately also nothing as it is indiscernible. If it cannot be discerned, it is no-thing. This is partly why we do not see things themselves, but only the surface of things. The non-all is beyond as the horizon of all contexts. One can only apprehend a divine name and not its referent. Its referent is unpresentable. This is why the generic subset must have a proper name.

The name 'Chaitin's constant' is but one example of that. That is because the non-all itself is unique and thus there is a unicity at work in the indiscernible. There can only be one indiscernible no matter how many times we name it and how many names for it we construct. The one which has no name is thus paradoxically never fully subtracted from the order of the proper name. One could never force out the unnamable itself, but only the lettering of its proper name, a proper name left behind after the unnamable's withdrawal. But the unnamable refers to itself because it is omnipresent in all. We add one divine name after another without ever reaching the divine itself fully. But even so, we are here lead again to the mind of God. In the mind of God, there is nothing that cannot be thought and nothing is excluded. One need only address and supplicate before the radically transcendent in order to discover the hidden and to plumb the depths of the veiled. The divine mind is that hidden light (the 'or haganuz') that makes for a lack of confusion. Any name can be articulated and even the lettering of the nameless can be spelled via its illumination. One need only turn to the absolute itself to solve the conundrum. This is where the divine poetry itself starts to articulate itself. Out of a number of words, we find a single word that names the nameless itself. In each word, we find hiding the nameless itself as an endless infinite incantation. We thus fashion a world foreign to any human language via a proper name. It appears as if by chance–the random selection of elements. But chance itself is fulfilled since even hiding in the random is the hidden divine light itself that illuminates the non-all and the absolute. Chance is vanquished letter by letter to paraphrase Mallarme.

If with the model upholding the continuum hypothesis we saw ordinality, here cardinality reasserts itself. Cardinality is duality as it involves two orders (one-to-one correspondence for instance) whereas ordinality is one dimensional. With Cohen's work, we see that cardinality allows us to move from the one-dimensionality of ordinality to the two-dimensionality of cardinality itself. It is by cardinality itself with its difference established not in time, but in space that we are able to crack open things and find their connections.

§10. Undecidability and Deconstructionism

Cohen of course believed that ultimately one day with the discovery of new axioms we will see that the Continuum Hypothesis (CH) "is obviously false".34 No such axioms have been offing, and strong axioms of infinity have not done the work of proving CH obviously false. We cannot at this point imagine such an axiom, and it might be unimaginable for us. Such an axiom would probably imply a logic unlike any we are familiar with. It would be revolution perhaps more profound than the one indicated by the difference between Aristotelian classical syllogism and the revolution in logic since Boole, Frege, and Cantor.

At this point, we have to accept the strict undecidability that we are faced with concerning CH. That undecidability however does not mean we choose one side or the other—at least not philosophically. Philosophically, we need to think both sides at the same time. That is, we must affirm both sides as characterizing reality as such since we cannot avoid thinking both. We cannot avoid both sides in thinking and thus cannot make simply a choice to operate as though the other side did not exist. Rather, we must think both as irreducible pictures of reality that at most cannot be explained one by the other. At most, we might want to find a way of saying that the model upholding CH is somehow a swerve within the model denying it. This would be like saying that the truth of being is the failure of CH, but mind projects onto this failure a veil that allows to see things by way of CH. Mind here would be what well orders an inherent inconsistent non-all. If mind itself is irreducible, then we would forever be removed from the truth of pure divine being.

Another model might be one of levels or dimensions. At the one-dimensional level, CH appears to hold, but when we move to a new level we see that in the previous one it fails, but not from within our own new dimension. In other words, philosophically, given the unavoidability of the logic of both sides, we can either try to think the two as irreducible complements or one as some sort of species of the other.

CH cannot be proven or disproven using the Zermelo-Fraenkel axiomatic system. But the decision here is not for or against CH as a result. Something that cannot be disproven or proven cannot be wished away or ignored. I do not see for example Badiou arguing this line. That is, Badiou's rejection of the One-Whole is not simply a choice of the failure of continuum hypothesis. Rather, Badiou insists that what he calls 'the state' is a real and unavoidable part of his ontology. The state attempts to order the non-whole, but one cannot avoid the state. This is how Badiou accepts the undecidability involved. If one cannot prove or disprove CH, then one must act as though it holds and as though it does not hold and draw both sets of conclusions at the same time and when needed.

Now, Cantor on the other hand did simply accept the truth of CH. But this was because he had a more classically Platonic realist view. Sets for him were isolated and autonomous ultimate entities that did not interact. He thus did not grasp the Leibnizian truth concerning thinking that Cohen's work exposed for us. Cantor did think the absolute infinite was a radical transcendent field that did not touch upon the world itself. God is not omnipresent in a direct way for Cantor. God does not intervene in the world. This is the difference between Cantor and Badiou. It is one of acceptance or rejection of the actual being of the absolute infinite, the non-all. It is a question of how to render the immanent nature of such a radical transcendence.

For us to think the irreducibility of both the insights of Gödel and Cohen, to think the undecidability involved, means again thinking the formula: Ω equals $\emptyset$. This means in particular proposing how existence itself enters the picture here. Wolfgang Pauli is reported to have said: "Just because something is infinite doesn't mean it's zero".35 But here we say that the absolute infinite is just that for us in one sense. After all, CH appears at first glance to at most be a question of where the thinkable touches on the real of being itself. That is, it seems to deal with a purely conceptual universe of what can possibly be thought. In existence, we do not seem to meet up with infinities. On the other hand, in existence, we do have recursive procedures and choice functions for expressing in a reducible way an infinite set. However, before articulating and emphasizing the existent's role in the triad, we should look at other ontological ways of dealing with the undecidability of CH.

The first is the recent work of Paul Livingston where he articulates what he calls a "paradoxico-critical interpretation" of the undecidability of CH.36 For Livingston, "it is not justified...to hold that the excess of the power set is measured or measurable at all (that is, in any determinate way) by the succession of transfinite cardinals".37 But it is not clear how this is either saying that neither Cohen nor Gödel are correct (and we do not have another model to show that and propose another reading) or simply restating Cohen's view that the excess is immeasurable and thus can take on any aleph cardinality (and thus denying the fundamental nature of the model upholding CH). To say the excess of the power is "simply indeterminate" is to claim that CH is obviously false without providing the new axiom(s) that would legitimate such a view.38 This is odd because later on that same page, Livingston says the issue of indeterminacy involves how "widely we may take...predicable properties to range through the whole universe of sets", but indeterminacy is truly radical and not measurable, then as we have shown it means that all sets are connected in a Leibnizian calculus. However, if Livingston is claiming that we have explained what sets are constructible and which are not, then he has collapsed back into a model affirming CH.

Livingston believes his own paradoxico-critical orientation should be contrasted with what he calls Badiou's "generic operation". But here Livingston attempts to reduce mathematics to linguistics, denies there is anything outside of language, and that language is simply self-reflective and self-limiting.39 In other words, Livingston's view is premised on denying anything beyond the linguistic itself. Livingston would thus deny our view as simply unthinkable. Platonism is rejected in any form by him. For Livingston, one can only note various paradoxes formed by the symbolic order when it deals with its own self-reflexivity. Where language itself came from is forbidden as a question. That language itself refers to something beyond itself would apparently be a self-generated illusion. Thus Livingston is interested in finding places where thought finds something refractory to its own conceptual framework and interpreting that refraction as some sort of residue of its own incompletion. We are left only thus with "equivocal paths of hermeneutics".40 In other words, Livingston accepts no transcendence beyond thinking itself. It is purely immanent to itself. Any impasses within thought are thus points where we need to engage in analysis, but never posit anything more.

Also, it is clear that Livingston has no space for existence or any functions of reality that would not be reducible to the linguistic sign. Livingston's position is thus ultimately a variation on Wittgenstein and Derrida (of whom we will speak presently). Livingston at best argues that the undecidability of CH requires an adoption of a deconstructivist attitude. Deconstruction itself must police any attempts to formulate a "doctrine of being" by performing the "critical work" of enacting the constant failure of thought to truly find anything that might exceed itself.41 Thus, Livingston believes his model works by "affirming the existence of a totality (of all that can be said, or of the world, of Being), and tracing the contradictions and antinomies that thereby arise at its boundaries and its reflexive center".42 A double game is thus always played in which one takes it that all can be totalized conceptually and then shows how that totalization itself fails.

But our task after Cantor, Badiou, Cohen, etc. is not to pretend that a totality exists, but to think that failed totality as non-all. This is not the same as seeing how totality fails and what contradictions arises due to inclosure, but rather to understand how we are caught in the non-all and always in relation to it. It is a strange game where we presuppose a totality that can never be rather than admitting the unavoidability of the absolute infinite itself as a necessary reference. This double game fails because it must admit at some point that "we are both within and without the totality we think" when we try to think being as enclosed in a totality.43 It is that vanishing point where we find ourselves outside that we realize there must be something more than our linguistic prison.

Livingston attempts to contest Badiou's' "generic approach" as saying we can think "from the perspective of a truth, which is always essentially beyond any specific situation", but such a Truth can only be thought from the very perspective of the divine infinite itself and acceptance of its as the Truth of Being itself.44 It is Livingston's disallowance of what is constantly unavoidable that is the problem--a confrontation with the divine absolute, which is why he thinks theology can only eve be a "position that sees the totality as complete and consistent in itself, though beyond the grasp of finite cognition, which is located simply within the totality".45 We have endeavored to erase this caricature of the theological in all we have laid out here and before. To say the divine absolute is consistent in itself would be an attempt to contain both divine omnipotence and omnipresence itself. What Livingston is thus blind to is that there exists a post-Cantorian theology.

It is actually Livingston in his Wittgensteinian deconstruction that needs to accept that totality since all is caught "in the One of totality" which encloses all paradoxes and cancels all else beyond the linguistic sign.46 Part of the problem here is the focus on reflexivity. As we will see with Gödel, one of the lessons of computationalism is that existence knows completion via the permutation and numbering of letters in a way that does not match the skeptically accepted totality of the deconstructionist. This is why we do accept the position of the generic in part when Livingston characterizes it as "recognizing reflexivity and its paradoxes, denies being of the totality and sees these paradoxes as traversing an irreducible Many".47 But part of the problem here is that Livingston uses the terms inconsistency, completeness, and incompleteness in way that is difficult to understand or recognize. He appears to be saying that if one accepts a complete totality (such as the totality of all being thinkable via the linguistic sign), then that completeness implies some sort of inconsistency (paradoxes, contradictions, etc.). On the other hand, if one accepts that a system is consistent, then something is always missing and outside of it. Thus, consistency implies incompleteness. Livingston identifies the former with his position and the latter with Badiou.48 But this view does not understand how computation conceives of completeness in the sense of for instance the universal Turing machine, the complete computer. There, completeness does not involve inconsistency in the sense of paradox or contradiction, but incomputability. If existence is itself computational, then it is not a matter of saying that all is captured by language. This is to take language at the level of the signifier-signed relation, but not to recognize what it does at the level of the letter. We believe Lacan is also a thinker of the letter along these lines and thus reject his inclusion by Livingston as a paradoxico-critical thinker.

Second, it is only a model that upholds CH for instance that would advocate consistency itself. For Livingston, all of truth can be expressed via the linguistic sign which means there is no truth transcending language. But even when there is completeness, one is lead to the transcendent outside as the notion of multiplicity itself will show. The letter itself refers to what it names. God is not reducible to his unpronounceable name. Livingston seems to act as if one has to choose either a complete or consistent system. But thought itself can recognize both. In this way, it is not clear that Livingston is Derridean enough or that Derrida did not understand fully the implications of undecidability. The problem here is that to accept the undecidability of CH is to accept both that it is neither true nor false, either true or false, and both true and false at the same time. Such a formulation of course echoes with deconstruction. But one cannot overlook the part where one acknowledges the truth of both sides. Livingston ultimately wants to say it is not really true in any sense that CH fails since there is no truth beyond language.

In many ways, this is the position of Martin Hagglund, the main philosophical advocate of Derrideanism today and someone who identifies Derrideanism with radical atheism. Although I am not aware of anywhere where Hagglund engages with CH and its undecidability, his points are relevant here in order to think through the implications of accepting the radical undecidability of CH. For Hagglund, there is something called "the infinite finitude of difference—since everything is constituted by the trace structure of time".49 Her we already see that Hagglund (and for Hagglund, his view is identical with Derrida's) denies both anything eternal and that anything exceeds the conceptual. To say there is an infinite finitude I take it here means an infinity of finite traces or finite instants. But as we saw earlier, such a view can only mean the posting of the non-all itself. The problem is that the non-all is itself non-temporal. This would be the ultimate deconstruction, that even positing that all is caught up in time, there is the non-all and its eternal nature. Thus, at the same time that one claims "every notion of an absolute that exempts it from the spacing of time is a version of the metaphysics of presence. It does not make any essential difference e if one says that the absolute is absent and impossible to grasp for finite human understanding", one must necessarily posit such a notion as both necessary, unavoidable, intractable, and impossible.50

Deconstruction always necessarily deconstructs itself and must posit the very thing it calls impossible since this impossibility insists on itself. The work of atheist deconstruction then becomes one of policing any hint that this necessary impossibility refers to an ineffable outside that is more than nothing. That is, the impossible can only be the void here. The eternal can only be nothing and nothing more than a name. This is why Hagglund says that for deconstruction one should not "make God unnamable and unthinkable" since that is but "the most traditional metaphysical move since it posits God as absolutely absolute by making him independent form anything other than himself".51 This is why the deconstructionist must say the impossible is reducible to a name alone. The absolute is impossible since it would be independent. It must be necessarily posited, but then one must take back what is posited and insist it should not be considered anything other than a name or transcendental illusion.

This was of course the great nihilistic error of Edmond Jabes for whom Derrida felt such a deep connection. But to say the impossible is nothing does not mean it does not take place which means it is not simply a name and nothing more. We can see this since for deconstruction, death is also impossible. This is a focus of Hagglund given his insistence on the "essentially mortal" nature of everything.52 But it is ironic that given that everything is mortal in the infinite finitude characterizing all and yet nothing can die given the impossibility of death. As Blanchot and Levinas showed, one cannot undergo one's own death. But of course everything dies. However, deconstruction following its own principles must deny this. This is because deconstruction is trapped on the side of the living and in taking the living as all there is. All is mortal, and thus there is no thing beyond that. If one claims there is something immortal, it is dead and thus nothing. Hagglund makes this explicit: "If to be alive is to be mortal, it follows that to not be mortal—to be immortal—is to be dead. If one cannot die, one is dead. … God is death".53 Thus, this position must see God and death as equally impossible. But death happens. It is an event. And that is undeniable.

Deconstruction must therefore constantly be positing the very thing it must deny. It is a rather cynical attitude ('I know very well..., but....'). But it is mostly a skeptical attitude. Of course, recognition of the impossibility of death is an ancient. As Epicurus put it, "if one is, death is not. If death is, one is not". Epicurus asserted this idea in order to allay fears of death (as when it is, one is not). But deconstruction of Hagglund's variety must say death is impossible and never is. It never takes place. In this way, while Hagglund insists all that is is mortal and trapped in the trace structure of time, his position deconstructs itself as life becomes thoroughly immortal. One can never reach one's own death and die. Death is beyond and all and a void. Thus, one exists as if one is immortal. But of course again, death happens. Thus, to accept that I die is to accept the idea of death itself as more than just an idea and more than just a name for the unnamable.

It is not by coincidence that so many claim that we only see the 'face of God' at death itself. Deconstruction here constantly deconstructs itself which makes it appear as a fully self-canceling viewpoint (as is the case with all skeptical orientations). Part of the problem here is that Hagglund denies the very idea of a "positive infinity that reposes wholly in itself and grants a person an 'uninterrupted duration'".54 But this amounts to a denial of the actual infinite itself. Deconstructionism is thus on this account a wholly pre-Cantorian skeptical orientation. In lieu of positive infinity, Hagglund only accepts "negative infinity" which means he only accepts the potential infinite as did Aristotle, the endless progression from instant to instant.55 Duration for Hagglund can only be a finite duration. There is nothing eternal. Of course, there is nothing eternal in the world of flesh and blood as they say, but Hagglund denies it in any sense. Time can only mean progressive succession. There can be nothing that is actually infinite and all given at once. Eternity would imply that all happens at once and thus nothing happens one after the other.

What is denied here is that what is impossible from the viewpoint of living is possible at another level or dimension. But that is because again being is identified with thinking. To say that thinking is inherently finite due to its self-reflexivity is to say the same. Thus, Hagglund's infinite finitude is never a positive infinity, but it is not clear how it is then infinite in any actual sense. If one admits an infinity of finite instances one being transcended by another, then the problem of the continuum arises and with it the apeiron, the non-all. But given that there is no finite whole for Hagglund, it is not clear how one can claim there is an infinite which is then not potential.56 The claim is that there is an open progression that never ends, but that means there is an infinite regress (unless there was an origin) which again presuppose an actual infinite. The denial of a positive infinity is thus another point at which something that cannot be denied by the very logic and conceptualization at work is denied thus again deconstructing the deconstruction. Hagglund thinks that the flux of finite things is itself enough to make things absolutely other to themselves, but something can undergo change while not being reduced to nothing or dying and being reborn at each instant.

Also, there is no way that even radically becoming finitudes can fill up an infinite finitude. Hagglund thinks the "spacing of time" is itself the absolute, but it is an absolute that always presupposes that actual absolute of actual infinity that is excluded by the deconstructionist.57 If nothing can be what it is, then it is not clear how it is possible to even make that claim (since the claim is not what it is). How did instants that can never be themselves come into being and if they always were how does that not posit an eternity and an actual infinite? Nothing is impossible per this view. But every time we conceive of nothing it is not, but at the same time it is referred to. The logic of the aporia is left here as a purely conceptual move. But nothing cannot truly be impossible if all is finite since if all is finite each thing could not be. And then what would be left? What would be with this alleged pure spacing of time that is the true absolute?

The implications of finitude are not here truly accepted. Whether or not Derrida himself would accept Hagglund's reading is not my main concern, but in my estimation it seems to fairly directly articulate the Derridean line. Derrida to my knowledge never engaged with Cantor or post-Cantorian set theory.

§11. Gödel Numbers

Given the atheist failings of deconstruction as noted above, another model for thinking undecidability and in particular the undecidability of CH is needed. It s our gambit in part that by turning to Gödel himself we can get a clearer sense of the issue. But before doing so, let us make clear that undecidability is very clearly a model for engagement with the divine. We see this in Judaism via the image of the divine being expressed by the knot of the phylacteries. When God showed himself to Moses, Moses saw only the knot (*Berachot* 7a). No one can actually experience the divine absolute itself ('For no man may see me and live'), but Moses was allowed to see the reverse side of God (Exodus 33:20). The image of the knot here is of two strips of leather being interwoven together. This is precisely an image of the undecidable. It is the same as the image of the cross where two lines intersect. There, the continuum itself is cut by another line. Man is crucified on that intersection for the Christians. But this would be at best a model for the manner in which we impose order on the continuum and not for accepting the failure of the continuum hypothesis. The tefillin knot accepts the joining of two parallel orders into an interwoven point where their distinction is caught up. Thus, the knot itself is an irreducible point where two irreducible orders are joined. This knot is itself an image of the divine and sign of it because it shows that the divine itself (revealed at the time to Moses) is itself a knot of letters.

The letter in its working is not itself deconstructible. Quentin Meillassoux seems to have recognized a similar point:

> When all your signs are meaningful, you are in deconstruction. Now why can't Derrida's deconstruction say anything about mathematics, why can't it deconstruct mathematics? Because Derrida needs a sort of meaningful repetition, a sign that is meaningful that, if you repeat it, you have differential effects, by the repetition itself. By a decontextualisation the sign will modify its meaning, in one context, in another context, and so on. So you can always say there is a dissemination of meaning which is not just a polysemy, because it is infinite: the sign is infinite in its capacity for meaning. But if you take mathematics, you have signs without meaning, and you just operate on these signs. So if there are signs without any meaning, all deconstruction, all hermeneutics, goes out the window.58

The letter has no meaning in and of itself. It therefore is not yet caught in the signifier-signified relation. Derrideanism founders on the necessity of the actual infinite because the positing of the actual infinite involves an eidetic proof by the way of the invention of a name which is proper and persist by its lettering. While Meillassoux here consigns things to the mathematical sign and thus seemingly either to inscription or conception, the letter informs existence in its computational nature. The very computation of existence is an operation in its own iteration and operates on signs that have no inherent meaning. Such computation is complete insofar as it is universal and not deconstructible. It rather leads to another issue, that of the incomputable.

Derridean deconstruction thus only works on the order of eidetic being. It works on conceptual determinations where meaning is unfurled via the signifier-signified relationship. It works on sets, but not on the letter and on existence itself. This order of existence itself is the order of the letter. It was Gödel who first exposed it and some of the fundamental aspects of its logic as he penetrated to the meaningless level of the number itself prior to any reflexivity. For it is by reflexivity that we recognize meaningful repetitions of the same in different contexts. Then in a new context the sign refers to itself and thus speaks of itself. The signifier becomes signified and vice versa. But the letter works at a level prior to this in its computation.

Gödel, as is well known, was working within the framework set out for mathematics by David Hilbert.59 Hilbert wanted mathematics to be axiomatic in nature which meant a formalism in which all the truths of mathematics could expressed by a system of symbols properly arranged. But as we shall see, Hilbert treated axioms as sentences, but those sentences could in turn as Gödel showed be broken down into words and ultimately letters and numbers. While there is a level beyond which one cannot go (the meaningless sign itself), one can build up from that level. Also, the most basic level is not simply an atom, but the arbitrary relations of meaningless sign and its linkage (to a number or to a function). To discover mathematical truths one would then need only perform operations on this system of axiomatic expressions per a set of accepted principles. But the symbols of which the system was made would be in themselves meaningless signs. One then would permute and transform strings of meaningless signs according to the given rules and laws.

Gödel took these strings of symbols and associated numbers with each of them. This is the famous Gödel numbering. By encoding the meaningless marks in this way, Gödel endeavored to arithmetize theoretical mathematics itself. This is thus similar to Cantor's arithmetization of the problem of the continuum. Every sign then would be associated with a finite, positive integer. This would include marks like the open parenthesis '(' as much as marks like the equal sign '=.' That is, purely graphical marks that merely break up the space of inscription would be encoded as much as signs seemingly associated with a sense (after all, the 'or' sign 'v' seems to have a clear sense). But by taking up Hilbert's idea that formulas and axioms are at their most basic level a list of meaningless signs, one sees that the number associated with them is arbitrary, but also that any mark needs to be associated with a number.

Now, of course, the number associated with each mark appears to have no motivation. It would thus only be indexical as it were as is the number for one's "telephone number or…license plate".60 We of course do not associate any significance with the fact that one's license plate would be '7' and another's '5' and would take the numbers here as being purely labels such as the street number or address at which one lives. The numbers tell one then seemingly nothing more about the mark they are associated with then that a linkage has been affected. At the same time, we will see that numbers do have some sort of inherent significance that will re-emerge despite their treatment as cardinals. It would be here after all cardinals not in the sense of saying that a mark has particular size, but simply in the sense that one thing is marked with a number.

Hilbert had established that all the needed axioms of mathematics could be reduced to a finite list of basic signs. One then could reuse this list of signs over and over again to generate all the needed formulas. But now each formula no matter how long or what it seems to express would be associated with a number. This number is itself generated by taking the numbers associated with each individual mark and adding them together in a special way (one essentially makes each Gödel number the power of a list of primes such that the first mark in the list would be two to the power of that Gödel number, etc. One uses primes due to their very nature enabling each Gödel number to be unique as a result of the calculation).

Given that one can associate each sign with a number and thus an entire mathematical statement, one can thus read the statement in two ways as a statement about numbers ('1 is less than 2' for instance) and also as a number. That is, just like with any code, each every thing has two sides. One side expresses the inherently meaningless marks as it is associated with a meaning ('=' is 'equals') and from another side the statement can be read as simply a number because each mark has number (7 or 300 million or any other positive integer produce as a result of plugging the number into a formula based on prime numbers). The coding of course means one needs the key to decipher it. If one does not know that '=' is associated with the number 7, one will not know how to decipher the code if one is just given a number.

The code is on one side a signifier-signified that is unmotivated and on the other side a number. This is made possible by the finite list of letters on which all is based and through which all is inscribed. If one did not know the rules for associating each sign with a number and the creation of unique numbers by using primes and multiplication, one would never know how to translate back a particular number into a statement or the statement into the number. But this was precisely an expression of Hilbert's program that all one would need to know was the rules and the signs along with their associations. This system also meant that each mathematical statement just as each sign was associated with a unique number. Just as every person has a unique identity number in a governmental system, here each number and system has a unique identity. Gödel had to use the prime coding to ensure the unicity of each Gödel number. Given the unicity of each number, it means that one can again associate any mathematical expression with a number that no other expression will have, but also that one can see each expression as a proper name.

One expression is the proper name 'M' and another the proper name 'XY' for example. The uniqueness of each Gödel number means one can refer to and speak to them just as one speaks to and refers to a person by a proper name. When one calls out to 'John,' one knows that 'John' is only a rigid designator for that person. But in having a proper name, one can address and speak of 'John' in any number of contexts. Of course, any number of people can be called 'John.' Here, however, given the coding, one would always be referring to the same instance with the same proper name. That is, in this system, each name is associated with a referent and only one referent belongs to one name. Now, that each proposition, each formula of number theory, has a proper name one will be able to make statements about those statements themselves. The proper names thus become part of the list of signs. A proper name is after all a mark meaningless in itself linked to a referent. The name 'John' has no sense in itself. It is but a series of letters.

But for Gödel it was not enough to simply associate each proposition with a proper name. he also made it so that proper name is a number because once again, as we will see, numbers have an inherent meaning that is irreducible and not arbitrary and that especially comes to the fore when one is encoding number theory itself. Once one has proper names one can make "statements about statements of number theory".61 Thus, while we cannot say that the name 'John' is less than or equal to 'David,' we can say that one is less than ten and cannot avoid that fact. The ordinal character of numbers will thus be irreducible here. At the same time, in axiomatics, one uses different propositions to derive new ones. One thus needs to link a series of formulas in a list and thus from them derive and deduce a new formula. If each formula is associated with a number, then one can express how a series of formulas lead from one to the other using the number given. Thus, there is a way of using the value of each Gödel number for each proposition to compute a new valid formula within the theory. All of the logical relations that exist between formulas in the system are arithematized and computable. Each formula and expression has some sort of purely arithmetical relation between each other that can be computed.

We thus would not need to work out mechanically ourselves how one proposition taken with others entails a new one. A computer can do it for us. Of course, there were no such computers at the time of Gödel's work, but his work makes doing pure mathematics via computer partially possible. Each statement her has its own numerical property that the system can understand. If one can show how to compute new valid proofs, then "it becomes possible to show that all and only the provable [formulas] in the system, the theorems, have a certain arithmetical property".62 Given that the probability of a proposition must be associated with a particular numerical value and property, one will thus be able to speak about whether or not a particular proper name is itself provable by way of other propositions in the system. How is this done? Well, first obviously a particular mathematical statement can speak of another by speaking of its proper name. Thus, one can plug the unique Gödel number into a proposition by way of its proper name (in the sense of 'X' or 'A'–that is, as a variable). Since the Gödel number is always irreducibly a number with numerical properties, even when one plugs it into a proposition of number theory as a variable, it will not simply be a proper name or number, but also a statement about the statement that was encoded.

What is key here is that while numbers can be written in any number of ways (Roman numerals, Arabic numbers, binary coding, etc.) the numerical properties associated with the number cannot be reduced despite the fact that the particular sign one uses is arbitrary and its association with the number is arbitrary and unmotivated. Numbers have values and properties independent of whatever signs we use to express them. We do not simply invent them with our signs. The sign '1' does not invent the concept of oneness. Thus, even when we manipulate numerical signs in their status as marks, we do not eliminate or change basic numerical properties. The concept then persists despite how we express it. The meaningless sign then when it comes at least to numbers does not simply remain mute or valueless. Thus, even if as Hilbert desired, we manipulate meaningless signs to do axiomatics, once those signs are associated with numbers, the concept itself persists. At the same time, because the signs are in themselves meaningless and only ever arbitrarily associated with something else, we can always substitute one sign for another. We can encode things endlessly. This is why we can speak of the Gödel number as a name, but also having a proper name when used as a variable. Things can have names and names of names. But, as we shall see, when it comes to meaning there are always two irreducible series signer-signified.

The number as a concept and with properties is part of a different series that is independent of the series of marks--even if linked and bound to it. This is why when writing we only ever exchange marks for other marks and in doing so perhaps also have on the reverse side conceptual relations. Given that Gödel numbers thus can be spoken of but their numerical sense persists, we can then see how Gödel's' famous incompleteness results came into being. If the variable associated with the Gödel number is plugged into the proposition [F(n)], then one is saying that the Gödel number itself, this variable, does or has whatever the proposition F expresses. Now, if the Gödel number has that property actually, then the statement F(n) is true. If it does not, then it is saying that F(n) is false. Thus, it can be said about n that it has a property, but that property might contradict what n expresses. For instance, n might claim itself that something is not the case, but when plugged into this other formula it says that it is true. There is thus a conflict between the two—two conflicting tings are said about the same number and thus a contradiction arises. There is inconsistency in the system.

Another of way seeing is this is also that since n is both a number and statement, the number n with its properties might not match what n says about numbers. N would not then be what N says it is. We then have the expression 'the statement n is not n.' If that statement is true, it is false. But if it is false, it is true. Hence, it is undecidable. But if F(n) is making a statement about what numbers are associated with provable and valid statements and what is not, then if it says n does not match, it is saying that n is not provable or valid in the system. But of course, n was a statement generated in the system and used in it. We thus generate the statement 'n is not provable in this system.' We thus can either generate an inconsistent statement in this way or a statement that cannot be proven or disproven.

Even though the Gödel number is generated in an arbitrary way, we see that it can have associated with it different properties. The number 37 (such as in 37 Elm Street) is odd no matter if it is first and foremost a designation purely or if we use the number 37 when counting. Thus, if n is 37, it will be both statement where properties are asserted of 37, but also of the statement associated with 37. Thus, it can be the case that one can claim 37 is both odd and not. But also that 37 is not provable. The mark '37' could of course be associated with a different concept (not the concept of 37), but once it is certain implications are unavoidable.

Jaakko Hintikka famously said that the self-referentiality involved here is like famous people appearing in plays or television shows where they play themselves (such as John McEnroe playing 'John McEnroe' in a TV show) and commenting on themselves and how they are in 'real life'.63 The statements made by John McEnroe make sense and refer to John McEnroe himself even if they take place in a sitcom. The statements of McEnroe exist therefore in the universe of the TV show and are intelligible there, but also refer to 'real life' and are intelligible as comments on it. McEnroe along with his statements thus exist in two different areas at once simultaneously. One can switch back and forth between the two spheres of references. McEnroe plays both roles in being himself and is split at the same time.

Here, "number theory" "turns out to produce its own structure within itself" precisely because it has enacted the split between a sign and what it stands for.64 Without this split, none of what Gödel claims would in and of itself be possible. This split made it possible in the end to say that one cannot derive all arithmetic truths from the system involved. There is always a statement that is true, but that cannot be proven as such. Also, this spilt enables us to say that the system can also be rendered possible as inconsistent where one and the same thing is shown to be true and not within the same system. But we should not take this as being simply a function of the system. If number did not have qualities and properties independent of us, then the split would not work and finally yield incompleteness (undecidability) or inconsistency. Again, this is all because numbers have real properties that cannot but be conceived and are independent of us.

Many are often surprised to learn that Gödel advocated Platonic realism in his philosophical writings. But this realism is a necessary component of the incompleteness proofs. They would not work without them. And the mathematical properties here noted are independent of us and our language. Linguistic idealism would not be able to capture them. The arbitrariness of the sign here necessarily is involved with the independence of the conceptual truth.

Gödel has shown that number theory cannot demonstrate its own consistency. But that does not mean that we need to abandon it since we can show it to be consistent by using a larger system (for Peano arithmetic that larger system is of course Zermelo-Fraenkel itself which we have shown to be inconsistent via CH). This larger system will contain additional axioms and machinery to enable us to show why number theory makes true claims. Also, it is important that one can generate here inconsistency or undecidability because the system itself plays about the split between signifier and signified. A system that does not do that can exhibit a form of completeness without implying Gödel sentences.

Cristian Calude in a videotaped lecture entitled "Incompleteness: A Personal Perspective" exposes a number of myths concerning Gödel's work.65 Here, Calude notes that when we look at things purely from a computational perspective no Gödel sentence is generated. A universal Turing machine for instance does not in and of itself yield incompleteness. With such a Turing machine, we have completeness. Incompleteness arises from axiomatic systems. The true Turing machine offers the ability to compute everything except what is incomputable, but the incomputable is something that is infinitely and irreducibly complex rather than being inconsistent for instance. This is because computation involves only letters and numbers. Bits are associated with numbers which are associated with commands. But there is no split series here at this level where one can make statements about statements. Statements might occur at the level of software, but not at the level of the most basic compiled machine code. There might be a moment when a Gödel sentence is generated causing a loop, but that is not at the level of the machine code itself. All programming has to do with the assignment of values. That is, it is about at a basic level if0-then statements. If x, then y. But x has to be open to be given any value. If x=z, then something happens. Looping occurs when the same value is assigned to x. This is also why quantum computing has problems. Despite the superposition involved, one paradoxically does not truly leave x open, but always must collapse it into one value without leaving it open. Hence, quantum computing has only been capable of the most rudimentary of computations (e.g. 3 x 5 =15). In other words, in quantum computing one is constantly needing to measure things by collapsing the superposition. It thus has a large number of difficulties performing repetitive and iterative processes that makes computing work. Because quantum stats are unknown before the measurement, on is not able say x equal something new because only itself comes into being with the measurement. But quantum computing is probably ultimately not that important because one can simulate using classical computing anything a quantum computer could do.

A universal Turing machine can produce itself and can simulate any possible computation. It is thus complete without yielding inconsistency. The incomputable might be thought as something like an incomplete sentence, a statement that cannot be proven. But that is due to the sentence's infinite irreducibility rather than self-reflexivity or self-reference. Computation therefore is not involved in undecidable propositions as it is a permutation of numbers and letters and sets of numbers rather than axiomatic statements and propositions. Even when a certain binary code is associated with a command, there is at that point only the association of a meaningless sign with a number and nothing more. CH proved to be an undecidable proposition from the perspective of Zermelo-Fraenkel, but that is because axioms involves. In this way, Gödelian issues do not affect computation according to Calude. And thus, computation itself at the level of the machine code, the binary, introduces a field of existence that is not deconstructible.

Deconstruction itself is about generating Gödelian like sentences from conceptual networks. But computation illustrates its own form of completeness. When we look at something as just zeroes and ones we will not find a deconstructible moment and not see Gödelian incompleteness. Even if things have numerical values, there will not be a way to comment on those numerical values. There is not yet the type of dual articulation needed. As Deleuze would put it, we have here two series as part of the same structure that are divergent.66 Each series has autonomous and independent properties and can even develop to some extent on its own. In this way, even though a text like the bible can be seen as generating Gödel sentences if we want to so articulate it, when we reduce the Torah is reduced to pure gematria, to pure numbered coding, it will not prove itself incomplete or inconsistent, but rather operate more like a universal Turing machine in this regard. But in this regard we have leaped ahead of ourselves.

§12. 0/1

Turing of course was the first (or at least among the fist) to say that 0 and 1 are signs of the first kind. Binary digits were thus first and foremost a basic level of computing machines. Any other signs involved in computing were called by Turing symbols of the second kind. Turing thus saw the most basic code as in itself a meaningless binary code of 0 and 1, on and off. It was not associated with any possible meaning. If a computing machine will only ever print a finite list of binary code, then that machine is said to halt. But if it will print binary endlessly, it never halts. We of course cannot know in advance what will be done. But the issue is halting or not halting and thus computability and non-computability rather than self-reference. That is, when a checking and tallying system for instance keeps arriving at the number that indicates it must do its procedure. A loop is thus created. But notice this is not self-reference as much as repetition of the same numerical value and thus of the same instruction. While one can build additional checks for this issue, one cannot know in advance when it will happen (only after the fact in software creation). This is why people like my wife are paid to do Q & A even if humans did not make frequent typographical errors.

Another way to connect Gödel with Turing here would be to say that a Gödel sentence will produce an infinite number of 0's and 1's when computed. Another way to put how computation is complete and not Gödelian is to say that in computation 0 is never 1. On and off are always a difference and differential relation purely. That is, there is a relation of pure difference at work. Only when we begin to relate signifiers to signified can 0 possibly equal 1 and inconsistency be signaled. Zero is of course the number that is not the successor of any positive integer. At the same time, if it has a property, any of its successors have the same property. However, there is a problem in establishing how zero can lead to successors. Zero essentially has to be counted somehow for it to lead to a successor. But that means somehow zero has to be a unity, it has to be 'owned' somehow. It does so by taking the power set of itself. But in doing so it is thus being said that zero include the subset zero. Thus, the empty set and the inclusion of the empty set are here differentiated. But that is like differentiated a and not not-a. It is a difference purely of inscription and differentiality, but it at the same time says (just as a and not not-a do) that the two are the same.

In this way, to generate successors (0 -→ 1) zero must be one at some profound level. The set containing the empty set is not empty as it contains the empty set itself. But that set is as it were included, but not belonging to zero itself. The empty set has no element at all. Thus, the axiom of extensionality says the empty set and the set containing the empty set are different. But at the same time, it is simply the zero unified as 1. We saw this again with ω where the action of the one was reproduced. Thus, there is a fundamental difference involved from the beginning that involves a spit between the two that at the same time are in some sort of fundamental identity. It is this contradictory identity that is responsible for all the later generations of undecidability, incompleteness, inconsistency, etc. Thus, when we say that God withdraws as absolute into the proper name, w are saying already that 0=1 for the proper name is already one thing and can be seen as such even if it marks the void itself. That very origin explains the further incompletion of the world. All other inconsistent statements are variations on the initial point of departure.

One sees this as well in the equation $\omega + 1 = \omega$. Even though we are not allowed by the rules of set theory to subtract ω from each side to yield $1 = 0$, the very inscription itself implies this formula and the possibility of subtraction.67 One cannot help to see the paradoxes of the transfinite thus rest also on $1 = 0$. But at the basic level of coding, this paradox of $0 = 1$ is not apparent. It only becomes apparent at a new level. At the level of bits, three is only the difference between 0 and 1 and that pure difference says nothing about 0 and 1 as such. 0 and 1 are just a division and difference. This is why 0 and 1 are other names for on/off.

The logic here is strictly Boolean. 0/1 as themselves do not yet say anything about other numbers. 0 and 1 before encoding sets of integers simply name two differential states. The difference in a computer for instance is the differences in voltage. When a certain voltage is achieved, a gate is opened for instance (and closed at another voltage). The voltage difference is the very substance of code here. We would not learn anything about it if we looked at the electrons involved in the voltage since there the difference between on/off cannot be found. This is why it is at this level of pure difference that we must begin. There is nothing in between on and off here. It is only ever one or the other. Any seeming intermediate states (such as a continuum of voltage between the two values) are rendered null. It as if it does not exist. This continuum will only reassert itself when it comes to the incomputable nature of real numbers themselves. Otherwise, something is always in only one of two states.

For Boole, the two values 0 and 1 were also said to be the empty set and the entire universe. That is, for Boole, these two values were precisely like the 0/1 at the heart of set theory itself except that now the issues was not one of building up sets through acts of inclusion, but of repeating the pure difference between the empty set and what differs from it. Thus, it is more so a play of presence and absence than belonging and inclusion. However, the two are ultimately two sides of same coin as ultimately they issue in the positive integers and their expression. For just as we can express all of mathematics with sets, we can do so using the code of 0 and 1. That is, even though we only have two states to work with, we can elaborate those states into whatever we want. This is because each state is itself a letter and those letters can be linked to others via the combination and in that permutation creates sets of letters and numbers and letters as numbers.

As Dale Jacquette notes, the issue is not simply the production of bit strings (strings of zeroes and ones), but the transformation of those bit strings:

> What is remarkable about Boole's algebra is the fact that the bivalent limitation of its numerical domain to two values, 0 and 1, makes it applicable to whatever phenomena can be modeled in a binary system. Computers are precisely devices of this kind. Machine languages function in a binary code whereby strings of 0's and 1's taken as input are transformed a coding to rules by machine program into the strings of 0's and 1's issued s output. The programming instructions that effect these systematic transformations are made possible by Boolean algebra, as are the electronic circuits that mechanically implement the programming instructions.68

Jacquette reinforces the idea that Boolean logic is found here at every significant level: "Boolean logic thus pervades the thinking, the software and hardware design and operations, that make possible the most fundamental aspects of modern information technology".69 0's and 1's here can encode anything. They encode not just numbers, but also can encode what occurs with an electron when it changes states or what happens inside the workings of the biological cell.

All of existence can be seen as a computer since any state of the universe can be rendered as 0's and 1's and then a transformation into a new string of 0's and 1's. That transformation of one state into another is then the product of immanent rules and procedures that allowed the phenomena to develop as such and take on the form they did. That is, there is always algorithmic transformation from input to output, from state a to state b. This happens with everything that is in our finite, existent universe. One bit string becomes another and the rule for doing is immanent within it. The bit strings are of course themselves numbers and sets of numbers, but these numbers do not mean anything at this point. These numbers perform operations and name the very materiality of things. That is, these numbers are simply letters and just as letters they have not yet spoke of anything. Just as in a computer, the bits are nowhere in particular because they are themselves circulating constantly throughout the universe itself. They are not stored in any place because that which remembers them is nowhere in particular. There is nothing permanent and lasting about them and thus there is no site or memory storage as it were. One can always say that this is a matter of presence or absence, 0 or 1, at this particular stat at this particular instance and then a transformation into another state. Otherwise, all things are circulating around the universe itself. It is not a question of a solid and fixed state.70

This code makes it so all has a telephone number and address. One can only confuse thus code by making an error such as when one reads a telephone number incorrectly. The telephone number has no meaning itself except as the index of where to reach a particular voice. Bit stings are themselves also not readable by us. It is a code that is doing and indicating, but it is not for human eyes in its pure form. One would for instance need to remember how each binary sequence represents a number and move from there which is very difficult. This is because we are used to meaningful signs, to signs associated with a clear sense. When we add two positive integers together (such as 7 and 5 to get 12 to use the Kantian example), we perform the operation by memory or ordinally by counting from 7 to 5 or cardinally by thinking of something representing seven (such as figures) and putting them together with a set of things with the cardinality of 5. But the binary code reads seven and five both as bit strings and then combines and differentiates the two bits strings. In a computer, the electrical voltage itself arises and is switched using logic gates until a new series of voltage variations elicits the desired number. This is not a process we can truly internalize and intuit.

It is important not to think there is anything essential here about 0 and 1. One could just as easily switch them around to achieve the encoding. 0 could encode on instead off for instance. Thus 0 and 1 are not a difference in kind between two things, but only eve a question of two stats in relation. There are thus two states and inherent relationality between the two. It is the relation itself that makes for the bit. One should not think here that one can actually separate things and treat them as distinct and autonomous objects. That would not occur until one achieves a set of bits and thus essentially a number. Until then one has a difference that exists in itself and has less to do with what 0 or 1 are in their charged states than the very differentiality itself. With computers, everything is stored as numbers. But any finite computer can only contain a limited aggregate of such numbers. In other words, there is only available so much space or so much memory. In an 'ideal' mathematical model such limits are not met.

Thus, the difference here is pure and thus one could say transcended the two states themselves. It is an actual, but formal difference. This is again what occurs with 0 and 1 in set theory. The two make the number one only be repeating the first emptiness. 0=1 in one sense and that is again why there is a systemic difference between them. But only that difference is here recorded. While 0 and 1 are thus like a and not not-a, it is only the difference written in that relation that operates here and not the identity. Now, many of course here will insist rightly that bit strings mean nothing without something to interpret them. Any number of bit strings are identical but within their own context refer to something else. At the same time, that two things are expressed by the same bit string mean they have some sort of fundamental identity between them despite their diversity at another level. That is, it may be very simply that the way stars revolve around a black hole and biological phenomena are intimately identical precisely because if the universe is a computer, the same program can be run in different instances. At the same time, there is nothing in 0's and 1's to tell one what they are about and what they are doing. They meaningless in themselves and can only speak of transformations at best from one string to another. The binary is always a code which means it is always the cipher text of something else.

This encryption is also linked to the very act of programming being enacted as Wolfram notes:

> The basic idea is just that in many systems the process of evolution
> through time in effect so 'encrypts' the information associated with
> the initial conditions for the system that no feasible measurement
> or other process can recognize what they were. So in effect, it
> would take a Maxwell's Demon of immense computational power
> to unscramble the evolution.[71]

What this means is that when one sees phenomena unfolding, one does not see the code for it precisely because its elaboration and articulation encrypts the meaning it was t first. Thus, one would only be able to find the code for the system by reproducing its evolution since its encryption such that it cannot be simply deduced or extracted.

Thus it must always be linked to something that one can decode if it is to operate at more than just the level of the number and letter. For us, there is no interest in a computer insofar as it is pure electricity; we want to see things displayed on the monitor and to move about with our mice. We thus make use of a dual structure where the code itself is transferred from electrical signal to meaningful signs, from voltage to commands. The code in and of itself does not refer to anything but itself. It says itself directly and only itself. It does not represent anything until it is linked to an interpreter and thus to a dual structure where the code can be a signifier for some signified. The digital code is in itself anything one wants. It is completely generic. This is why one and the same code could be for the galaxy and the whirlpool.

At the same time, the binary code is not just meaningless letters but also numbers which enable them to function as such. Lacan said:

> What Descartes now introduces, and which is illustrated at once, for, at the same time as his discourse on method he introduces his geometry and his dioptrics, is this—he substitutes the small letters, a, b, c, etc., of his algebra for the capital letters. The capital letters, if you will, are the letters of the Hebrew alphabet with which God created the world and to each of which, as you know, there corresponds a number. The difference between Descartes' small letters and the capital letters is that Descartes' small letters do not have a number—they are interchangeable and only the order of the commutations will define their process.72

Lacan here refers to the Kabbalistic concept of creation of existence through the letters that we are both implicitly and explicitly attempting to articulate. But also we see that with the digital code's letters are now again associated with numbers. Cartesian science only saw letters as without any numerical significance and thus considered them to be meaningless until spoken to one. But now see that at the level of the letter itself and in its permutation, there is not the same interchangeability and rather a relation of difference itself that yields laws, rules, etc. Bit strings are floating signifiers, but at the same are caught with differentiality and numerosity itself. Thus, with the bit strings we need to understand how they are at one level signifier, but later function as signified that is, computation itself involves a process where data is manipulated by recognizable patterns and rules. There is thus a program that is immanent for us to the transformations. But when we reach the level of mind itself, of the human subject for instance, there is a more direct processing of this data. The computer thus reflects our own minds more so than the universe and its form of computation when it comes to seemingly non-conscious processes.

The computer is constantly shifting form one level to the next switching between data treated as input and data treated as output. Because there is no motivated relationship between any bit string and what is assigned to do or represent, any bit string can become linked to another command and at one level the bit string can function as the meaningless code itself but at another level as the name for what hat code does or means. This is why we see fractal patterns so often Such facts are found when input leads to output and then that some output becomes the input for the next step. The iteration of this process yields the self-same pattern on differing levels. Here, the process is looped. But it need not be so regular.

Coding will yield ambiguities if one does not have another code for saying what it does. This is especially here the case since 011000 could mean one thing in one code and another in another. One thus often needs additional bit strings to clarify previous ones. The bit string is thus tied to another bit string that decodes it. It is always either the cipher text or plain text. The binary coding is the universal code, but also in another from the plain text. Only for us, when it comes to mind and what it cognizes, there is another language at work. This is also why one cannot simply focus on an isolated bit string. The issue is always to show one bit string yielding another. One wants to know the immanent rule for the transformations and not just the outputs. At the same time in a computer, one must have a split between a set of instructions and another the action itself. For instance, one needs the electric current and the logic gates interacting and at the other level the coding itself related to each step. If one does not have that split, one would have an infinite regress. But the split is two sides of one and the same thing. The electric current and its adventure is one and the same thing as the bit string that instructs. There is thus an internal split of the same thing into two faces. Only this allows for a basic level that cannot be gone beyond further.

One does not need to ask what the electric current means since it is the same thing as the 0's and 1's. There is no need to regress further. Thus, one and the same this split such that is a one-to-one correspondence between itself in one state and in another. There is already an internal split between the thing as it is in its electrical adventure here and its being as zeroes and ones. This is the same for any phenomena in the universe. It is always split itself in its identity between what it does as an organism for instance or as a stellar phenomena and its being as bits with each being two faces of the same. We can thus say that what we see when we see stars revolving around a black hole is but a higher level language that is always already compiled. The acts we see are themselves a semiotic language, but that language is already converted into the machine code of the universe itself. We simply are trapped in the imaginary of phenomenal perception and only intuit one side.

It is like a computer screen. We see the pixels and the colors, the photos and the images and do not see the coding that it is as well. There is no need for a translator when it comes to the universe since it is running on its own. Our computers need translators only because without our programming they would remain inert. On one side then things are the appearance and another they are their encoding. But that is the same as saying on the one side there is the cipher text and on the other the plain text. The cipher text itself devoid of meaning and has no reference since it is but the reverse side of the other. This is why the bit string is itself a set. It is as a set having no referent, but as a set of bits it is a structured set of integers and thus not removed from the principles and properties of numerosity. Bit strings thus refer only to themselves and also have another face, but it is not a referential relation between one side and the other. It is more so like the lining of a garment.

At the same time the bit strings as sets are identical if they have the same sequence. The bit string 01010101 is the same as 01010101 not matter what each is linked and what each is the other side of. Because any linkage is arbitrary, each could be linked to two different things because one and the same program can run in two different places. The axiom of extensionality here works on two different sets with two different names. The set is itself an act of belonging to a name without reference beyond what it collects, a proper name and a designation. Many will reject this vision since they want to things as being solely on the side of appearances or on the side of perception. That is, they want to see only the computer screen and forget about its reverse side. They thus believe that there is a material media that is decisive here. But what they are calling a material medium is but the manner in which one bit string transforms into another. It is only the program itself and not some ether. They believe that one and the same thing written in blue ink versus blue pencil is important different given the difference in writing device. But what they do not see is that each is lined by a code. It need not be the same exact code, but that it is the code which is its reverse side and would tell us if the two things are truly identical.

Part of the vision being articulated here concerns the idea that all of existence is mathematics since all is in its materiality bit strings. However, some object to Pythagoreanism. I am told that Markus Gabriel for instance in a lecture argued that the world cannot be inherently mathematical since when I add together two distinct drops of water it does not yield two drops but rather one.73 However, this object presumes that all things are simply positive integers and that when one says all things can be mathematized it means that any unity is an integer-like unity. Water has a continuous aspect to it. Thus what we call a single water drop is not a simple unit like a positive integer. For this reason, when we add two drops together we get one drop. All water drops are thus somehow related in a continuous way. Water's continuity probably means it needs to be conceived as being like ω and aleph –null rather than one (that is, by transfinite numbers). Each water drop is connected to a continuous being. Thus, water may be more likes ω times ω thus yielding the same aleph-null cardinality.

Or, we see in water that one drop is not added to another but it s more so a relation of multiplication (1 x 1). In either event, we can calculate both relations using an electric computer or other forms of computation. In other words, the fact that water drops do not act as positive integers does not mean there is no mathematical structure to the world but that we need to unearth that right mathematical structure informing it. Mathematization thus teaches us something fundamental about the properties of the water we will not otherwise understand. We see that for instance water while it might appear numerically discrete as does a positive integer is never really discrete in its very being as drops. Or it shows us that two distinct things merge into one because their relationship results not in one of addition, but rather multiplication. Even if we have four water drops it is only ever 1 x1 x 1 x1. Thus, the difference in things is precisely the difference in their mathematization and thus in the relations that inform them and form their substance.

The point of saying that the world is mathemitizable is not that one tries to force the world to fit one specific model of mathematics but that one accepts for the world how it speaks of its own mathematical nature. A calculator after all does not just have addition and subtraction buttons. And yet the calculator does all it does ultimately by making use of bit strings. Whole numbers do not apply to water directly, but in another context the phenomenon will show itself to be like whole numbers. We have to accept the phenomenon itself and show the specific mathematics that express it rather than trying to saying everything is made of whole numbers. Not surprisingly, mathematics is not just a theory of whole numbers.

§13. James Gates and the Programmed Universe

Scientists are only now today realizing the way in which the universe is a computer and how all phenomena are in their very substantiality made up of zeroes and ones, of information. At the forefront of this discovery is the work of physicist James Gates. Gates claims to have discovered computer code at work at the most microscopic levels of reality itself. In an article entitled "Symbols of Powers" Gates shows that in supersymmetry particle physics (SUSY) he has unearthed how phenomena operate just as error-correcting software code does.74 Error-correcting codes are codes sent along with a bit string to ensure that the bit string is received as it was intended at the other end and not in some jumbled form. When one sends a message down a signal, that message can be altered by is called 'noise.' Thus, if one sends the bit string 010101, nose might flip one bit and thus the message 011101 might be received instead. By adding bits that can check to make sure that what one received is the same as the original (this is done using Hamming distances as invented by Richard Hamming) one can correct for any errors produced as the message was set. Without error-correcting codes, many of the emails we would receive would be garbled.

Hamming codes are of course also used in spellchecking software since there the Hamming code suggest the correct word based on distances between what one has misspelled and correct words from the software's dictionary. When data is sent by computer it is always in the form of bit strings, thus any word or sentence sent is coded into binary. Thus, there the plaintext is one's sentence and the cipher text is the binary code. But the additional error-correcting bits are added and the software knows what the function is. In fact, there is a particular algorithm that does this by adding up 0's and 1's from their place in the bit string to see if the sum is even or odd (0 or 1). A few bits are used to add up different places in the bit string. This way one can check different sums and based on discrepancies find out which particular bit was flipped. Hamming codes can only work because a binary code is used.

Gates took equations related to supersymmetric phenomena and translated them into what are called 'Adrinkas,' which are visual representations of numerical relations. The point here is that Gate took mathematical equations written out as methodical formulas and then discovered by way of translating them into Adrinkas that these formulas can be expressed not just in binary form, but in the binary form of error-correcting code. Thus, equations that express how a particular fundamental level of reality works are shown to work not only as computer code does, but the type of code that corrects for errors. Part of the way Gates did this was by addressing different points on the Adrinka with binary codes and then seeing how the different segments of the drawing related to transformations in the bit strings from one to another. The use of Adrinkas is here secondary as the key is the manner in which the equations and their relations are rendered in binary. Thus, what the equation expressing about a phenomenon itself is renderable in binary code and its transformations.

Gates then offers a model for expressing any physical phenomena that we can analyze using mathematical equations into a programmable event. Most science today is done on computers, but this is often taken as some sort of accidental fact. Only when we realize that any phenomena can be rendered in code in this way and thus understood to be part of a universe itself that is computer will we begin to understand that we can simulate any phenomenon on a computer and also thus discover its basic properties and functioning. What Gates' groundbreaking work shows is how information theory itself will be the fundamental theory of Physics and other sciences as in particular these sciences are more and more so done using computer simulations. Only because existence itself is computational will we be able to discover how it works simply by putting the basic binary code that forms its substance.

Our reality is coded and controlled by it. We must not simply go from 'it to bit; as Wheeler wanted, but to see that it is bit, and bit is it. Gates explains Wheeler's view well:

The idea of "it from bit" is a complex one, and Wheeler's own description of it is probably still the best. In 1990 he suggested that "every 'it' – every particle, every field of force, even the space–time continuum itself – derives its function, its meaning, its very existence entirely…from the apparatus-elicited answers to yes-or-no questions, binary choices, bits". The "it from bit" principle, he continued, "symbolizes the idea that every item of the physical world has at bottom…an immaterial source and explanation: that which we call reality arises in the last analysis from the posing of yes–no questions and the registering of equipment evoked responses; in short, that all things physical are information-theoretic in origin and that this is a participatory universe.75

We must accept with Gates that not only can codes be found in nature, but that nature is itself code. Existence itself is computation, and we can do with any equation whether it is those for Quantum Mechanics or General Relativity what Gates has done with superstring theory. In fact, we should begin doing so because we will discover something about the very nature and function of these phenomena precisely by learning how they function as software. One phenomenon might work to correct errors while another might work like a random number generator while yet another might simply show itself to iterate the same pattern in a fractal-like algorithm.

At the same time, by discovering the informational substance of things, we can both better simulate them on the computer we have and thereby project into the future how things will develop. We can thus make predictions on how a particular phenomenon will unfold because we will have the very coding (as long as the computational time of our computer will be faster than that of the universe in this context). We should accept that reality is inherently mathematical and this is why equations could teach us about it in the first place. Systems that are expressible by the same equation or the same code are related if only in these sense that they run the same program.

As Gates notes, Eugene Wigner argued in his famous article "The Unreasonable Effectiveness of Mathematics in the Natural Sciences" that we should not think there is any special relationship between two things just because the same type of mathematics explains them.76 But with computer code and programs we cannot continue Wigner's attitude. It leads us of course more and more to believe that two things have the same coding and thus program because they were designed to have them. But also that these two systems with same program while perhaps not directly affecting each other can tell us something about how reality functions insofar as they have the same coding. Gates writes: "The number pi, after all, occurs in the measurement of circles as well as in the measurement of population distributions. This does not mean that populations are related to circles".77 True enough. But the issue is not showing that both are related to circles, but would be for instance showing why populations have the same program as the motion of certain molecules. This in itself when take together with the idea that the universe is a computer will help to shed light on why things function as they do.

Gates here also asks whether we live in the Matrix, but the issue is not whether we live in a simulation that is being run on a computer located in some other dimension. Rather, we should take things for what they are and they are on that score computational. If we do exist in a computer simulation then as Edward Fredkin has argued, that computer is located in any entirely transcendent dimension (Fredkin calls it 'Other'). It must be because the computer running the simulation must be more powerful than the simulation itself. It would thus be the mind of God that would form the very computer itself and we would be a reflection of it. But that presumes a mirroring relationship between a world of essences and this world rather than the divine form of creation we have suggested via contraction.

We should look for code in the laws of Physics and in doing so plug them into simulations. For instance, if we measure how electrons in particular changes states, we have the measurements of the whole process. When we look at this process as a bit string, we will not know what in the bit string the electron is since it is a process itself. We should not think that there will be a simple code within the code for electrons. We only have the bit string for the process itself. When we measure another process an electron undergoes, we will have a different bit string. The important thing is how the bits flip and how the bit stings are transformed. The important thing is the program and not looking for some 'object' called 'the electron.' After all, we rush all too quickly to reify the measurements science offers us. We also rush to reify the equations and the signs with them. An electron is first and foremost a measurement. Since it deals with measurements and then explains those measurements using equations. To think there are always discrete things like the perceptual objects we are familiar with is a step too far.

Also let us say something here about noise. Noise is often taken to refer to the pure entropy and randomness that pervades all things. Thus, the fact that one needs error-correcting codes would indicate that one is fighting against an inherent lack of order and randomness in the universe. But that error-correcting codes seem to be built into the fabric of the universe should lead us to see noise as having the same status. Noise in one context might cause disruption, but in another might lead to diversification and thus functions like a random number generator that can produce new content and avoid the repetition of the same. Thus, when we want to send a message the random noise that flips bits from 1 to 0 interferes and thus needs to be corrected for. But given Gates' discovery, we should expect that this occurs in nature as well while in other cases the random or quantum noise works in a constructive way. The point is that even noise need not be purely random, but rather the function of programming itself. The discoveries of Stephen Wolfram show us precisely how a program can generate randomness.

The divine plan is concealed in all things as their reverse, their binary coding. But few have so far attempted to discover them. Recall the earlier Wolfram quote here. Part of the problem here is that the code necessarily encrypts itself as it unfolds. We forget that we are only looking at the screen. We think the picture is the whole thing, but hiding behind it is not a Platonic realm of objects. Behind the stars are not really real stars shadowing them, but rather there are 0's and 1's forming their substance. If each thing is a bit string, the string is a set of letters, but what is then associated with that bit string is arbitrary. It is not necessary. One cannot show that the linkage between the string and its phenomenal face must follow. One could only show if one know the very most basic code of the universe itself and then one could show from its unfolding that the linkage was necessary. The compressible core program would then decide how things are and why the express what they do in the manner they do.

Leibniz too thought there would be one rule for determining such things. But he did not have the same developed sense of computation we have today. Thus, it is not clear that Leibniz would see the arbitrary relation between one example of a certain bit string (no matter how long as long as it is finite) and a process occurring with what we call electrons. At the same time, even if we have all the bit strings, we do not necessary know how to read the book yet. If we were given the bit string information for a process associated with electrons, we would not know just base on that that it referred to electrons. One cannot eliminate empirical investigation quite so quickly. The next step is thus to learn the language of how the generic elements arrange themselves into sets and why those sets. Doing so might require us to know the compressible code for things themselves and then running it. We thus can have at one time either the plaintext or the cipher text, but not yet how one goes from one to the other. But seeing transformations themselves can tell us the code regardless.

The issue for thought today is simply of code and its decipherment since we know now that code can encrypt itself and also undergo transformations on its own following rules. Thus, if we have a sequence of letters, we could once upon a time translate that sequence into the pluses and minuses of Morse code for example. We would then send it and reinterpret it. But today we see pluses and minuses assets transforming into a new sets of pluses and minuses. We have discovered that computation via our invention of the computer, but the universe was all along doing the same. We on the other and were caught up in questions of meaning and reference rather than taking the letters themselves as the heart of the matter because we knew they were somehow meaningless. But now we know that we can learn for the letters themselves even if we do not know how to decipher them. We can simply ask how many letters it takes to do something. We can ask what numbers are associated with those letters. We can simply look at the sequence of the letters themselves. We thus are thus well beyond the age of Morse code.

For instance we do not simply what the info in the pluses and minuses, in the dots and dashes. We do not simply want to know how to render pluses and minuses into a signified and into a semiotics. We want to know now the bit string itself and its transformations. We want to penetrate beyond the screen and understand the pure logic of dots and dashes rather than rushing to learn only from the screen.

§14. Did Leibniz already say it?

This is as good time as any to differentiate what is being advocated here from what Leibniz claimed. It is often said that Leibniz already argued certain ideas. Certain, already I have argued that Leibniz's idea that each singular monad expresses the entire universe in its own way can be substantiated in a new way. There, it was argued one could show via the failure of CH how the thesis that each thing is a mirror of God and the world within which it exists. For Leibniz, it was only a question of what something includes. But there is no conception of the notion of belonging. A concept is only ever an intensional whole for Leibniz. But because he emphasized the relation of inclusion (predicate included in its subject), he was able to discover intuitively the infinite hiding within everything. However, we have offered a new grounding for his point. But the issue was not one of events or a line of cause and effects, but rather one of belonging and inclusion. It was also about a relation to the non-all rather than a totality and to a name for the unnamable rather than a complete language.

This view was also restricted, at least in our previous discussion, to the realm of eidos. For Leibniz, every real unity is like a city resident who has their own perspective on the city where they live. Leibniz certainly saw that each thing is marked by the divine in itself and by God's power of creation, but did not see them as containing a relation to God's omnipresence, to the omnipresence of the absolute infinite. Leibniz's position here is derived from a combination of the principles of identity and sufficient reason relative to subject-predicate logic. Therefore, inclusion for him was a matter of properties included in a subject, rather than subsets included in a purely extensional set. Also, in Leibniz there is no clear sense that there is a way to reduce to all of existence to a single program (no matter the length). This is not surprising since in Leibniz's age there was not a clear sense of what computation was and what it was capable of. In this way, we would also argue that one section of the universal program does express a perspective on it. Sometimes a perspective on a program is like a fractal where one particular segment is a microcosm of it. But in another a selected set of its iteration is its own irreducible expression.

Now, Leibniz was the first to think that all of the rules of logic could be expressed using numbers and that logical arguments could be tested relative to their validity using a binary or numerically expressed logic. But Leibniz, despite being one of the most important progenitors of digital philosophy, never connected his work on digital expression of numbers for instance to his most detailed and important work on metaphysics, *The Monadology*. There, one would not get any sense that it was Leibniz who in scattered texts said that all might be expressed using only 0's and 1's. Part of the reason for that is that monads while being metaphysical points are still perceptual beings in some way. They are therefore would not simply be bit strings, but at most something like machinic processes that engage with other such processes.

Also, while Leibniz said that things are their complete concepts, he at the same time rejected the idea that a mere aggregate of things was a true unity.78 Such a rejection shows that he takes a conceptual unity to be a real and natural thing rather than a product of thought, but such a view forces him to restrict what a monad can be without any clear principle to do so. Thus, Leibniz is far from being a forerunner of extensional set theory on this score. This is because here Leibniz was willing to admit that when it came to atomic corpuscles that anyone can find in it an infinity of divisible parts and thus did not know from any true unity, he would not accept such a view when it came to the true indivisible whole making up pure unities. That is, Leibniz would not accept that the whole did not precede its parts, that a part could be equal to or larger than the whole, etc. Thus, Leibnizian monads necessarily precede their parts and only later organize them. They give them unity. Unity only comes from these wholes. It is these wholes which must be some sort of eternal objects created whole cloth by God.

Despite being a dedicated student of the Kabbalah, Leibniz here has not taken to heart what it means to create the world with letters and numbers. It meant that prior to a unit such as dog, there is only d, o, and g. Monads as simples for Leibniz meaning the whole is the indivisible unity. This is in contradiction to a view where the indivisible itself is a without relation or the empty set. One cannot go on infinitely for Leibniz and also cannot end in emptiness, but there is no empty set, no void, for him either. There is a complete world and complete language for deriving it and thus there can be no vacuum or purely supernumerary name that explains things. This is because Leibniz did not realize you can only have a complete language (insofar as it is possible) using 0 and 1 and not using subject-predicate logic as such a logic involves intensional sets and self-reference, which are always a secondary development of the computation of the meaningless sign.

Leibniz never argues that YHVH is the pure name that forms the program for the computation of all things. Leibniz never would claim that at the heart of sense there is non-sense, a string of letters. Such a non-sense at the heart of things decompletes them and in a radical way. Leibniz would need to say it is something else, purely the mind of God issuing the right amount of monads in the proper relations. Leibniz's model is thus, as man have noted, closest to that of Indra's net rather where indivisible wholes are networked. For example, in a text entitled "Two Studies in Logical Calculus" Leibniz speaks of discovering how different numerical values can be associated with concepts directly such as the concepts of "man" and "ape" and then arguing that the concept of ape "does include that of man" solely based on the numerical relationship.79 The problem here is that it is not clear that Leibniz would ever accept that the numerical values have been derived arbitrarily.

I have already mentioned Leibniz's view on the ideality of the continuum. Not only did Leibniz not see it as real ,but as not divisible "into points" or "in all possible ways" showing that Leibniz would only accept a model in which CH was upheld since he was against there being anything other than "a certain infinite progression of" things.80 It is also not clear that Leibniz can be designated as a realist rather than a pure ontological idealist. To my knowledge, Leibniz never speaks of the resurrection of the dead in actual physical terms (outside perhaps of one text from the last few months of his life we will engage with later). Monads after all cannot be created or destroyed. They are not ultimately material things in any essential way so it is not clear why they would need resurrection. At most Leibniz could claim the monad still persists as the organizing principle of our bodies as they dissolve in the ground. The resurrection of us back into our very bodily existence would seem strange to Leibniz insofar as the monad is on its own sufficient without any reference to materiality. Now, clearly Leibniz did for all that on isolated occasions entertain the idea of infinites of infinities, but never systematized this view in an away. Leibniz also believed that even "in the smallest particle of dust, there can exist a world, in which all things have the same rational properties" as in the larger world", but it does not appear here that Leibniz means anything more than an infinitely self-iterating fractal. That is, while Leibniz could agree with the vision of all things being self-similar at each level, he did not see that repetition could lead itself to difference. This insight would have to wait until Wolfram in many ways.

Leibniz also opposes very clearly the notion of the void. It is not simply a matter of there being no void time, but that there can be no voiding of "forms" as such.81 This is not to say we cannot find a text where Leibniz does not discuss the void in positive terms. In the oft-cited "On the True Theologia Mystica", there is a central passage that does in a few sentences what the title of the text promises:

All creatures derive from God and form nothingness [Nichts]. Their self-being [Selbstwesen] is of God, the nonbeing [Unwesen] is of nothing. (Numbers too show this on their own fully, and the essences of things are like numbers. No creature can be without nonbeing; otherwise, it would be God. Angels and saints must have it. The only self-self-knowledge is to distinguish well between our self-being and our non-being (and so to prevent our straying from the way of light. But one must make use of sensual things [Eergetzlichkeiten] and must view the shadow pictures only as an aid or a tool and not rest in them). Within our self-being there lies an infinity, a footprint or reflection of the omniscience and omnipresence of God.82

The Pythagoreanism evoked by this passage is profound, but it is not clear that it ever reappears in the Leibnizian corpus. Could one say that the notion of nothingness or numbers articulated here has any impact on the *Monadology* which will be composed 24 years later? Nothing in the letter of the text indicates as much. But this is precisely the problem with Leibniz. One will find in an isolated text of a few pages or a few sentences expressing perfectly what we would agree with, but then no evidence that this view informs in any systematic way his most direct and detailed expressions of his philosophy. This is why our text is not simply a commentary on Leibniz since there is no sustained text that engages in the issues at stake here (except in one obscure and relatively unknown text which forms a specific case where Leibniz anticipates our key issues in surprising detail—a text from near the very end of his life where suddenly the letter makes its appearance).

Instead, to be Leibnizian today is to write the text that Leibniz did not write, to connect the dots that are left scattered in the Leibnizian opus. To be Leibnizian today is to take key theses of the Leibnizian worldview and to articulate them using the tools Leibniz would not have had available to him (Cantorian set theory, computationalism, the notions of undecidability and incomputability, etc.). For instance, when Leibniz speaks of the divine footprint included in all, we have discovered it by name via Cohen's intervention on CH.

Also, Leibniz here does not see that the nothingness is itself in one sense the absolute infinite. There is also no notion of the empty set here that can form a bridge between God and nothing itself. Things are made of numbers and non-being, but it is not insinuated that the numerical substance of things implies its computational nature. It is not clear that it is not more so a Platonic relation of mimesis and mirroring between the eternal and appearances at work. Numbers might be expressible as 0's and 1's for Leibniz, but there is no discussion of bitwise transformations or bit flipping. This is why those who say Leibniz has already said this or that imagine a text that we would very much like to read, but has not existed until perhaps recently and has been signed by names other than 'Leibniz.'

In addition, while Leibniz is able to express how numbers arise from 0 and 1 and articulate each bit string, Leibniz rejects the idea that "number arises only from the division of the continuum" as the "Scholastics falsely believed" which means he thereby overlooks several key ideas amongst them that numbers are related to questions of limits and partitioning of the infinite itself in the realm of existence and the finite. This is because Leibniz sees God as a mathematician, and thus sees an external relation obtaining between God's calculation and execution of thought and the creation of the world rather than seeing God's creation of the world as outside the realm of thought itself, pure contraction. Thus, Leibniz does not distinguish between God and his thoughts and thereby one can agree with Badiou when he says that here "God is the constructibility of the constructive, the programme of the World. Leibniz is the principle philosopher for whom God is language in its supposed completion. God is nothing more than the being of the language in which being is folded...." (*BE* 317).

Because Leibniz cannot see the split between God and his thoughts, the withdrawal of God from his very thoughts, he thinks that God is language itself and the calculating and programming of things without realizing the gap between this program and the programmer. The erasure of this gap also leads to the notion of language as complete with known external reference or without gaps, without undecidable statements and any problems of self-reference. Badiou also argues that Leibniz's rejection of the void is connected to his belief in a complete language as the void would be an excessive difference in its very indifference and indivisibility (*BE* 321). This excessive point of the void has a name, a pure proper name. Leibniz, to my knowledge, never discusses God's proper name despite his immersion in the Kabbalah (that it came to him via Lull and what is often called 'Christian Kabbalah' is not relevant at this point)--for it is the Kabbalah that imagines a space wholly empty of God that God himself creates. That empty space shows the very contingent nature of existence itself.

Leibniz is worried about the indiscernibility of the void and God's not being able to notice it, but that is because he also misses the void's relation to the mark and point. This rejection of the pure proper name and the void shows us why Leibniz is not a true Pythagorean or Kabbalist despite his belief that nothing cannot be numbered and search for a kabalistic calculus of names. When Leibniz wants to resolve all things into a set of indivisible and ultimately unanalyzable, primitive concepts and show that those concepts are the very elements of human thoughts, he does not think that this arises as a result of lettering in any fundamental sense.83 There are for Leibniz fundamental concepts, but they are like names. These names are not further analyzable into anything, especially not letters.

This is why one should not think that the Leibnizian universal characteristic would be written in 0's and 1's and via the permutation of letters. Rather, it is mostly likely he had in mind a pictographic language where each sign is a pure expression of a name. In other words, Leibniz looked at Chinese characters and their lettering rather than a purely consonantal or phonetic language as model for his universal characteristic. Writing for him should be done with signs that seemingly express their signified in a natural symbolic way in order to allow the imagination itself to do the work of thought and for thought to move silently and without a reliance on the verbal.

Leibniz's ideal langue is inherently significant and does so with images that are themselves pure and axiomatic concepts. There is nothing here meaningless in and of itself. There are only signs that are immediately sublimated into signifieds. One then of course allows for the combination of these fundamental signs. But the signs are inherently meaningful and essentially related to their signified. The linkage between them is not arbitrary in any sense. The concepts themselves and the relations among them are human thought made flesh insofar as they would be written. It would only be a projection and mimesis of what goes on silently within the mind. Thus, the elements here are not letters in the sense we understand them or bits. It is not from the meaningless sign that sense or thought emerges for Leibniz. Leibniz thinks that the idea language has nothing to do with sounds and only involves concepts. He is looking for a language that dispenses with sounds and inscription as such.

Thus, while there may be a symbolic calculus here, there is no real computation. For computation, one would need the permutation of letters themselves. One cannot compute with ready-made and indivisible concepts that are unanalyzable in any further sense and have no arbitrary linkages with their inscription. Hegel himself identified this in his criticism of Leibniz's celebration of Chinese pictography.84 Only on the basis of an appreciation of alphabetic and phonetic inscription would one would discover computation as such. Only in the idea of inscription can concepts be represented by meaningless signs and arbitrary linked to them. Thus the concept on this score is exiled to another order where in its irreducibility it will return, but not due to its being expressed by inherently significant signs. There is an alphabet repeating all possible concepts, but it only obtains completion via the permutation of letters.

This is why one has to object to Martin Davis's attempt to see Leibniz's work on a universal characteristic as the very foundational text of the modern computer.85 Davis here misses how computation is itself based on symbols with no inherent meaning. It is also to mistake the nature of human thought. It would lead us to believe that human thinking consists of a series of imagined pictures rushing around in a theater of representation. But human thought as we know now is neuronal in action and stuck to the signifier. Thus, Leibniz's view does not relate to the computer or to the human mind.

§15. The Birth of the Letter

We rush to attribute things to Leibniz that he never truly said when we think that by a universal characteristic he meant 0's and 1's. He means rather a perfect notational system where each notion is itself a fundamental and irreducible concept. Thus, if computation was done with hieroglyphics, Leibniz's work on a universal characteristic would be the first attempt. But hieroglyphics never lead to computation because their very natures as pictures lead people to look through them and believe that they present via this transparency perceptual objects and ideas. Human thought is opaque and really just pluses and minuses and bitwise transformations insofar as what occurs occurs in a universal computer. The relations between our thoughts are not simply rules, but themselves immanent in the bitwise transformations.

The problem here is that manner in which Leibniz conceived of Chinese (regardless of its actual status) would make it only a partial writing system, as John deFrancis argues in his book *Visible Speech*.86 Any pictographic system would be a partial system of writing that can convey only part of what is thinkable whereas, as we shall see, phonetic writing can be used to express any possible thought. In particular, such a complete system requires a dual articulation between a series of meaningless differential elements and signifieds to which they have been arbitrarily linked. Leibniz in creating a system to express all human thoughts did not take this into account. Of course, in its spoken form any natural language can express any possible thought. But this is because via the phoneme all languages already have the necessary meaningless elements to permute into all possible thoughts. Thus, all the natural languages we know about are capable of articulating whatever can be said of our mental and physical experience. We can discuss in them all our experiences and engage in philosophy.

But of course the spoken is restricted to the oral. It was only recorded in memory. When it comes to graphical writing, one can only begin to match this notion of completeness with phonetic writing. Pictographic writing involves symbols attempting to represent a distinct thing or signified idea. Of course, these images were not purely mute as they already were readable out loud. But their focus on the things themselves meant that they were about attempting to articulate the world rather than the letter. They painted language out as a series of names that were assumed to be inherently meaningful. The signifier was seen as being directly linked and caught up with the signified without gap or difference. Thus, nothing about the pictograph was taken as non-signifying or meaningless in itself. The image is taken as whole which is not reducible to its parts immediately.

Of course with pictography every shape of the picture is important, but one does not pay attention to the curvature of the line or the sheer coloration of the hieroglyphic face. One experiences the sign as transparent. One passes directly through it to the thing. The picture disappears into the thing which it represents or the idea that it is meant to impose on one. To use a stark example, but one that will one make the point. Often, in pictography, 'woman' is represented by a triangle with a line moving upwards from its bottom vertex. One cannot of course not look at such an image and not immediately see the shape of a woman in one's imagination knowing that it is linked to 'woman.' The sign here as it were directly affects the imagination and offers one the illusion that one passes through the sign to the thing itself. Of course, a woman is not truly shaped like a triangle. She is not a geometric shape. But once the symbol and the thing become associated there is an immediate association of idea and image. An image in the mind and the pictographic itself are immediately intertwined.

This is why pictography is itself intimately related to paganism. One might not be able to say it is the very cause of paganism itself, but it is the spiritual substance of that form of being. Paganism is locked inside the imaginary. This is why Plato's 'Allegory of the Cave' despite being written in phonetic script reflects Plato's existence in the pagan world and the very metaphysics of paganism itself. There, a relation is established between the thing itself as idea, the thing in flesh and bone, a picture of the thing, a shadow of the thing, etc. All exist on a scale of imaginary resemblance where the thing in itself is always represented by something that is allegedly identical to it and yet fails to match it perfectly. But that is precisely the pictographic sign in its signifying quality. When one looks at the word 'woman,' one does not see the image of a woman or imagine one without concerted effort, but rather hears immediately the sound. With hieroglyphics, there is no recognized non-signifying element. This is why hieroglyphics are not made up of letters, but are indivisible symbols. They are wholly semiotic in character. They represent something to someone. They have a determinate meaning to which they constantly refer.

It should be emphasized here that whether one argues pictograms refer to ideas or sensible things in the world, the result is the same. This is why noting that pictograms of clouds did not simply point to a cloud in the sky, but also to feelings of sadness or darkness would not change the issue. Like any symbol, the meaning had to be fixed by a trans-individual code. Associationism is at the heart of the pictograph. At the same time, there is always a system one must be educated in to know the meaning at work. No one should suspect that we claim here that the meaning of a pictograph is obvious or natural. Pictographs are linguistic symbols through and through and thus part and parcel of a code. The writing system at work could articulate many sophisticated thoughts, but not every possible thought. This is because one was always combining whole names rather than permuting meaningless signs. The signs are not mute and do not yield a deaf writing as Hegel claimed, but that does not mean the writing in itself offers the same possibilities as phonetic writing.

Pictography is ultimately universal in the abstract sense. It has difficulty referring to a particular sun on a particular day rather than the sun itself and its immutable properties. This is again whey despite existing in a culture of phonetic writing Plato's view is still very much a product of a pagan, pictographic culture in which the universal is itself prominent. But the universal is always connected to an image. It is not for instance an extensional set. The universal is a pattern or archetype. It is of course the emphasis on this aspect of the universal that separated Plato from the Pythagoreans who already via their view of numbers had grasped more fully the new alphabetic culture that would emerge. This emergence is simply a brute, empirical fact of history that cannot be overlooked or argued away. That means one must trace the manner in which pictographic writing became phonetic writing.

And linguists have put forth a powerful theory for how this transitioned occurred. Linguists, such as the aforementioned DeFrancis, argue that this transition was made possible by what is called the 'rebus principle.' Pictography already referred to sounds and could be read aloud. When one saw the symbol of the sun, one said aloud the corresponding word. Thus, it was almost always that pictography was about the thing, the idea, and the verbalized word. But the verbalization of the sign opened the door for a further transition. The pictographic sign could now be taken simply for its sound alone. Thus a symbol for the sun represented the articulated word 'son' as well and functions as its written sign. Taking the symbol for 'sun' to be related to 'son' is already an example of the rebus principle at work The pictographic symbol is taken to be solely a sounded signifier independent of any idea or thing it might represent. It is also a sound in itself. When this sounded literalization occurs, the pictograph has its perceptual relation with the thing it allegedly represents broken and becomes at least in one context a wholly phonographic sign. It now represents only the sound of the words spoken and nothing else. Sound can function beyond any intended meaning here. Thus what might appear to be a purely referential sign, like that of the sun pictograph, becomes caught up with its homophone.

DeFrancis notes how the rebus principle took a step forward when "a pictographical symbol was used not for its original meaning value but especially to represent the sound evoked by the name of the symbol" such that one could write out a sentence now using symbols irregardless of any ideas those symbols represented or things they were meant to resemble. Here, the resemblance between sign and thing signified was bracketed. The sign now functions not as a picture, but as a signifier. DeFrancis offers the following example: "The change in function that results from using a picture as rebus can be illustrated by the use of a picture of a bee followed by that of a leaf to express the sounds of the word belief".87 The concept of belief here is immediately inscribed in writing whereas before one had a combination of the ideas of a bee and that of leaf. What occurs here with the rebus principle is the transformation of pictographic signs into letters. For instance, in Hebrew, the fourth letter is 'dalet' which once was the symbol for 'door" (most probably a "three-cornered tent door).88 Today, the letter 'dalet' has no meaning or sense. It is a letter. It does not represent a door any more. It only represents its name and its sound. 'Dalet' today does not represent anything.

Pictographic writing "could write only what the limited part of thought was clearly picturable", but with the invention of the letter via the rebus principle, the new phonetic writing would be more complete.89 This is not to say that phonetic writing captures all things that are in speech such as "intentional stress, and tempo" or that writing does not have marks that have nothing to do with an attempt to represent sound (spacing, punctuation marks, etc.).90 That is, even in our own phonetic writing, there are still pictographic signs used whether when one is driving or otherwise. Phonetic writing is not something that can be simply be verbalized by the voice. It has its own two-dimensional domain, that of the page. That domain is a graphical one. It has non-phonetic aspects such as the line and its curvature. Phonetic writing is thus not controlled by the voice or the vocal. It is not a writing that is simply a pale image of the voice or that can be at any moment be purely translated into the voice that would read it aloud.

All phonetic inscription includes gaps between words, purely orthographical marks, etc. But phonetic writing is capable of articulating any possible concept such as that of 'belief' once the pictographic sign functions only in its phonographic aspect. Thus, while pictography was universal in the sense that it evoked Platonic ideals in the sense of patterns phonetic wiring is universal in the sense that enables the articulation of pure thought itself. After all, the rebus principle, as any reader of Freud would note, is the dreamwork, the unconscious itself, at work. The transformation of the pictograph into the letter was an example of how human thought was already literal in its own process. One only needed to allow humans to dream about the pictography system for them to finally hit upon the phonetic system in which they were already thinking. Alphabetic writing involves thus signifiers rather than signs since the signifier 'woman' does not represent any thing in the world via resemblance or imaginary representation.

It is always via the written letter attempting to affect a relationship to the phoneme itself—even if written language does not contain all the phonemes as its most basic material (for instance, in English there are 26 written letters, but 44 phonemes. It is also not clear that some letters do not overlap in their phonemic relation such as 'c' and 'k'). But whereas pictography was closed off in terms of a finite number of sign-words and their possible combinations, the completeness of phonetic writing seems to open up a relation to the infinite itself. One can see that phonetic writing is related to the infinite paradoxically precisely because it has a limited number of senseless letters. While Egyptian hieroglyphics has an endless number of signs, there is no clear rule for generating what the next sign will be. One can draw a picture of anything in the world, but it is not clear why one would. However, with 22 letters, in Hebrew, one can compute any word of any length on its basis. In this way, while Hebrew is limited in elements, it is related to the infinite whereas the open hieroglyph is confined to a closed world. Another way to put this is that with letters we get a clear ordinal system of counting while hieroglyphics only knew from cardinal relations. With pictography, one could only ever put things into one-to-one correspondence. But with phonetic letters, one has a clear first, second, etc. element and a reason for why they have that ordering.

At the same time, phonetic writing thus rather than attempting to immediately represent ideas and to associate in the mind a sign with a meaning, it reduces all first and foremost to the meaningless sounds, letters. Thus, phonetic writing makes more explicit the duality of all writing, the two levels of meaningless inscription or sound and the other level of meaning and linked sense. Phonetic writing also makes clear the unmotivated nature of this linkage.

§16. The Phoneme and the Cut

One might think the triangular symbol of 'woman' was somehow a universal or natural symbol for her; the word 'woman' seems to have no direct connection to her. The letter is related to the phoneme. But we need clarify what a phoneme is. A phoneme is not simply any physical sound heard. Rather, the phoneme is a concept. It is, as Roman Jakobson explained, "a bundle of differential elements".91 That is, a phoneme is a purely extensional set. It can include one sound or many (or even none as we will see). It is the bundling together of those distinct sonic elements. It is thus not any one sound in particular, but a collection of units. It is the unit collecting potentially several units. It is thus, as we shall see, more like a number than a tone.

The phonemes of language are themselves also differential elements. The phoneme illustrates the very idea that something cannot be made of itself. The phoneme does not belong to itself and is only a bundling of distinct phonological elements. The phoneme is the set to which things belong rather than being the element itself or the sound itself. But the phoneme is indivisible and a cut. It is for this reason it must be thought as negative, differential in order to isolate it as the fundamental level for sense itself even it is itself something that emerges from a continuum of sounds. The phoneme is an indivisible element of the continuum itself, but only by bundling together other sounds. They are sets that as units serve to differentiate words. One can with a single phoneme differentiate any number of words. We see this graphically often by varying a single letter in a list of similar words.

Also, phonemes as sets can not only have one member, but between two phonemes there may be similar sonic elements in their bundles. The key is that they are identically composed entirely of the same distinctive elements. Not every letter we have corresponds to a phoneme. In English, 'the' (which is not in and of itself a letter) corresponds graphically to two phonemes (as 'the' versus 'thistle'). Again, there are 44 phonemes and only 26 written letters in English. Thus, phonemes can only refer here to the basic form of sounds rather than written letters. They are sonic letters. Written letters relate to them, but there is not a perfect correspondence. Writing and speaking have their own domains. The fact that the change in one sound can change a word means that phonemes are differentiated from each other. They are their difference from each other. They are at one level nothing more than that difference. One does not hear the phoneme, one is only ever mentally aware of the difference between two words on its basis. This leads many to conclude that phonemes are only ever mental units and not heard or seen. But phonemes are never distinct from sound as such. One cannot hear a phoneme as such, but they do not exist distinctly from sound itself. They are not heard and only mentally perceived within the experience of sound itself.

Phonemes are also taken to be ideal since one can vary them using aspiration or lack of aspiration and still recognize the same phoneme at work. Thus, there are certain invariant qualities constant in all the various possible instances of a phoneme. Different speakers will put slightly different twists on the phonemes without the basic function of that specific phoneme being affected. The phonemes 'b' and 'p' will differentiate 'billows' form 'pillows' despite the varied ways in differing context one might say them as long as the key invariant properties are met. Thus, even though phonemes are bundles of differing sounds, the phoneme as such is not decomposable into those elements. The phoneme as the set is itself an emergent whole.

Jakobson calls the invariant aspects of the phoneme "distinctive qualities or properties" or "distinctive features", but notes that these features themselves are purely differential in the sense that they are differing sounds within the sound spectrum.92 The difference of the elements is like two distinct tones one might hear played by a musical instrument. One can clearly distinguish the two as not being identical, but when one plays the instrument there is a meaning effect that arises from the combinations or sets of combinations. The phoneme bundles together things such that when differing phonemes are combined there is a meaning effect that emerges out of their senselessness for the phoneme in itself has no meaning. With the phoneme we thus have an example of something with unchanged properties that persists though various instantiations that is in itself not meaningful. It is nothing but the bundle.

The phoneme is thus a very distinct example of extensional Platonism. The phoneme is necessarily trans-individual and thus cannot be said simply to exist as a concept or mental frame in one's mind. At the same time, we see here a Platonic-like entity that is but the reverse side of the existent perceptual experience: "The phoneme is not to be identified with the sound, yet nor is it external to the sound; it is necessarily present in the sound, being both in them and supported upon it: it is what remains invariant behind the variations".93 As a distinct set, "two phonemes cannot be emitted simultaneously" even though the sonic elements which they bundle could be.94 This is because, as we shall see, the phoneme is not found on the sound continuum itself as can the features which it bundles. The phoneme is an interruption of the sound continuum. This is because the phoneme cannot be divided. It is indivisible in its every essence unlike the continuum itself which appears to be susceptible to endless subdivision. The phoneme will be precisely the point where the sound spectrum loses its indiscriminate and continuous quality for us.

The distinctive elements that phonemes bundles together, but that is not the reason that phonemes have no intrinsic meaning of their own. Phonemes gain meaning only via their function to alter the sense of things through their substitution. This is why their differentiality relates to meaning whereas the sonic features they bundle do not. Phonemes are also combinable into words here as their units are not. If one combined the distinctive features phonemes bundles together in permutations, one would hear noise rather than intelligible sound no matter what language one heard except perhaps for isolated moments where one would think the static had spoken.

It is important here to note that phonemes are finite sets. They are not transfinite. While the set of all possible pronunciations of a phoneme is transfinite, the phoneme bundles together a limited number of features. This shows us how transfinite or finite sets are equally eidetic in nature. There a limited number of rules for putting phonemes together to form intelligible words, morphemes. There are obviously many sounds one can make using the phonemes of English that sound like noise to the English speaker. Only particular sequences work at this time. However, there are not truly rules for grouping together the distinctive features that phonemes bundle. Rather, each phone is an irreducible set that appears contingent. Other groupings of the same distinctive features are possible. Here, there is no clear rule for why English has the 44 phonemes it does. This is not say there is no rule, but on the surface and given that these 44 are each irreducible cuts in the sonic continuum there is no sense for generating more phonemes and no way to say why it must be 44. The number and the character thus have the status of a brute facticity and indivisibility.

Phonemes are the atoms of human speech, and their "limited number" is crucial for "these empty entities" to differentiate between words and their senses.95 If there were an endless number of phonemes the human mind would not be able to deal with them. If there were an infinite number, they would not be able to differentiate. 44 are just enough where each speaker can intuit them and also manipulate and remember them. In their negative and differential aspect, they need not be confused. If one were to find them indistinguishable, they would not function. But phonemes are not simply negative and differential since they are also sets, bundles.

The same can be said about the written letter. One can write letters in any number of shapes, ink colors, etc. The key is that the letter fits its pattern of distinct graphical features enough to distinguish between writing the word 'bat' and the word 'bet.' Except written letters here have a phoneme as part of its sense and referent. The letter 'd' has the phoneme d as its reference. Thus, the sound 'd' and the letter 'd' can have the same signified precisely insofar as the phoneme is itself a set, but at the same time the letter is itself already a set of graphical distinctive features. It is thus selected form the two-dimensional continuum of the blank page. Thus, the letter 'd' exists distinctly from any phoneme.

It is important not to believe that the phonemes in their meaninglessness have a relationship that is clear or even possibly existent. Insofar as each is an indivisible whole and selection from the sonic continuum, each phoneme stands by itself and its opposition to the others is purely external to it. The difference between phonemes is only ever a formal one. One sound does not cause another to appear. If we analyze phonemes into their distinctive features, we immediately lose them in a sea of sound just as if we were to analyze the letter 'd' in terms of the verticality of its line or the curvature of its lower part, it would disappear. Now, the vertical line in 'd' but might also be at work in 'b,' but that does not mean that the two were created intentionally or otherwise as mirror images of each other. There is no clear rule for how the 26 letters of the alphabet were generated graphically (the claim for Hebrew might be different given the apparent ability to generate all the letters using the letter 'yod'). On the other hand, it might be found that there are certainly basic lines for English that when permuted in certain ways yield all 26 letters.

If we were to try to understand the algorithm for how written letter are produced, one way to do so would be possibly to make use of the famous research of Torsten Hubel and David Wiesel. These two scientists found two types of simple cells. Each type of cell is set up to receive a particular type of visual input in the cortex. The input consists of different cells of straight lines with different orientations. If one sees a line of the right type, the cell fires. In other words, some neurons are attuned to lines of one angle whereas others are tuned into visual stimulus showing lines at another angle. The second type of cell is a complex cell that works at a second order. These cells aggregate a number of simple cells with their lines. Here, a number of inputs are brought together to form one image. In this way, all the various inputs are filtered into one. The basic image is thus deconstructible into simpler cells and lines. These complex cells are able to take the cells of various types and at different scales and thereby find what is invariant in visual stimulus. Visual sensory processing thus builds different hierarchical levels and differentiates between scales of detail. Our recognition of visual objects is coded in this manner by these cells. One can see that the manner in which these visual cells works is algorithmic. Thus, if one can know how the algorithm works one could also possibly build up the letters of our alphabets similarly from simpler lines and figures that work together to form all 26 letters by way of a basic or set of basic rules. Since visual sensory processing is already doing this with visual information, it is presumable that it is also at work with something as basic as written letters. One could see the simple cells here as the 'phonemes' of visual perception itself.

Of course, not all letters are written as English are. But it may be the case that all phonemes of any language have the same sonic distinctive elements bundled together in differing combinations. The idea here would be that the distinctive elements that phonemes bundle are actually less than the number of phonemes and thus can yield many combinations beyond the phonemes we have in any language. But we hear those distinct elements differently, since the phonemes would have a retroactive effect. Phonemes discern meaning form words, but also in doing so form a net for discerning and filtering all sound. Accents show us how there can be irrelevant features that occupy phonemes but are not invariant and essential features of them. Thus, two people with two differing accents can be understood since the phoneme still discriminates between words. In the same way two different handwriting styles do not make it so one cannot read letters sent back and forth.

Once phonemes discriminate meanings, we no longer truly hear the sounds they bundle together. This is the same as with reading the written word. There we pay no attention to the material aspects of the lines of the letters themselves. That materiality, as Jean-François Lyotard taught in *Discourse, Figure*, disappears and is sublated into the sense. We thus never see the lines and materiality of the letter when we read. If we were to focus on the curvature of the letter itself, sense would return to non-sense. The intelligibility of the world depends on the sublation of the sound and the line. The ground recedes yielding only the intelligible figure with its sense. If we look at the line all becomes opaque, just as if we attend to the sounds of the distinctive features of phoneme we encounter only noise. The materiality here resists us and must be rendered invisible or mute for sense to emerge. This happens whether we are looking at different typesets or handwriting. We look through the differences in writing style to understand the sense involved. Otherwise, we would be engaged in calligraphy.

Whereas the pictographic sign made use of its resemblance to a perceptual object, here one is in an either'/or situation. If one attends to the plasticity of the line in its shape, then one loses the sense. Thus, phonetic writing cannot work as art and painted voices in the same way as hieroglyphics. It is no longer an imaginary regime and culture, but a symbolic code. The letter or phoneme is not linked to any sense in the way a signifier is linked to a signified. A signifier always has a signified on its reverse side even if that linkage is unmotivated. They fact that the signifier 'woman' does not refer to any perceptual object in the same way as the pictograph does not mean that the signifier is not always linked to a signified. The signifier might be also negative and differential, but that can never rule its relation to its signified or multiple signifieds. It is not a meaningless and differential unit per se in the way the phoneme and letters are.

Deleuze for instance only recognizes the negative, differential aspect of the phoneme and thus never acknowledges its status as bundle.96 This is partly because Deleuze wants to relate phonemes to a Leibnizian conception of the infinitesimal. We on the other hand will relate the phoneme both to the positive integer and to the real number, the Dedekind cut. Deleuze was right that sense emerges from non-sense and is always an effect of the combination of things meaningless in themselves. But the phoneme is not simply a way of discriminating between two words. They are also sets.

When Deleuze emphasizes the differential relation of b/p he makes it appear as though phonemes only ever come in pairs. But the phoneme is itself an extensional set. This is why, as we shall see even more so, the phoneme is not an infinitesimal within the framework of 17th or 18th century mathematics, but rather relatable to the integer and real of 19th century mathematics. At the same time, in English, the letters do not have any clear numerical value. They are not associated with numbers as they are in Hebrew. Thus, at the level of the letter, there is no clear dual structure already at work where the letter is also a number and paralleled by numbers. One can flip in Hebrew letters into numbers. There is no sense that English letters are already coded as numbers even if a, b, c, etc. can be used in an ordinal fashion. When letters are linked to numbers, then they exist on their other half.

Letters are like numbers insofar as the issue is there pure, negative differentiality. 2, 3, and 4 are for instance only distinguishable in terms of the inclusion of the empty set. This is precisely why letters are numbers in this regard, positive integers (in another aspect they are reals, Dedekind cuts). When letters are numbers, they are still senseless. But, once linked to a number, given the irreducible properties of the number they are associated with, they are now linked with a sense. Letters can be iterated without any sense, because they are without sense in themselves. The same can be said of phonemes. But this is because they are bundles. Their repetition thus depends on their being marks, but marks that can always be recognized. The repetition of the letter and the phoneme is what makes mathematics possible. This is also why to associate letters with numbers is only to bring out how they are already the mathematical sign itself. When one lists a, b, c, etc. to number things, one is not giving the letter a new use, but emphasizing one of its fundamental properties. There is no repetition here without a Platonic-like entity involved both for the letter and the phoneme. Thus, repetition is always linked to a set even when it has one meaning in and of itself that would be seen in the repetition of the letter 'd' or the sound 'd'.

We also saw the signifier always has a signified as its reverse side. But a letter could in principle be a signified if linked to a signifier and also a signifier as a signifier without signified would function as a letter. The letter is the signifier outside of any linkage to the signified. This is the foundation of the arbitrariness of the sign. It is precisely because the sign outside of its relation to the signified is simply a letter or mark that the relation is arbitrary in the first place. To be independent of meaning is to enter the field of the letter, but to be completely outside the letter itself is simply to enter the continuum of the blank page and lines or the continuum of sounds themselves with their varying tones.

Now, it is only with the letter that divine names as understood in the monotheist sense are possible. Whereas pictography is essentially connected to paganism, monotheism is essentially connected to phonetic writing and the letter. God is not nameable in pictography. If one were to try to name God here, one would use as symbol. Perhaps, one would use the sun as the Egyptians did. Thus, one necessarily refers God to a thing in the world, to an entity. One is always picturing the thing or concept in the imaginary. Only with the letter can we find God himself as ineffable and transcendent. If phonetic writing had not existed, monotheism would have had to invent it. In fact, we can say that it was monotheism that itself was part of its invention. For God revealed himself to Abraham and Moses only on the basis of refusing pictographic signs and their inherent idolatry. Pictography is thus left in the past with phonetic writing even as we saw with Plato and would be the case for hundreds of years later the pagan worldview persisted as people continued to misrecognize the nature of the letter that stood against them.

In pictography, one can have an oval with 'x' as its tale to say 'fish.' Here, one pictures a fish. One might also then think of the fish itself. One can have a temple with a pool in its center and a fish inside. The god, Dagon, is then named with the pictographic. Dagon does not name anything beyond this world. Dagon names the essence of the fish. The pure idea of fish one pictures by way of the sign.

It is also important to note here that the name of God for monotheism, YHVH, is made up of the so-called vocal letters. These letters are the vowels of Hebrew that help a consonantal language to speak things aloud. They give voice to the body of the word when it might not already have it. Monotheism is thus also able to identify God with the zero-sign. The name YHVH is a series of letters that one knows not truly how to pronounce and, in any event, all are forbidden from doing so. Thus, YHHVH is a secret and encrypted name. It is ciphered away in a silent series of letters. It is a pure proper name and thus signifier, but without a signified. This way with monotheism we have the zero signifier, the one without a sense. There is no evidence of it in pictographic writing.

That God is related to letters is also the case because the letter or the phoneme always relates to the infinite itself. The letter emerges out of the continuum of the blank space of the page using the line and the curve whereas the phoneme emerges from the continuum of sounds. Each language differentiates out of the sound continuum a finite and usually relatively small number of discernible bundles. Of course, humans can only hear a very partial spectrum of the sound continuum. But that is no different from saying 0 to 1 is only one segment of the real number line. Despite its being only one segment, 0 to 1 has the same uncountable infinite cardinality as the whole number line itself. Here, the sound continuum refers to all sounds that the human voice can make as well as that the human ear can hear. While we have to be able to say a phoneme is a bundle of vocable sounds, those sounds must also be audible since if we were to listen to the sound of a river and hear words that would also be possible even though our own voice might not be able to imitate the sound of a river. Thus out of the entire sound spectrum, a particular language has only a small subset of possible phonemes. All else is excluded.

That exclusion returns after the reduction and is filtered by the different phonemes. Thus, the sound of a river now sounds to the English speaker like a very long 'shshshsh.' Phonemes thus divide up the sound spectrum, but we only hear part of the possible sounds. Even with what is possible for the human ear, we only hear a small selection of the levels of sounds that could arise. The sound spectrum is just as endlessly divisible as any other finite aspect of the continuum. It is because phonemes select out of the sound continuum, that they must be conceived as Dedekind cuts.

Dedekind reals are just collections of rationals specified by a cut. The cut is a partition of everything to the left and right amongst the rational numbers. With sound, those rationals are the very wavelengths of the sounds involved that are infinitely partitionable. The Dedekind cut shows that real has a greatest lower bound and a least upper bound. Take the square root of 2 which was the non-algebraic real the Pythagoreans confronted and thus perhaps the most famous. The greatest lower bound here involves the list of rationals such as 1.4, 1.41, 1.412, etc. The least upper bound of the cut is not in the set q that makes up the real. It is only a limit. The real itself is a cut, a partitioning, between the two series that involve the greatest lower bound and the least upper bound. The least upper bound cannot be in the set since one can always find a smaller numerical value. Thus, the Dedekind cut is not the last number of the first series or partition and not the first member the second series.

The square root of two is of course a non-repeating real with an infinity of decimal places. This is what causes it not be the first member of the second partition--say 1.42. The sequences of rational numbers of the Dedekind cut are a well-ordered series. The left side of the partition has no greatest element, but also is not empty of elements and closed downwards (that is, has a least element). The right side of the partition is also not empty and has a greatest upper bound. We also see here how the reals exhibit well-ordering in their status as cuts. They have for instance on the left side downwards closure and a least element and thus a limit. There is clear order and not chaos despite the non-algebraic real having an in finite and non-repeating decimal expansion.

The random real is thus defined clearly. This needs to be noted by all those who think CH is obviously false. Reals have a natural and obvious sequence. But there is split here between two parts. All that is to the left must be less than the square root of two. And all that is to right must be larger. The real number is just the gap between these two sequences. It is just the section removed. It is thus a gap and excision. We see how real numbers are sets of rational numbers.

Phonemes are sets of rational numbers also insofar as they bundle together sounds. But we should not think here that a phonemes are given one at a time as though one conducted one Dedekind cut and then another. As the Structuralists such as Levi-Strauss taught, language must be given all at once if it is given at all. All the phonemes must be given all at once and grasped as such. This is why, as Plato in his *Philebus* noted, it seems that they can only come from a divine source. Of course, we are born after their formation and are thrust into them. As children we are caught up in a pre-existing language. We thus absorb the phonemic relations and begin to babble them out. If one does not have all the phonemes, one cannot discern between them and permute them into words. If one only had part of the alphabet, one would be lacking an entire series. In other words, all the phonemes are given at once, but it is not clear how that occurs. It appears groundless.

At the same time, the letters have a musically pleasing sense to them. This is because in being selected from the continuum they fall into their own scale. They thus have a Pythagorean proportionality to them in terms of their pitch and tone. There are ratios between them. The phonemes are cuts in the unlimited and thus are sets as well in terms of the finite set of elements making them up. The phoneme just like the Dedekind cut is a partition of all that comes before and after. It gathers together a series of rationals without actual being any one of them or simply their sequence. Phonemes are cuts or gaps in the continuum and not reducible to the contents of the cuts and gaps. They are not divisible.

Existence implies the need for reals because of the continuum itself regardless of the need for real numbers to do Quantum Mechanics. Phonemes as indivisible gaps are distinguishable, but they are so only in relation to the continuum itself. This is what they expose in their indissoluble nature. Now as we know the set of reals, the set of these gaps is not countable. There are more gaps than rationals despite these gaps being themselves partitions of sequences of rationals and found within the cracks and breaches in the rationals. This is the case because these gaps are related to the continuous line. One then attempts to put together the real line together with a series of gaps lined up. That is, the line appeared to be complete and continuous, but we see here that the continuous line includes gaps within itself. That is, the purely continuous includes the discrete and that is what makes it continuous. If the continuous did not include the discrete, it could not be what it is.

On the other hand, the discrete is the same size as the continuous here as both are uncountable. We can say that each gap in the rationals is a letter, but the phonemes of any human language are only ever a finite set of such letters. These letters name the gap. The phoneme like the Dedekind cut is both the partition and what fills in the partition at the same time. The continuum has no spaces because it includes all the spacings. This is why a blank page is such a simple example of the continuum. It includes all possible spacings of the letters themselves. The blank page has no gaps, because it already includes all the spaces. These letters can be also be taken as names, as names for the cut they indicate. The cuts are not themselves divisible since they are divisions. The phonemes are the same they are not divisible because they are a division of the sound spectrum, a bundling of various distinctive elements. The continuum for us is of course indiscernible from the void. This is why in its other aspect the phoneme is pure negative differentiality like the integers. This is why any letter or phoneme is a name of the void itself and must include it like the whole numbers. Thus, there is no tension in conceiving letters and phonemes as being both as integers and Dedekind cuts at the same time.

We can also then see here why writing is about making cuts. The fist cuneiform letters were precisely the cuts and gaps that were made in the clay (the etymology of the term means 'wedges'). Letters like real numbers are set of points in the continuum. To every cut corresponds a phoneme or letter. The cut decompletes the whole via the phoneme or the letter. With the cut, we create a new letter or phoneme. The phoneme is like a cut also because when one hears a sound there is a certain point at which the phoneme would disappear. Thus, we reach a point a limit and then the phoneme no longer holds. This is why it is about reals and not rationals. The least upper bound of the phoneme is not included in it. And the greatest lower bound marks a limit before which we would not experience the phoneme doing its discriminatory work. Thus, even if the phoneme includes sounds, it is not like a set of relations that make up a rational since the phoneme is not simply proportional sequences of this kind.

Some might here think that the continuum is only retroactively posited. They would say that these cuts and gaps that are supposedly punched into the uncountable infinite are actually the discrete decision that allows us to posit the continuum. The continuum per that view does not pre-exist the cut. We would have the first cut, the divine contraction itself and then a retroactive positing of the absolute. The problem is that the cuts are themselves sets of rationals and one cannot ignore that. This is why the continuum must be presupposed here.

We can see now why Deleuze went partly astray in trying to say phonemes are in their pure negative, differentiality like infinitesimals. We say that this corresponds to them being numbers. After all, letters are already ordinals. Infinitesimals must be like zero (since one can ignore them) and also more than zero (since they are related in divisible relation dx/dy). The phoneme is functionally zero insofar as it is not a sound. It is also when related to another phoneme like the relation dx/dy. Bu infinitesimals continue to disappear ad infinitum as they approach a limit. It is not clear how that relates to the phoneme itself or its differential relation with other phonemes. Deleuze thinks that phonemes are neither undetermined nor indeterminable, but only determined within a relation with another phoneme. But that overlooks the phoneme as bundle. I don't see why one would say for instance that the phoneme is a vanishing quantity that disappears at a limit near or at zero.

Infinitesimals in their 17th and 18th centuries' definition also mean they are a relation that vanishes but still persists and must be accounted for. But it is not clear why even the negative, differential relation between phonemes persists despite the terms disappearing. The difference here does not vanish as a relation persists when the terms are no longer present. When 'bat' becomes 'bet', there is a difference between a/e at work. But it's not clear how that is a vanishing difference where a and e have disappeared. Clearly 'e' is at work still and only one half has been erased. One would not recognize 'e' without the phoneme qua bundle. This is again why the difference between integers works better here as a model.

Deleuze also relates phonemes to ordinal and singular points. A square has four singular points and all the rests of the points that make it up could be called ordinary points. This analogy might work to discuss how a phoneme is made up of distinct elements. Deleuze seems here to be saying that insofar as phonemes have no inherent meaning, that they are meaningless, they are like dx/dy. Thus, phonemes have no determinate value in and of themselves and determine each other only in there being linked together. The symbolic order is for Deleuze made up of such differential rations. In this way, Deleuze can relate phonemes to infinitesimals best when it comes to their being meaningless in themselves. Without any particular value or signification, phonemes thus determine each other only in relations. But it might not be simply two relating in this way, since we would have to see how letters come together to form morphemes. At the same time, one cannot discern how letters and numbers and thus the elements are real, and the relations between two letters can hold on this view. We then must see them as being like positive integers.

When we put letters together it is like 5 +7 yielding 12. Something new emerges from the combination. At most we can say that Deleuze's discussion of differential relations and singulars here relates to phonemes insofar as each phoneme is indivisible and there is a finite number of them selected from the continuum and that they are also are meaningless in themselves and related to each other differentially.

Here, we should also examine Jakobson's notion of the zero phoneme. The zero phoneme is not any of the other phonemes, and also not the absence of a phoneme as such per se. It is the empty set when it comes to phonemes. The zero phoneme could thus not truly be anything other than the spacing of the phonemes themselves. It is the silence that each violates. Jakobson may have meant voiceless vowels here, but such vowels ultimately come down to the unmarked in the voiced itself. They are thus a gap in the voice itself simply marked as gap. This gap marks the excess of the continuum over the limited number of phonemes selected out of it rather than the excess of the signifier over the signed as did the floating signifier. It is not a question here of something having no symbolic value, but of something not being a phoneme itself and yet functioning as such. It is thus a great mobile element because it enables the other elements to be distanced from each other.

The phonemes do not sound one at a time because they are indissoluble and distinct, but linking them to a zero phoneme is needed so that the sound itself does not become wholly discrete. The zero letters thus would be the analogue of very space itself used in writing letters. The zero phoneme is an empty set (had no distinctive features) and thus bundles no sound. It is pure aspiration. They are no-thing's that accompany all vocalization. One might want to connect it with silent letters in a word or with an 'h' that for instance drops out when pronouncing 'hello,' but I think that covers up how the zero phoneme is acting as white space and breathing itself even in those examples.

§17. The Permuted Book

Today, the zero phoneme is the bit itself. The bit (0/1) is the zero letter itself that marks a new era of writing and inscription. The bit reinforces the connection between letters and numbers. Bit strings are themselves numbers. Also, one can say here that one has only two letters (0/1) or any endless number of letters (any irreducible bit string). Lettering in the latter case would no longer be restricted to the finite. It would immediately raise issues of the infinite via infinite bit strings. The bit itself can encode any speech, but also any sound. Thus, it is no longer a matter of selecting only a few cuts out of the sound continuum, but of being able to reproduce anything audible.

The bit is not a set of distinctive features. If one wants, a bit is a set of electrical voltage and switchings, but mostly they are sets of numbers. Any set of letters can be encoded as bits. ASCII of course encodes all bits, but also encodes any orthographical marker. It thus has a bit string for every letter of every alphabet, every mark, etc. Today we can if we want render any book written in the past into a series of bits. The bit is thus not limited in the number of combinations it can produce in principle. With English, one has twenty-six letters and a very large number of combinations, but not all combinations will be meaningful given the current or past English lexicon. Also, it is not clear that English words can truly be much longer than 20 letters. It is rare for a word to be much longer than 10. Insofar as we speak of spoken words, one would not understand a word beyond a certain length since one would not be able to mentally unify the entire word as a whole, to hear the whole. In this way, we enter with the bit directly into a form of writing where inhuman intentions at most are often at work.

Bit writing entails a transition from the page to the electric circuit itself. It bypasses the screen itself insofar as the screen is only a realization of part of the bits one might have encoded. Thus, while the page is a confined and limited space seemingly, the bit is always pointing to its infinite expansion. Coded text is rendered as bits; we have text as pure numbers and only letters outside of signification itself. It can then be searched and manipulated, explored and computed, only at the level of the a-signifying letter. When we render a text written in English into bits, we void it of its explicit meaning. As a result, we have only a series of letters. Those resulting bits themselves can compute any other book. Thus, each book as a result of its resolution purely into letters can become any other book. Each book thus becomes a mirror of the total possible library of books (one thinks here of Borges' library of Babel). Despite being a specific bit string (no matter the length), the entire library could be generated from the permutation of this one book. Thus, in some sense, every book will be contained in every other book. The only thing that will mark the book is itself an extensional set of books. The book is only divinely articulated in this way as an extensional set. It is its own unique perspective on the entirety of possible books. If another book had the entirely same elements, it would simply be the same book by way of the axiom of extension.

Each book is thus a number, a sequence of 0's and 1's, a structured set of integers. What does that number mean if anything? Perhaps, it is only the telephone number of the book itself, an address and a designation, but it would thus be at the very least a name for the book, a name no human author (until perhaps recently when the tools were available) had every made for his book. It is a name that arises out of the letter itself. The rendering of the text as bits is also its encryption. This is a step beyond previous forms of inscription in which letters were substituted with numbers or other letters since here with the true and empty universality of the binary code one is able to permute and compute on its basis. In this way, for instance, perhaps the bit string of a particular book matches a program, one for doing something in particular. A book that per its expressed meaning is about birds might as code be the program for producing images of birds on a screen.

One of the key ideas behind encryption is that "two messages with the same number of letters could be considered 'encryptions for each other, just as any two stories with the same number of narrative elements could be considered encryptions of one another".97 The key point here is that the same number of bits or letters means the two texts could be a transformation of one into the other. Thus the bit strings need not be identical for the texts to be identical. Any two bit strings or letter strings of the same length are mirror images of the other. Thus, a bit string if long enough could encode one text, but also be an encryption of other texts of a smaller length. Ultimately each text is connected to the uncountable infinite, to the divine and pure silence, that none could in themselves ever fully express and only perhaps name. All texts refer to the uncountable infinite, because not all texts are uttered and all sounds spoken. And yet one is aware that there is more that could be said. It is the excess of the uncountable infinite and what it names that shows how each text is but a partial expression of a whole that cannot be given.

In the sequence of the uncountable infinite, one would not even know what a sound is. There would be no way to distinguish and discriminate between one sound and another. It is not a place for phonemes, but of silence itself. We have used already names of God to differentiate the pure divine, the absolute infinite. But each text itself is also related to this absolute. Each text is related to God as He is Himself withdrawn, a pure silence.

One of the questions here is whether given a text as a set of letters, if there is a rule or program shorter than the text itself that will produce that text. Of course, today with programs and computers, one can imagine authors (insofar as they have not already) producing texts simply with such programs. But a text from 100 years ago was presumably not made in this way. In that way, to discover within a text a shortest program that would generate the text would speak to the fact that text itself was not irreducibly complex. It was not a random text. It would show that there is a rule.

Now, that there is a rule might itself simply be a result of language itself. Each language has certain letter frequencies, grammatical rules, word frequencies, etc. that would make it so one would expect the text not to be completely irreducibly complex. Let's think here of Zipf's law. This law teaches that the world frequency in any language (no matter what words happen to be most frequent) always has an ordered scale to it. That is, the second most frequent word is always half as frequent as the most, the third one third as frequent, etc. What we see here is order created at a scale that certainly no conscious human mind would have access to. One finds Zipf's law in all human languages. But what cause it to occur? It appears that it shows us something about the computational power of the human unconscious itself. For meaning to arise out of things, they need to be ordered. Zipf's law shows us how that order arises on a large scale and in fractal patterns of self-similarity made from the repetition of similar laws at lower levels. We keep applying the same rules for symmetry and proportionality to all we understand. If things do not have an order and ratio, they are then noise. Zipf's law is then an emergent effect of the way in which we all must unconsciously order things in order for them to be meaningful even if this ordering takes place on things that taken independently are senseless.

Zipf's law is not simply a statistical phenomenon where we would expect these frequencies in any aggregate of data. Some think that Zipf's law is just a product of randomly generated information. But the data here is already ranked and ordered in some sense since it is about language. Also, this randomly generated information is usually taken from already formed texts. It thus jumbles up a text with order. It is then not surprising that the order found with the language is reproduced in the jumbled text since the order affects every scale including the letters. For this reason also, when we permute a book we expect various ordering relations to pertain even if the text is purely a jumbled mass. But that it has that ordering means there is meaning immanent it just as in the original plain text since the meaning is itself part and parcel of the ratios.

All data that is not pure noise will have some order and immanent meaning to it. It will be well-behaved in some sense and show statistical distribution. It will thus express rankings and scales whether these be fractal in nature or of another type. Part of this is true because all data is expressed as numbers and numbers inherently have patterns in their relationships to each other. Within the positive integers, we can find there patterns of odds, primes, cubes, etc. If reality itself is inherently mathematical per the Pythagorean thesis, then we expect to find time and again the allegedly remarkable result that all phenomena have well-ordered series like that of Zipf's law. The frequency distribution of the raw data is not probable since one can imagine any number of other relations in the scale of terms. Zipf himself contended that human language users all have the same basic minds and thus find the same proportions and ratios pleasing and intelligible. What happens is that across the various scales form one text to a language one sees invariant relations being maintained. This implies that meaning itself is about putting various sounds for example into specific ratios and that these ratios resonate universally for humans.

Zipf's law thus taps into the grand symphony of meaning. It is an expression of the song we as humans are singing. Therefore, we would imagine that if whale songs were analyzed we would find similar patterns although perhaps less complex or less pronounced. The smallest level patterns then could be correlated to basic whale concepts. Many here might point out that some natural phenomena act according to Zipf's law. But that only shows that these phenomena are already computational in nature and programmed. If we find the same relations at work in language in the population sizes of cities in one region or incomes, then that is because we are ordering ourselves too at each scale. We are programming our own world as much as the world is itself programmed. The repetition of this programming on each miniature scale has long range effect that build up and yield distributions such as we see in Zipf's law that express self-similarity.

Texts are of course built up from letters, words, sentences, etc. They thus at each level exhibit the arrangement of meaningless bits into patterns and then the aggregation of those patterns on top of each other. Natural phenomena are also programmed. They are not simply randomly occurring and chaotic. It shows us following Gates again that the universe expresses a code. The universe is thus singing and a harmony of scales since the distribution at work is equivalent to harmonic series. Even if we spoke for an infinitely long time, the distribution indicated by Zipf's law would hold.

Let's explore this issue of distributions over large scales more so. Part of the reason humans require ratios and proportions at every level and scale is so that the information is compressible. This compressibility is what makes the information both meaningful and also enables one to add new information with minimal effort. If with each word, sentence, text, etc. we had to compress a large amount of information it would take too long. It is precisely because we unconsciously find repeated patterns that we can compress quickly and anticipate what is to come next, what is new, what is new and interesting, etc.

Jurgen Schmidhuber has been attempting to determine intelligence as such in some of his most important work. One could say here that Schmidhuber is attempting to rewrite Kant's *Critique of Judgment* using computational principles. For Schmidhuber, the data intelligence encounters is interesting only when we are able to compress it and on its basis predict what will come next. For Schmidhuber, we take pleasure in finding order in things which means our ability to compress the information given into a smaller form.[98] Whereas beauty for Kant was about how our mental faculties harmonize when we see something symmetrical, for Schmidhuber beauty is what occurs when we subjectively express a set of data as compressible and are able to predict what will occur next on its basis. We are incentivized to look for more things by experiencing the pleasure that comes with beauty.

Schmidhuber is of course interested in these features because he wants to build artificial intelligence on its basis. In this way, by building something that rewards the artificial intelligence for finding compression within a data set, the AI will have an inherent drive to learn more and built on the compressed things it learns. Artists on this reading use elements that are compressed to create a new and interesting new objects on their basis that are interesting because we have to compress them anew. Art is interesting and beautiful because it is compressible and not simply random, but at the same time not familiar. We want thus to discover in the world more and more non-random and non-arbitrary regular patterns of data. We want to be surprised by it. We find it beautiful to find it. We find it inherently pleasurable and rewarding. .

One can discover here a rule was at work beyond any individual human intention for generating a text or data set. The issue is not just a matter of textual analysis. We also need to look at textual generation. One imagines authors of the present and future writing programs to generate texts. This is a new form of automatic writing that depends not on the psychic unconscious, but on the vast unconscious of the letter in its transfinitude. Textual generation here might operate only on letters and their numerical values. One has a program which would necessarily be the shortest possible program for generating the text. But that does not mean the text will be a fractal and self-repeating pattern. It can issue in any number of permutations and include random sequences.

We can also use the generating of texts to mine the computational universe and discover what programs lead to what. Given the principle of computational irreducibility, one cannot anticipate what pattern arises from a program. If we find a program that produces the first five books of the bible (we will return to this), then we need to ask what that name is and if that program is used in other contexts for other purposes. Just as Gates found error-correcting code at the level of supersymmetry, the code for a specific text might itself be at work in another way. The code for text is not then just limited to it but might be doing things in other places. We can only discover the sequence by repeating code of longer and longer elements and waiting to see how those programs unfold. Some might terminate after a few steps. Some might lead to pure gibberish.

In any event, even if a human is programming, human intention is no longer the issue. We need to begin to ask about a different form of intention, the intention of the letter itself or a divine one. We thus create texts here from a-signifying elements. This would be the same as taking the 26 letters of English and permuting them to produce a text. Such a text as letters is not deconstructible, to return to Meillassoux's point. It is a computation. And computation runs into problems in terms of loops and the issue of incomputability rather than deconstruction since it is only dealing with letters and numbers. However the iteration here does have differential effects. It is not a question of new meanings, but new emergent properties that come as a result of the permutations themselves. It is not a question of a dissemination of meaning, but rather one of exploring the transfinite capacity of the letter itself.

Meillassoux showed us in his latest book that Mallarme counted the syllables for his poem and attempted to arrive at a specific number.99 We do not doubt that Mallarme was capable of such a calculation. But when we reduce the text to bits or ask about how the text itself can be encrypted or permuted, we enter a terrain where such simply human intentions cannot follow. Meillassoux of course leaves it open as to whether Mallarme truly did count the syllables to arrive at this number and also discuss it obscurely in the poem, but human intention seems to have control over the number or syllables in a text. In fact, one can compose an entire novel without using the letter 'e' as Earnest Vincent Wright did in 1939 (thus depending only a typewriter) to write *Gadsby: A Story of Over 50,000 Words Without Using the Letter 'E'*. The lipogramic word game here makes it all but certain that it was intentional. The high frequency of the letter 'e' in English makes the probability of such a text being produced unintentionally astronomical. But when we enter the text and analyze it or generate it using bit strings, we lose this level of easily accepted intentionality.

The problem here is that there is a transfinite (aleph-null) set of names which can be produced by letters. But with 0s and 1's, if one was able to write them out in finite strings, one would always be able to produce through diagonalization a set of bits not appearing in the transfinite list. Thus, there are an unlimited number of names that we cannot write and that we cannot even imagine. Even if such transfinite considerations remain only realistic in the non-all and the mind of God, they still relate to each text for the countable set of meaningless and meaningful names is already implicit in the repetition of the letter itself. Even if we only look at an infinite list of names, the number so exceeds human calculation without the aid of the machine that we see how our alphabets are exhausted by the very prospect. We should thus see all texts as addressing themselves to both the countable and uncountable infinites that language implies. Each text is thus addressed to the very power of language itself even if in this world it is always restricted to some finite form. There is an infinite power in the letter itself even if we are able only to recognize it as transcending the sets of letters we have witnessed and produced. The infinite disappears beyond the letter and within it. It transcends the letter while also always informing it. That infinity is for us always the unnamable, the nameless.

The book that all books point to then is transfinite. The book beyond that all refer to is uncountably infinite. We only have fragments of that Book. Every text, whether it is acknowledged as such or not or intended as such or not, is part of it. The uncountable infinite can never be a true whole. It is either a continuum or transcendence. It is never a totality. Our human speech and writing then is always a speech that speaks to and of God. But God, as noted, contracts himself into the word itself and exiles himself there. Our human speech is an echo of that. It is not however separated from the holy name but always striving for it. It is not about a total ignorance of the Book. Each book is marked by the omnipresence of the absolute infinite just as we showed with each eidetic essence. Our human speech is exposed to the absolute infinite which it notes as an empty and missing point.

Thus, a single book can include all the possible books. How so? It is only because we can treat a book as transfinite set. That means the book is all possible repetitions of itself or all possible permutations of its letters without any limitation put on the length of words or a list of letters. Then, a single book refers to both the transfinite universe of names and also the non-articulated non-all of the book itself. But at the bottom of this is the bit itself (0/1) It is like aleph itself, the number 1, which the Kabbalists said was the origin of all the phonographs. The bit itself is the root letter of all the other letters. Aleph is one, but as we saw zero is already intimately related to one. Aleph would thus be split between itself and its numbering. The entire alphabet would follow from this point, but the bit alphabet is only 0/1 or a transfinite or more.

A text also insofar as it can permute into the other books is like a Turing machine. A universal Turing machine, as all know, is precisely that Turing machine that can emulate any other Turing machine. A text is thus when connected to the infinite power of the letter a Turing machine capable of computing all others that are computable, all computable texts. One text can if computed properly turn one text into all other texts and books given enough time. It is not a matter of presence since it is itself becoming all those texts. It becomes identical by the axiom of extensionality. This becomes apparent once we make the text bit strings. Once we admit a way to see a text as an infinite binary sequence, we then encounter the problem of the incomputable. Since we can list all the infinite binary sequences in principle, we can then diagonalize to produce one not appearing on the list. There is thus always at least one incomputable text here once we enter the transfinite, and an infinity of incomputable ones.

However, it is not clear that that all those incomputable texts are not ultimately indiscernibly identical. This is what the Kabbalists called the Torah in heaven, the one that is pure black fire on white fire. It is not readable by us. We only ever have the computable texts. We have the Torah of this world and not the one from heaven. The incomputable shows why there is no closure, no total book. The Book itself is always a book beyond all the books and uncountably infinite. That is why the Book itself must ultimately point to the absolute infinite and God. The Torah we have in hand is a seemingly finite text of a little over 300,000 letters which is why to understand its divinity we will need to connect it to the Book itself and the uncountably infinite.

Another way of putting this is that all texts we have seen are at most expandable to aleph–null names (if we do not restrict the names to a certain finite length), but the power of the continuum is bigger. Even when we conceive of things like phonemes as cuts and thus reals, we only spoke of a finite number of gaps. We can approach the uncountable itself as the unnamable, but we cannot name each non-algebraic real. We rather will have to force out specific names from the absolute infinite and the continuum even if we will always be lacking names. We will be able to force out of the uncountable a countable number. There is thus here an excess of the signifier to the point where we have signifiers that will never be written or said. This also means there is always something missing from any book, the absolute infinite itself, the unnamable holy one. But it is the missing one that enables the text itself to be a play of exchanges and permutations.

We see here, as Derrida did, that the issue is not that the finite cannot encapsulate infinity, but that the infinite itself causes an exclusion of totalization.100 Even if the infinite leads to the non-all, to God, it means nothing is excluded from the non-all. Nothing escapes it as there is no outside for it and thus no book could be outside. This is why even in the Book God is not represented, and God despite some Kabbalistic expressions is not identical with the Book. For Derrida the book was endless as there was no totality, but that only meant the book was always connected to the uncountably infinite Book that resides in heaven and is heaven, the non-all. It is important to note here again that we are speaking of texts as pure letters without limit. The divine as book is both impredicative and ineffaceable. It is not the Platonic idea of a book since it is not one set amongst sets. We will connect thus the scared scripture we have to it.

All these considerations take place prior to the linkage of the signifier to the signified. There are no Gödelian sentences yet here as no duality of series has been ordered. That the book can be rendered as bits and permuted means that within any book is something more than it is. The greater is contained in the lesser. This is the paradox of the bit and its permutation. The book elaborates itself in its permutations. But that paradox of the greater in the lesser will only be realized by way of the letter and not the signifier in its relation to the signified. The signifier and signified are two continuums that are linked and in their linkage split into two. They do not fully match each other. One always is deficient or in excess relative to the other. The letter and the number are always perfectly linked and thus avoid this gap. This is why the letter is directed to the issue of the transfinite and the incomputable rather than the Gödelian and the undecidable or the deconstructible.

The floating signifier is not the same as the zero phoneme. The zero phoneme or letter is itself the substance of all letters. But one floating signifier like 'mana' does not make up all other signifiers. There is thus when there are two series a signifier without signified and a signified without signifier. But there is no letter without number--even zero is the first element of a progression. Thus the letter communicates only with itself and the transfinite whereas the signifier communicates with the signified or lack thereof and the signified with a name that cannot be named (and thus a name that is returned to the letters). With the letter one does not reach a too many until one touches the uncountable transfinite, but with the signifier there are too many signifiers since one can always have a signifier without signified, a pure lettering and non-sense.

Let us examine these issues by way of the permutation of the finite text in its lettering. A typical novel or other book will have a very large but not infinite number of permutations possible. That is, the number of ways of re-arranging its lettering are not infinite –especially if one always ends up with a text of the same length. Mallarme, in his 'A Throw of the Dice' poem is actually contrasting the random throw of a dice where one has a 1/6 chance of each throw and the permutations that he wanted to create with his project of 'The Book' (Le Livre). The pages of Mallarme's ideal book were supposed to be detached to the point that one could rotate them and pair them in new ways. Mallarme even counted the maximum number ways this could done. If one permutes all possibilities for instance on a dice, there is no chance. One gets all six versions of the dice—the abolition of chance. Thus, chance could only truly never be abolished if there is an uncountable infinite at work here or if one can only have a partial number of the possible permutations.

We see then for Mallarme a throw of dice means being given one possible permutation when many others were possible given the system. In a reading of his book, one would by way of a pre-designated system arrive at a new combination of the text. Thus, a meaning effect would be achieved by receiving that sequence on that day. Now, in the poem, 'A Throw of Dice' the sailor is caught at sea in rough waters. The sailor has not forecast the weather and now has lost his bearings. The throw of dice is a way of calculating which course to take since he has no idea where he is. But he will not throw the dice to give a sign and thus direction. The sailor does not want to receive a determined number and direction. Hence, a throw will not eliminate chance—as he resigns himself to whatever will happen.

But there is no indication that Mallarme's own poem is anything other than a carefully arranged text. There is no evidence that it is a text that was written by way of permutation or dice throwing. At most, Mallarme might be saying that his text is but one possible combination of French words, one possible text of the French language. Thus at the end of the poem, Mallarme hints that the arrangement of certain stars in the sky is itself like the poem and a reflection of it. The poem is thus the constellation of stars. The constellation is that which is supposed to guide the sailor caught in the storm. I take Mallarme's message here to be that one must accept the permutation one is given of possibilities rather than going down with the ship. One must thus be guided by nature itself, the stars that are themselves one possible combination of all the possible combinations of material existence. One cannot abolish chance/fate by receiving one combination because there are still other combinations that were not realized. One is always subject to receiving only one possible permutation rather than them all.

But the problem is that with a finite text, we can today permute and calculate each possibility and explore it. We are with texts at least not left with a singular text as we are with the one world we live in—at least for now. We can explore the computational dimension of the text by treating it just as letters. We can then search that space using our computational devices to discover what is included in it. This is a purely inhuman search that requires algorithms and other devices to be performed. We can thus reduce all aspects of the page into bits such as letters (if we really wanted we could also include punctuation marks, spacings, etc.). We then have a count of elements--and a number to correspond to each element. We could then find if we wanted how many words begin with a particular letter in the text. We could know the frequency of a certain letter in the text and compare it with the frequency of the text in the language by looking at a randomly selected list of words of the same length as the text or selecting texts randomly from the social archive. Knowing the word frequency in a text is of interest. For instance, a love story might have its highest word frequencies relating to words with mournful connotation thereby showing the story is at another a story about mourning rather than just love. If a large percentage of love stories showed this type of frequency, this might tell us something about the connection between love and mourning.

Since the text is here only an example set of elements, any combination is permitted. We are simply looking at the power set of the text. Such a power set will not look at that fact that the vast majority of permutations may have no sense in the language written. The excess of the power set over the original set is enormous. What is included in the text transcends what belongs to it. Take a set of only three letters [d, o, g]. That set as extensional in its power set knows no ordering. There are eight possible subsets that one can spin out form it using axiomatic set theory. Of course, differentiating here between dog versus god is not possible extensionally. Only one set of three letters is possible since the extensional sets know not from order. Odg is also not a word in English. In Hebrew, a consonantal language, any list of letters is a possible word. Also, in Hebrew, one can take any list of letters to be an acronym and ask what word each letter stands for. However, this is not a usual convention in English.

However, when order becomes important, we can rearrange a set of three letters into 14 possible subsets where now god, dog, and odg are all permuted possibilities. However, the empty se is no longer a subset. The empty set is not included because we can only re-order the given elements. Thus, the permuted book excludes the empty set from it when it is conjugated. This also means that difference between two sets is always also ordinal in nature and not just cardinal. Dog and god have the same cardinality (3), but the issue is ordinality. Thus, even if we had an infinite number of letters, if we permute in this way, we only will get aleph-null number of permutations. In this way, when we want order and meaning in permutations, we will always be stuck at the level of aleph-null and unable to go beyond.

The excess of the purely extensional is larger than the ordered. This is because to look at the difference between dog and god is to look from a finite perspective. The difference between the two is the difference that a finite mind searches for. We want not a purely extensional relation but an ordering of elements. The purely extensional on the other hand is blind to god and dog being two different words with meanings. The extensional speaks of every possibility such that some possibles are rendered inert.

We have to choose how to see, from the perspective of the one who interprets or from the perspective of the absolute itself. The axiom of choice is of course what ordered things and noted a least element. But that is because the axiom of choice is always connected to mind, to finite mind. It is the work of the finite mind's intuitive ability to interpret and make choices as to what counts and what does not count as meaningful. The purely extensional and the power set is indifferent to meaning as such and thus to order. Once meaning enters the picture we only have aleph-null and well-ordering. If we want to think from the perspective of the non-all there is no order and no discrimination in this way. It is the eternity of the *aion* and of time itself (chronos), and our finite minds cannot exist as they are now there.

From the perspective of the non-all any two things are the same as long as they have the same cardinality and elements. But from our perspective, which is that of the self-referential mind, we want order and finite groupings that can be linked to a signified. In this way, to have the signified is to fall short of ever reaching the non-all.

§18. Apokatastasis

In a text translated as "Revolution" in English, but called by Leibniz using a combination of a Greek word in Greek letters with his French "Apokatastasis, La Restitution Universelle", Leibniz anticipated much of what we are exploring here.101 In this text form near the end of Leibniz's life, 1715, Leibniz attempts to calculate the "number of all possible books." However, in doing so, he restricts the possible length of a book to an arbitrarily finite size (no more than "100,000,000 letters".) Thus, the number of all possible books will be large, but finite. Within this very large, but finite number of books Leibniz notes that we would even be able to see a book that differs by one letter from another. In this way, a book like *Moby Dick* that differed due simply to a printing error with another version of the same novel would be two different books since we are looking at books initially as sets of letters.

Leibniz assumes one could write out the entire history of the world in a book of this length. This leads him to the conclusion that the number of possible alternate histories of our world can be calculated. After this, Leibniz works out his own notion of the 'eternal return of the same' long before Nietzsche. After all, that is what the term Apokatastasis is about. It was a Stoic idea that given enough time there would be restitution and restoration of things to an original state, and those things that were past would return. Leibniz notes then that if the history of the world can be coded and expressed in 100 million letters and if humanity endures long enough, then humanity will be restored to a past state. Just as Nietzsche would later claim, there will be an eternal return of the same given a finite amount of matter or states and an endless amount of time.

One does not even need an endless amount of time. As long as humanity were to persist beyond the amount of time taken to go through all the permutations of history, there will be a restoration of a previous form of humanity, This would mean a resurrection of the dead necessarily. This is because Leibniz imagines that in each book, in each alternate version of world history, each person's entire set of thoughts and experiences will have been encoded. A book of enough length would thus be able to record all that concerns a particular human. Leibniz has no doubts that a book of a 100,000 million million letters will be enough to do this (and calculates it based on humans being only one billion in number, what is possible in one hour, etc.).

However while Leibniz seems to have apparently established the eternal return of the same, he then states:

> However, even if an earlier century returns as far as sensible events go, or those things which can be described in books, it will still not return completely in all respects, for there would always be differences, albeit imperceptible ones, and no books could adequately describe them since the continuum is actually divided into an infinity of parts, and indeed there is a world of an infinity of creatures in each part of matter, which cannot be described by any book no matter how long it is.102

For Leibniz, this idea demonstrates that the world cannot be made up of discrete atoms. If the world were made up of Epicurean atoms, then the eternal return would be a certainty. Rather, it is the power of the continuum itself which wrecks the idea of the atom. This is because the continuum is an infinity beyond any infinity that could be counted. Because the power of the continuum informs every aspect of being, even the infinite, and leaves its imprint on it, the eternal return is not possible. It is the power of the continuum itself which ensures there are going to be differences in things and that nothing identical will return. The continuum is always somehow both continued in things and also ever exceeding them such that there is always more in the things, an uncountable infinity. Looking at the world as discrete atoms hides this fact. Thus the continuous space between atoms must also be accounted for and this continuous space, the continuum, contains an uncountable infinity of reals, an uncountable number of gaps that would never be able to be coded in any book.

Leibniz thinks evoking the continuum here is not problematic insofar as God as absolute infinite could comprehend it since any infinite being could perfectly know and understand the world in its entirety. For Leibniz, thus there is no possible return of the same. Rather, there is only a "progress towards the best". Everything will return with some differences, with each return there is not a return of the completely identical, but rather staggered sequences of figures indicating improvement. Leibniz asks whether those who would return in a slightly altered form with the same souls (thus the difference would presumably be at the level of matter itself only somehow) would truly be the same or new and different human beings without any memory of what had come before. However, Leibniz cannot answer this question except to say that whatever would occur would be what God deems best in this regard and whatever would be for the best in the world.

Here, Leibniz envisions an endless series of rebirths of the entire world with only slight differences occurring. With each rebirth the world itself is somehow improved. Leibniz is optimistic here insofar as for him this vision is one of the constant betterment of humanity. However, it is not clear given the continuum if humanity could ever reach a stage of absolute perfection. Nonetheless, humanity's knowledge will also grow in the same direction. Humanity will slowly be able to understand more and more axioms and theorems until they are infinite in length. With such improved knowledge, humanity will be able to predict more and see that what is contained in larger and larger theorems expresses more clearly the nature of things.

Essentially with this vision Leibniz sees the world itself as text. However it is a text that always can include more thanks to the power of the continuum itself. The continuum is the only available mechanism. It is included in all things and thus all things are capable of unlimited change. There will be no identical return of the same since the continuum guarantees that each thing contains within it imperceptible and indiscernible differences that will affect it in the future. There is something then for Leibniz in the uncountable infinite absolute or in materiality itself that cannot be captured, and this uncountable infinite means we cannot truly ever have a complete concept of a thing. While all things are able to be formulated and encoded in mathematics, the formulas needed to truly capture things are endless. We will constantly discover new and more detailed aspects of these formulas, but not complete them. We will thus remain finite and yet unbounded. The power of the continuum saves us from the eternal repetition of the same.

However, if our world is infinite and if only a finite number of things are possible as in the permutations of a finite text, we are doomed to experience the same things over and over. Understanding then how the continuum informs all things and also leads to imperceptible differences in things even if we seem to repeat them in all in their elements is important. Many things are left unexplained by Leibniz in this short text such that as we have asserted before it is our job to work out the problems Leibniz left. In this text, one of his last, Leibniz seems to offer a radical new view of the continuum without even noting he is doing so. He also anticipates Cantor on the nature of the infinite without having many details for this view; nonetheless, Leibniz for us here anticipates how Cantor's work put an end to the inevitability of the eternal return. Part of what Leibniz is here insisting about the continuum is that even if we try to encode all the information for a particular hour in letters, then there will still be the minutes, then a way of dividing those minutes, etc. That is, it is the indefinite divisibility of time for him ultimately that makes it impossible to encode all the information.

But the continuum is now here obviously present in any set of letters. As we saw, it can only be unearthed through the construction of the generic subset. Thus, to understand Leibniz's points we need to understand how the non-all is included in each thing and how it affects differentiations in things. It is not clear that Leibniz has fully abandoned his notion of the ideality of the continuum. And if so, it is not clear why the continuum here is relevant for comprehending things in their very materiality. Leibniz has not for instance shown why the continuum if ideal affects the material thing rather than only the concept of the thing. At most, Leibniz would here be refuting his own idea that there can be a complete concept of a thing. But it is not clear why that would show that the world in its very materiality is not Epicurean. To do so we would need to see any discrete point as being itself like the phoneme, a cut. Anything discrete would thus be a gap, a Dedekind cut. Each discrete thing, any letter, would itself be elected from the continuum and the continuum would be continuous only insofar as it included the uncountable number of gaps and cuts.

Thus, we need to see things as being written elements selected out of the continuum by cuts as irreducible wholes. The phoneme was for instance an indissoluble whole. The continuum includes singular and irreducible wholes (wholes that are holes) in it, but an uncountable number of them. But each one is itself a mirror reflection of the continuum. The singularity of the letter as a gap in the real continuous line means that all of existence is made up not of Epicurean atoms, but letters, of the discrete. It is therefore not contradictory to claim that we live in a discrete world because the discrete is ultimately what makes up the continuum on this reading as long as there is an uncountable infinity of discrete singularities.

Lucretius already signaled this insofar as he constantly needed to discuss his atoms in terms of alphabetic letters and their combinations. We can still see the world as made up of atoms as discrete things, but only if those atoms are themselves Dedekind cuts. With language, we saw that it is made up of a finite number of them. This means we always subtract from the continuum and build on it. What makes something singular is not that it is withdrawn from us or exceeds our perceptual abilities, but rather that it is a gap in the real itself. Clearly, we can only understand Leibniz's early 18th century formulations with late 19th century mathematics.

Also, Leibniz is here implicitly running into the problem of the incomputable. While Leibniz has given us a rule for computing all possible texts, he is hinting that there is a text that cannot be computed and that that text has the very power of the continuum itself to make it possible. Ultimately however even these considerations have not yielded what Leibniz needed--an explanation of why the inclusion of the continuum in all things and all things in the continuum means that there is never the return of the same but always imperceptible differences. And that is because only God can explain this. God as the absolute infinite with an unlimited power of creation must cause all things to happen. Thus, God has the resource of his omnipotence to vary things as He wishes. Given the continuum, only the hand of God can move our hand since otherwise per Zeno it would need to traverse an infinity. Only God also can have complete knowledge of things through the continuum in their very being, and the continuum is connected to the non-all, the mind of God.

Leibniz claimed he can show how our conception of a thing differs from what it is due to the continuum. But a thing is on one level only the extensional set of what it contains. Only God can draw on the generic subset within it to add to it new elements. Only God can makes use of the power of the continuum, we can only name that power. When we permute a text, we are not drawing on the power of the continuum. We are drawing rather than on a finite world and its very large possibilities. We are capable of acknowledging the imprint of the absolute on things. The absolute is beyond any numerosity we know. The continuum is then only the unbounded space in which we conduct our permutations, but not a reservoir for the permutations themselves. There is always a gap between us and the power of the continuum. That gap ensures that there is always space for more, but it does not in itself ensure that we will be able to draw upon the continuum for new differences.

We draw on the letter itself for it. We would have to say the latter insofar as it is cut out of the continuum and thus is marked by it can lead endlessly in its permutation even beyond what it seems to be capable of. If we don't wonder why things seem to exceed themselves, that is because the power of the continuum informs all. That means though that God himself is informing and marking things with his omnipresence. However, we do not need the power of the continuum itself to appreciate the permutations of a text. A text of even just 30 letters has an unimaginable number of possible distinct arrangements when we look not at the extensional powers so much as the ordered set of permutations. One could never check all those permutations unless one lived for much much longer than the universe has existed. This amount of permutations is itself overwhelming. What this means is that if we have a text of 30 letters, we can encrypt it in so many ways that one could not guess what the original text was since one would never go through all the possibilities. One would need to know the rule for how the cipher text was constructed.

§19. The Shofar Blasts and the Revealed Text

When it comes to a sacred text, that construction of course occurs at an event of revelation. Since for us there is only one sacred text (the Torah--the five books of Moses), its event of revelation is at Sinai and comes from the voice of God. That it is a text spoken and received from the voice of God will be of decisive importance. Up to this point, there would be no way to differentiate one text from another. One could only differentiate texts in terms of their extensional sets of letters and thus by the number of letters involved. But any text we have (including seemingly the Torah itself) is finite and thus connected only ever to a finite number of permutations. One can of course envision repeating those permutations but given enough time there will be simply eternal return of the same. To differentiate the sacred scripture from secular texts must in part then being in finding how the continuum is at work in it (since as Leibniz noted it is only the power of the continuum that can save us from the eternal return). To find the power of the continuum we will be to find again how this text was received from the voice of God Himself.

This voice, as the Torah itself, explains, came from the fire. This fire is not the same as that of the burning bush where God revealed himself to Moses. There, only a divine name was revealed whereas here a text as a whole (which is also a name) is given. The burning bush spoke and concealed itself in giving a sign. The crackling of the fire reveals the divine voice, but it is also interpreted as the ever increasing (never waning) blast of a shofar. The prayer book of Rosh Hashanah explains what is stake here in a section of the Musaf called 'Shofar Blasts' that itself comes immediately after a series of shofar blasts are sounded:

You were revealed in the cloud of Your glory to Your holy people to speak with them. From the heavens you made them hear Your voice and revealed yourself to them in thick clouds of purity. Moreover, all of the world in its entirety shuddered before You and the creatures of Creation trembled before You, when You were revealed, our King, on Mount Sinai, to Your people. Torah and the commandments, You made heard to them the majesty of Your voice and your utterances of holiness from flames of fire. And in thunder and lightning to them You were revealed and with the sound of a shofar to them You appeared, as it is written in your Torah. And it was on the third day when it was morning there was thunder and lightning, and a cloud that was heavy on the mountain, and the sound of the shofar was strong exceedingly, and tremble did all the people who were in the camp. And it is said: It was the sound of the shofar progressively stronger, exceedingly; Moses would speak and God would respond with a voice. And it is said: And all the people saw the sounds the flames and the sound of the shofar and the mountain smoking, and the people saw and shook; as they stood from afar. And in Your Holy Writings it is written, saying: Ascended has God with the last; Hashem, with the sound of the shofar.103

The voice of God Himself which comes from the fire is also the voice of the lightning and thunder and also the voice of the shofar. When the shofar is sounded on the Day of Judgment, it is itself an attempt "to imitate" this voice, as Theodor Reik noted in his analysis of the shofar.104 While Reik thinks this use of the ram's horn to make noise and thus imitate the voice of God is not unlike pagans who would mimic the voice of their gods using such devices, the issue here is not imitating the voice of an animal or of a limited and defined pagan deity. However, Reik is correct insofar as when it comes time to hear the voice of God and for God to reveal himself to the people of Israel at Sinai, it is the voice of the ever-increasing ram's horn they hear: "We are only told of the sound of the horn, and nowhere is it said that the people heard the Lord's voice. Yet the people say they heard this voice, and God Himself said that the people would hear His voice".105

The fact that the sound never wanes indicates to them that it is not any human act of trumpeting. Of course, such a horn blast is itself a-signifying. One does not on the face of it hear any intelligible words or sounds, but only the blast itself that seems to increase without limit until it exceeds the spectrum of human hearing. Mladen Dolar has attempted to expand on Reik's psycho-analysis by attempting to show that voice of God here is voice as object, what Lacan called *objet a*. The shofar notes the presence-absence of God in the excessive voice of the ever increasing ram's horn blasts. The sound of this blast overwhelms and causes the people to tremble given its transcendent nature. As Dolar notes, the presence of the radically transcendent God is designated in the Lacanian algebra as S(A).106 Thus, the imposition of the absolute and impossible Other on the world is a point where there is always something lacking. Here, it is God himself who is absent despite the exorbitant sounds associated with His voice. This lack of totality, the non-All, signaled by the voice will itself play a critical role in the voice at work.

For Dolar, the voice as *objet a* is "a senseless remainder of the letter" that is in itself-a-signifying as it what is left of the voice after it has been mapped by the differential network of phonemes.107 This object voice must be detached from the network of meaning itself made by possible by phonemes and be something like a horn blast in order for its full power to be made present. It is "an act" and not a signifier.108 It is through voice as pure and senseless act that law is founded as the law has no force by way of its content, but by way of the fact that it is heard as a command, as a pure voice.109 And that pure voice is an object rather than a spoken message, the object that supplements the intelligible network and content that might be in the law.

However, as an object, the voice "covers the lack".110 Here, we can say it is the lack of the transcendent Other. Of course, Dolar thinks that God is dead such that all that is left of God is his voice; the voice is the presence of a total absence.111 But this declaration of God's death confuses God's withdrawal from the world with God's being a voice and nothing more. While the voice does "stand-in for an impossible presence", that impossibility is its necessary reference.112 The Law can only here have as its origin some radically contingent and divine moment. The law itself in its lettering seems to have already existed, but here we see that the law had to be instituted by a voice, the very voice that accompanies its articulation and gives it its force. This a-signifying object voice is "the Law itself in its pure form" at its foundation and to obey the law is to heed this voice and accept it as related to a divine and transcendent Other.113

The voice appears as though out of nowhere and thus notes something lacking, but at that same time comes from outside and seems to have no ground and to emerge and be based only on itself. It is thus a pure enunciation and pure command. But we would be we wrong to simply accept this formulation as the final one since from this senseless and terrifying voice the entire law, the Torah, is extracted. In other words, the law in its pure form may to our ears have no intelligible form, but there is an actual a text itself hiding in the voice in its seemingly deafening noise. It was Moses (and only Moses) who could discern the text hiding in the voice itself. Moses spoke to God which means he could investigate this divine voice and render from it meaning. The people only knew this voice was itself the presence-absence of the divine Other. Thus, the people only understood in it in the basic idea that it was the voice of God and that God is unique (there is no other) for there can only be one absolute infinite.

Moses himself ascended Sinai to receive and discern from the voice itself the text that was included in it. While the voice seems to arise only as a supplement of the differential network of signifiers and meaningful terms that make up the law, in its senseless sound there is still information within it. The voice is thereby indiscernibly singular and at the same time a transfinite encoding of information. As we know today, sound is made up of waves. Any sound we can hear can be expressed as a wave. As Manil Suri has noted, any waves composing a sound are themselves composed of "simpler components" called "basis functions".114 Thus, the voice of God heard at Sinai could also be represented by a voice analyzer and be expressed as a wave. But as Suri notes, we can take a wave and show it is for example broken down into a number of simpler regular waves. The sound we hear is essentially a super-position of all the other waves since different sounds as waves are additive rather than subtractive (canceling each other).

If one hears, using Suri's example, a small burst of wind, one can break down the wave expressed by it into four simpler components that if superimposed compose the wave. But each simpler wave itself is made up of a basis function. The basis functions are blending together to form the overall wave. The continuum of sound itself thus can be expressed and represented by a series of basis functions. A less regular wave, one of the wind blowing, is made up of four very simple and regular waves. One wave here is deconstructed into four waves, four basis functions. In other words, a sound we hear is a stack and sum of multiple other sounds and waves.

The wind is of course a senseless and a-signifying sound. As Suri notes, an electric synthesizer used today to produce popular music depend on this idea of producing sounds by stacking and blending simpler wave patterns. In another example, Suri notes that the sound of an orchestra is made up of many different instruments and many different components. The instruments are the basis functions of the orchestra, the simpler components, but of course any of the instruments in their sounds can be decomposed into basis functions. The sound of orchestra can then be seen as the sum of all the simpler components. One creates a Fourier series here to produce a piece of music.

Suri also applies his model to images and painting. Any pixel of a computer screen for instance is made up of different intensities of overlapping red, blue, and yellow. Thus, one can say that any image is itself when magnified properly a series of pixels of various intensities that here compose the basis functions for a painting. One can then show how a painting itself contains the information involved in basis functions being stacked together to produce it. Seurat's pointillism for example would not be one specific movement in painting, but a movement that reveals the underling basis of all coloration. Even when one paints with a broad stroke, the image left is itself analyzable as a pointillist work and by way of the mathematics of a Fourier series.

With the voice of God, then we have a very large number of basis functions being stacked one on the other simultaneously and thus producing a ram's horn blast, a senseless never waning sound. Since the torah itself is made up of over 300,000 letters, we would think that the voice heard was at least 300,000 basis functions sounded at once. Thus, Moses needed to decompose and analyze the voice of God into over 3000,00 basis functions and revealed the information contained in it. But given this idea of basis functions we see that different wave patterns and functions are all composing it. One sees here that the basic building blocks of the voice of God were phonemes, letters, themselves all superimposed at one instance on each other. While with paintings, one's building blocks are red, blue, and green, with sound it is ultimately wave patterns and thus more directly numbers.

Letters as we have seen are numbers themselves. The key here is that one has some series of numbers, letters, etc. that expresses the basis functions making up the senseless voice. Moses extracted at least part of that sequence. Moses ultimately listed a sequence of numbers (which is what the Torah is insofar as each Hebrew letter has a numerical value). One question here is of course whether the sequence is purely random or not. However, if the sequence is somehow compressible, then there is a code for producing it. Even though the voice of God is some exorbitant voice that seems unintelligible and exceeds our capacity to understand, the singular prophet Moses was able to render the fundamental experience that forms its expression, the superimposed basis functions making it up.

We should contrast this analysis with Leibniz again via his notion of micro-perceptions. For Leibniz, all conscious perception was only a partial rendering of an infinity of minute perceptions that things are made up of. His example her famously was hearing the sound of the ocean roaring. That sound is made up of very many water molecules oscillating and banging into each other, but we only hear part of that whole. Hence, the object we hear, the roar of the ocean, is only a partial object of some vast oceanic body that exceeds us. All the other micro-perceptions that we do not hear are still composing the sound, but are unconscious. All the sound waves of the ocean roar are not heard--only a select part. It is an interesting property of waves that they sum together rather than cancel each other out. Thus, waves can become and be simultaneously in a way perhaps other properties cannot.

But of course the entire world is making noise at all times. All is in motion. If we could experience all possible sound waves occurring now everywhere, what sort of wave would we have? If we speak of the entire universe in principle, then there is staggering number of waves that would need to be stacked on each other to form that sound. It would certainly seem like pure, white noise. We do not of course experience this entire series of waves. Just as we do not see or experience all possible numbers being computed at once, we only see a finite segment of even a transfinite series. We only grasp part of the series, but that does not mean the series is limited to what we grasp. For us the sound of the ocean is confused, but that does not mean there are not individual waves.

If we ask what sound the ocean can possibly make in the past, present and future, then we have a transfinite series of individual waves. The sum of that transfinite series would itself be an infinite sound. When we hear the ocean, we are only hearing one finite series of it. This is the same with the voice of God. God is not simply transfinite, but the absolute infinite. Thus, God's voice would have the power of the continuum. To hear only 300,00 sounds simultaneously here is as if to hear nothing compared to the uncountably infinite individual basis functions and sound wave patterns making up the divine voice as it is in itself. I do hear individual waves, but only ever as a finite aggregate. The infinite aggregate I hear is a fragment of an unpresentable and ever absent transcendent series. These waves are only made distinct by way of numbers and numerical expression, by way of letters.

Deleuzians think that the unheard micro-perceptions here exist virtually, but that only can mean that they transcend our conscious perception. Our conscious perception is always participating in a continuum of elements that are not conscious, but that continuum is actual. It is actual in the transcendent eidetic realm relative to God. It is not some potentiality that needs to be activated. It is not some netherworld of patterns that must be actualized. It is already here in the continuum and continuity of the world itself and its being marked by the divine omnipresence.

We should also not think that the sounds and perceptions we have indicate something transcendent such as a shadowy object double that is over and above them. Our perceptions occur within a field of letters and numbers and are limited and in sets of finite sequences. There is the continuum that transcends them, but no individual unities that does so. It is our experience that is made up those unities. Thus, we should not project from our conscious perceptions shadowy transcendent objects doubling them as Plato seemed to do in his allegory of the cave. We should only ever allow Plato to be a Pythagorean. Rather, we should recognize that what transcends us is the non-all of the letter itself just as what transcends our experience of the sound of the ocean is a very larger number of individual wave patterns that we do not hear. It is not that there is some great virtual memory at work outside of the mind of God himself and the continuum. This is why the continuum is included in each individual unit and set and also the continuum includes each possible unity and object.

Of course, when we try to hear the ocean or the universe itself we hear noise. One is the stacking of all the sound waves together. It is noise to us since we do not hear intelligible words and voices in it. It is also does not seem to have any recognizable pattern that is melodious to our ears in the way music is. We do not enjoy the sound of noise and find it often painful. But when it comes to hearing the infinite and continuum itself, we have actualized a sonic spectrum that is always sounding itself without end and assaults us in our very materiality. When the voice of God was revealed at Sinai, one heard what cannot be enclosed in intelligible human speech, but what exceeds it. However, paradoxically, that voice resulted in a text. The voice was spoken all at once. It is to hear the continuum as much as that is humanly possible which means that only a finite series was extracted from it.

Now, of course based on this analysis, one could say that the Torah could be extracted from the roar of the ocean itself. Simply by listening to the universe, we could then spell out what it is saying in letters. The very noise of the universe itself would be a text. I am not aware of anyone composting a text on this basis. In particular, it would be interesting to see if the text made any sense in any language. What is remarkable about the Torah is that it makes sense. That is, the sequence of numbers and stacked wave patterns formed itself into an intelligible text. There is a Torah to be heard in the waves of the ocean for instance, but it might not be a text anyone would try to read and appears only as pure noise and a wholly random sequence. If we say this text is based on all the possible noises the ocean itself could make (and thus transfinite), we would say it is itself already included in the Torah. After all, if the Torah is a finite series of the uncountable infinite of the power of continuum and is related to the absolute infinite, then any Torah we could extract from the sound of the ocean would already be included in the permutations of the Torah. Even if the sequence of letters and numbers we found in the ocean's roar was purely random and irreducibly complex, it could be generated from permutations of the Torah. Thus, once we have Moses's act of extracting the sequence from the divine voice, we need not search for in the noise of the universe itself or some segment of it any more.

Of course, it is also the case that no pagan ever produced a text in this manner to my knowledge. This is because their gods are finite and limited. Any text they would inspire would be completely indiscernible from a finite poem composed by a poet. The God of Sinai is thoroughly and radically transcendent God. Because the Torah is connected to the divine voice and the voice to the power of the continuum, it is possible to differentiate it from other finite texts even though the Torah we have is made up of a finite set of a few hundred thousand letters/numbers.

For Leibniz, as we saw in the end, each monad must be connected to the continuum and thus be mirroring and expressing its own perspective on the absolute. However, each monad only sees the continuum in a confused manner. God transcends all and thus is only seen through a veil, the void itself. We hear the infinite in all that we hear, but we could not recognize this fact until Sinai itself when the divine voice itself was collectively witnessed. The event of Sinai as this collective witnessing is then passed down via the generations. For Leibniz, God would hear the uncountable infinite in itself. But God would not hear it as noise, but rather be able to discern every simple component making up the sound. God would thereby in hearing himself speak know and hear each part of it since no part would be excluded from his mind, the non-all. What Leibniz shows us here is that the non-all itself is impressing itself upon us and that all our finite perceptions are themselves partial perceptions of God. In all we perceive we are seeing God and in all we hear once after Sinai our eyes and ears have been opened. The event of Sinai has not ended as this event continues to reveal to us that we are still hearing the non-whole and how it impinges upon our sense.

We would only recognize the non-all as noise, but given that our own experiences are part of it, we can see that what appears as noise is itself made up of discrete parts. This is of course the nature of sound itself for us. Our ears are always taking the mechanical movements of the sound waves and transforming them into electric currents of varying intensities. These electric currents travel through the eardrums to the brain where we by way of the brain hear them as sound. All sound for us only exists because it is rendered discrete as electric pulses. To say sound is ultimately for us electric current is to say it is made up of bits (0/1) and thus numbers. Hence, in all we hear we are hearing bit strings without realizing it. If we did, we would see the encoding of all auditory experience. This auditory encoding would reveal the program.

Perhaps the roar of an ocean even though it appears to be noise in its bit string is expressing the very program for articulating ocean waves. One of the interesting differences between sound waves and light waves is that sound waves need a medium such as air to function whereas light waves (especially as photons) need know such medium to undulate. The air of course can slow down the sound wave or speed it up. Things at night sound louder because the air is thinner. That means the bit string we hear is different at night than at day. The bit string in its encoding already includes the airs as medium. We are wrong to think that media in this way do not affect things, but at the same time we are wrong to think that the effect and nature of the medium cannot also be encoded into bits.

As Richard E. Berg and David G. Stork note in their *The Physics of Sound*: "In fact, at any point in space there is in general an infinity of waves; all space is filled with a limitless number of waves of all kinds and wavelengths, none of which is affected by the existence of the others".115 While sound waves can superpose on each other, not all waves do that. However, we exist in an endless sea of waves of varying differing kinds. In fact, what we often think of as 'particles' are actually fields made up of waves. We thankfully are only conscious of a small fraction of this roaring ocean. Just as the sound continuum is the background for any specific act of human speech and out of which the phonemes are cut out, there is a background noise that we only hear partially. That background noise is in itself unceasing, but we could not handle being fully immersed in it.

Noise is thereby the materiality of all sounds. The continuum itself would be a noise, one indiscernible from the divine voice. The unlimited divine is the very continuity of the continuum itself that marks all things. Phenomenologically we would never know of this noise or the continuum since phenomenologically we consciously only experience things in a restricted form. We must step outside of Phenomenology to encounter the very materiality of existence itself. Every sonic phenomenon is cut out ultimately from the continuum and is a gap in this background. It is not just the phoneme. But that should not be surprising since the phonemes were themselves to be combined to form intelligible words. The senseless background noise is no different in its unending emission.

We can of course discern nothing in the non-all unless we make it finite, but that does not mean we are only with the finite and that the only thing that transcends the finite is a thing-like shadow of it as though what transcends a tree is a more perfect tree. Rather, since existence is made up of the letter itself, the letter is able to enter into differential relations and thus produce meaning and sense. We may have a set of endless sound waves, but as numbers and simple units that are superimposed those sound waves can at some point differentially relate the one with the other and become audible and clear senses. It is a system of waves itself that allows for noise, but the differential relations between the basic units enables meaning. Sense and non-sense are then intricately linked.

Of course, today we know that the one of the pieces of evidence that helped to confirm the big bang theory is the background radiation that is everywhere around us. This background radiation is famously heard as static noise and can be picked up by a radio. Given that God is the divine cause of the being bang; when we hear that background radiation in its crackling, we are hearing again the voice of God. It would be interesting to translate its basis functions into numbers and then letters and see if it matches the Torah itself or one of its permutations. It would also be interesting to render it as a bit string and see what program it offers us. When we listen to the background radiation we turn to the voice of God itself and hear it addressing us again just as it did at Sinai with the crackling of the fire. Only after Sinai would we think to find such things in radiation which is itself part of the basic noise of the universe.

When God hears his own voice divine in its infinite form, he does not hear noise, it is not confused for him, but rather he hears his own divine name being spoken. We have said that the divine voice at Sinai speaks the 304,805 letters of the Torah at once. All are superimposed on each other. The Jewish sages taught that this 304,805 letter sequence is itself one name, a divine one. The Torah is a single word and name per this view. The set of letters here, this 304,805 extensional set and string of bits is itself one of the most important divine names. It is certainly the longest discussed. We cannot of course recite all 304, 805 letters at once on our own. But we can perhaps compute mechanically them all together at once and superimpose them forming a single wave. It is probable that would be noise, but this is an experiment worth trying to see what the actual result would be. Would it sound like a shofar blast? Or the crackling of the fire?

At the burning bush, God revealed his name YHVH, but at Sinai he revealed the 304,805 letter name. One of the questions we need to ask about this divine voice and the name it spoke is whether it is in any sense compressible. Nose itself as pure randomness seems incompressible. White noise is thereby irreducibly complex. But that does not mean that any noise we hear in its a-signifying and senseless nature is so incompressible. The question here would be if the Torah itself is somehow incompressible into for instance the first 42 letters. We know those first 42 letters form another divine name via specific encoding and permutation. The High Priest would speak this name on the holiest of days and thus it would not be wrong to think its pronunciation all at once is an imitation of the divine voice. It would be when spoken all at once produce an unintelligible sound like the shofar. While there are an uncountable infinity of real numbers and thus irreducible forms white noise, each has its own frequency spectrum which also all look to us as flat line and thus are relatively indiscernible. But if one relates them to non-algebraic reals (which are themselves infinite and non-repeating), then one sees how each real could be its own version of white noise.

But not all infinite reals are incompressible. Pi is an infinite real and seemingly random, but it is compressible. We should thus not believe necessarily that any noise we hear is incompressible and knows of no pattern. Even if the universe thus emits white noise, it may be the kind that is compressible. It may be a real like pi. In fact, if we are right, it must be. Thus, even though we are engulfed in a sea of noise, it is itself a function of some compressible pattern. That pattern is found in the background radiation and thus in the divine voice. Once we had this sequence and program, we would be able to predict what thing would come next simply by running it and waiting for it to unfold.

We know that with finite human speech that given the redundancies in what we say (the high frequency of certain vowels and sounds for example) we can in many cases easily predict how speech sound patterns will unfold. With this in mind, sound engineers can compress speech sound patterns and only add to them what is new in what will be spoken. They therein conserve bandwidth and resources. This compression allows one to foresee how the sound waves of the entire sequences will unfold given the current ones within the context of human speech. Divine speech is somewhat similar. It is compressible via a divine name. This divine name then unfolds such that one cannot so much predict what the pattern will lead to in the next moment as show what it will unto into by way of the program itself iterating and executing itself.

Here, we see the reverse of what we saw with the phonemes. Whereas the phonemes being cut out of the sound continuum reduced noise itself into finite segments that would yield sense, here we see a pattern itself in its iteration building back up the continuum to produce all possible noise sequences via permutations. This is not to say that one cannot articulate noise using phonemes, but that they allow us to exclude all these noise sequences by sticking to the rules governing human speech. Without them there would only be a-signifying sound patterns and noise.

At the same time, we know that the divine voice itself yielded the text since the Torah itself teaches that people saw the voices (Exodus 20:18). When the people saw the Torah written out, they knew that it was the divine voice made visible in writing. To see the voice is to see letters, the sound waves transposed into a sequence. This sight is a mark of the final step in the exit from Egypt and the pagan universe. In Egypt, they only ever saw hieroglyphics. Hence, they saw pictographs that were referring to things in the world and to imagined ideas. But after having heard the divine voice, they now could recognize phonetic writing and see the phoneme in its relation to the letter and see the voice itself. The blank page is now reduced by the letters in the same way the phonemes reduce the sound spectrum and filter it. They were unaware of these letters before because the signifier is always slipping into the signified in speech and the hieroglyph is always evoking an image of a perceptual object.

They also now see that the crackling of the fire is itself a sound made up of phonemes in its noise and that this is only possible on the basis of the name itself: "The voice of YHVH divine as the flames of fire" (Psalm 29:7). God is invisible but leaves behind his voice and the letters it is made up of. In this way, whereas the Egyptians had painted images of their sun-god on the walls of their temples, the God of monotheism is radically transcendent and as a result must leave behind a visible book, a series of letters. The voice here disappears and contracts into letters. The divine voice and with it the power of the continuum withdraws into the Torah itself.

The divine voice articulates the entire Torah at once. This means it is for the divine one single utterance, one divine name. In human speech and writing, we only encounter one sentence of the Torah at a time, one word at a time. However, the divine voice in being all at once can thus intend multiple things at once. While for us we see the Torah saying one thing and then another that seems to conflict at another stage, for the divine voice all things come at once. For the Divine there is then no contradiction, but rather for instance a particular principle and a possible exception noted at once. We do not see then the connection between two passage because they seem to come some at a distance and removed from each other, but in the divine voice all comes at once and thus there is no contradiction as much as clarification. We are separated in time and space from one section and the other of the text and forget this. The divine voice spoke about multiple dimensions of the same thing at one and the same time.

There are many rules connected to the Sabbath for instance. We cannot speak or hear all of them being said at once, but the divine voice did just this. In Judaism there is the expression 'God has spoken once, twice we have heard this.' We hear things that were done all at once in stages. While Moses was able to transcribe the divine voice, Moses still presented us with a text that was intelligible on its surface to the human eye and ear and composed in the language of men. Moses himself was still very much human, and even if he was be to hear in the divine voice as a sequence of numbers/letters, he heard it as a human and not all at once. It took him time to extract things slowly bit by bit. God's language can be heard by the singular prophet, but not as a single utterance at once. It could only for Moses be written in the language of men. Rather, he is able to discern from it a series of statements that seem to conflict with each other when spaced out.

§20. Torah Codes

Simultaneous divine speech also does not know from any of the paradoxes of self-reference we are familiar with. It sees all permutations at once throughout eternity. In other words, the divine language is the incomputable itself rendered at once. But we can only have a finite sequence of that incomputable real. We have tried to link the divine book to the transfinite via the divine. If the sacred scripture can be linked to a number like pi, then it can contain all possible information. However, in another context, the idea of connecting a poetic text to the transfinite was called 'ridiculous.' In their *Fashionable Nonsense: Postmodern Intellectuals' Abuse of Science*, Alan Sokal and Jean Bricmont chastised Julia Kristeva for arguing that poetics is related to the power of the continuum.116 In one of the isolated sections where Sokal and Bricmont do not simply quote a passage and call it 'nonsense' without attempting to interpret or deal with the concepts articulated in it relative to the author's system, Sokal and Bricmont note that the idea continuum of continuum is related to "infinite sets" and ask "Where does one find such sets in poetry?".117

Our claim is one finds only such sequences relative to the divine text. Otherwise, one would have to agree with the following contention of Sokal and Bricmont:

> Let us note that the set of all texts ever written in the entirety of human history is a finite set. Moreover, any natural language—for example, English or Chinese---has a finite alphabet; a sentence, or even a book, is a finite sequence of letters. Therefore, even the set of all finite sequences of letters in all conceivable books, without any restriction on length, is a denumerable infinite set. It is hard to see how the continuum hypothesis, which concerns nondenumerable infinite sets, could have any application in linguistics.118

But of course, we know of no books without some limit on their length. It would only be a text related to the divine itself that could be ever be uncountably infinite. But as we have argued elsewhere, once we have denumerably infinite set, we can find included in it as a generic subset that relates it to the continuum and the uncountably infinite. Thus, while a secular text produced by a human author has only ever be seen as finite, a divine text because it is related to the divine mind and intellect itself, to the non-all, is related to the power of the continuum. It is always with the infinity of language that the divine text is involved precisely because it is divine in origin.

However, given that the Torah as we have it is only 304,805 letters it is only by first permuting the text that we can see further how it is related to the infinite and the continuum. First, when we permute any finite text, we enter a scale that no human mind could ever experience or capture. It is only with computational devices that we can even begin exploring such an exceedingly large space of combinations. Even if we were to try to permute the text of *Moby Dick* to find for instance how many other texts of the same length using can be produced, we would never argue that Melville intended these texts or authored them. The meaning of the words of his text already exceed Melville's intentions due to the fact that the linguistic code is trans-individual, but to reduce his text to the letter and permute it is work at a scale that he could have no knowledge of.

Only today would we expect that an author might have been able to experiment with his/her text using a computer program and thus be capable of producing such a text. But even here, there is a limit. A computer would have to run an indefinite time to enact certain computations. In some cases, it would have to run longer than the universe has already existed. Thus, at a certain point, there is a place where only the intervention of the eternal one, the divine, could ever possibly allow for all such permutations and to foreseeing and intending them. And if a text is collectively witnessed as given by the divine voice, then one necessarily accepts that this text is capable of such endless permutation and all must be intended in it. This means the Torah must be encoded and ciphered and connected to all the possible permutations of its letters.

The divine mind is in itself unlimited and non-all. Thus, nothing can be excluded from it including any thought or any permutation of letters. One does not look for codes in Melville because anything one finds other will already be attributed to the symbolic Other and to the logic of the signifier and not to any conscious intention of Melville's. But in a divine text, anything one finds there must necessarily be attributed to the barred Other, the divine other, the symbolic in its transfinitude and inconsistency. In a text by Melville, finding that a particular section can be transposed using a rule into another would be taken to be simply a word game that one can perform on any text, but in the divine text this act itself is a unveiling of a divinely intended aspect of the text. For the human author, he/she did not intend anything insofar as their text can be permuted into saying something else. It is only at best part of the unconscious structure of language. But the divine is that unconscious power ultimately and thus it is all intended in the sacred scripture. This is what makes a text sacred.

And there is only one such sacred text. One can also see here why a sacred text needs a sacred language. One can write a sacred text only in a language capable of being so permuted. Before computers, that meant a language where meaning could arise out of the permutations of the written phonetic letters alone. In Hebrew, each letter has a numerical value and also any combination of letters can be meaningful since it can be read as acronym or as a word yet unspoken, but easily pronounceable. This is why the sacred text is written in a consonantal language like Hebrew. In such language, one need not have vowels in order to have a word. Any combination of letters is in principle a word regardless of what is included in the currently available dictionaries and lexicons.

Of course, such a sacred text could not be written in pictography since there one deals only with the signs and not the letter. We can ask here if the Torah itself was the first text of any length written in fully phonetic, consonantal writing since it is the first text to clearly tap into the infinite permutations of the letter that phonetic writing announces. Also, a consonantal language opens up multiple possibilities because one can pronounce one and the same string of letters in multiple ways since the vowels are absent. One simply looks at the word and knows that the sting of letters itself has a series of permutations. Were one to permute pictographical symbols one would never think the permutations could ever be anything but limited, and it would not be clear the new combinations produce meaningful effects.

In the vast computational universe of the pure letter, one encounters the divine necessarily since one ultimately must ask about whether there is only a finite number of permutations or an infinite number. One leaves behind a finite human author's intentions and enters into the ultimately divine space of the non-all. One also must here leave meaning behind. The pictographic text completely ignored any of its a-signifying elements, but the letter itself is a-signifying on its own. It is thus simply a matter of rearranging elements. Also, given the numerical value of letters, one with permutations and listing of numbers begins to see how the numbers grow infinitely larger and thus is necessarily related to the question of whether there is an infinite number. When one does render a secular text by a human author as numbers, it does resonate with the divine, but only as a text that would be included in the divine text.

This also means the divine text is necessary encrypted. While Mallarme may have counted the words in his poem, the Torah is encrypted which means all that can be found in it using permutations, letter transpositions, letter counting, etc. is intended. The divine text however also says it is not exhausted by the operations we can invent for discovering what it is saying when we decode it. The divine text says there is always another way to transpose it or to discover something in it since nothing is excluded from its true nature. In his *Reading Machines: Toward an Algorithmic Criticism*, Stephen Ramsay notes techniques for detecting word frequency in a secular text.119 But even here there is no suggestion that the author knows how frequently he/she uses a specific word or set of adjectives. It is taken as something that in being counted expresses and characterizes their own linguistic unconscious at best and offers in being taken together their stylistic tendencies.

Ramsay also discusses what he calls "the entropic poem".120 Such poem involves spelling out all the permutations of the text. Since a poem is often a very finite set of letters, one can see all the permutations on a page or a few pages. But there is no suggestion that all the permutations "provide data about the original" as much as simply show the inherent power of language itself.121 Here, we see that any finite text is always one finite sequence leading to the power of the continuum of the divine text itself. Each text is already included in the divine text, but in being finite and human-derived obscures that until we ourselves reduce it to the letter and transpose it.

We should also not look at the divine non-all as a potential realm. It is a transcendent realm, the divine mind itself. It is not present in existence, but as we will begin to suggest it is the always already final endpoint that existence is unfolding into. This is why the Torah itself is only a finite number of letters in its present form. It will only unveil its full nature in a future that is already actual in the divine intellect. But since creation means the contraction of the divine into a finite series of letters, the Torah is here no exception.

Of course, saying the Torah is coded is not original to this text. In their *Torah Codes: A Glimpse into the Infinite*, Robert M. Haralick, Eliyahu Rips, and Matityahu Glazerson presented their own argument as to how codes can be found in the Torah although beyond the title of their book they do not in any way connect their ideas to infinite, the transfinite, the continuum, etc. Instead authors of Torah Codes focus on finding a connection between two different words (for instance, 'Rabin' and 'murder' in Hebrew) in one and the same table (one particular slice of text) by choosing the lowest possible numerical value for the letters of each word being spaced out and yet in the same table. For the authors, the issue involves deriving the probability that one would find both words in the same table using the lowest possible number of letter skips. One then checks the probability the two words would be so connected versus the probability they would be connected in any randomly selected text or population of randomized texts of the same size in Hebrew.122 If the text has a high probability of being in any text of that size, then "there is a chance explanation".123

The authors here think that they have shown that the Torah is divine since the probability of finding the two words linked using this system is slightly, but significantly lower than in the random text. Given the low of probability of the two words being so connected, it is said not to be simply a chance occurrence. That is, there is a law of probability of finding the two words connected and thus their connection seems to be non-random. Also, the authors look at the specific passage where the two words were connected to see how that passage with its contents can shed light on things. Presumably, they are claiming that if one knew what name and what word to connect to it and found the table where they are most connected one would be able to predict events. In any event, one for them can retroactively see how the Torah already predicted the event and commented on it.

Of course, this system was immediately criticized by showing how one could construct tables and find the same words connected in a text like *Moby Dick*. The authors of course claim that the connection in *Moby Dick* is only made using much larger jump sequences such one does not see the same low probability that the two words would be connected. One strange part of this system is that the words and their connection are taken from current Hebrew newspapers. It is thus determined that in the newspapers covering a current event the name Rabin was most connected with a particular noun or adjective. It is the authors who decide what words were most prominent in the discussion. But there are of course any number of words used in describing current events. There is no clear methodology here for determining how one links word ('Rabin' for instance) and the linked word. One could use the word 'murder,' but also assassination or shooting. If there are multiple possible word linkages, one can compute many different slices of text and find which word with which name has a low probability, but the leaves aside the other associations that appear at a chance frequency. If things appear at chance frequency, then all is random. The laws of probability then determine why two things are connected in the Torah as much as in any randomly selected or generated text.

A code is not found because two words appear in more than one newspaper article. This is strange because if one is talking about a code one would think that one could just from the name 'Rabin' for instance using the numerical value of the letters and some set of rules one would be lead to a particular passage in the Torah itself. Of course, the passage one would find by such a system would be open to interpretation, one would then if the Torah is prophetic, find some description that seems to relate to what happened. But instead of such a code, the authors take their specification from newspapers. Why these newspapers are themselves a tool for finding things in the divine text is unclear.

This focus on historically connected terms seems to indicate a lack of a true code. Now, of course one might say that if Kabbalists like these authors had such a code revealing prophetic statements they might want to conceal it for fear of what revealing future predictions might have on history and humanity. The problem here is also that by focusing on probability the divinity of the text itself is put into question. Anything one can permute in a divine text is intended because the text is itself connected to the voice of God that revealed it. Hence, one only needs to show that is can be so permuted. To differentiate it from secular texts requires looking at intentions for instance rather than probabilities.

However, the low probability of relatively compact arrangements of coded cylinders of words where the two key words are found using letter skips is fascinating. But ultimately, one sees this low probability as being meaningful because one thinks one can find such connections in this text. Interestingly the authors take into account the possibility of errors copying the Torah and suggest "that God put an imperfect code in the text of Mount Sian and that after any alleged copying errors, the imperfect cod becomes perfect".124 In other words, copying errors were already anticipated by God himself when revealing the text to Moses. In this way, when we would look back after the Rabin event to see if it was encoded in the Torah, any errors that had accumulated would help to elicit a table more compact than could be find in any randomly selected text.

Another issue here is that the number of letter skips one needs to use is not clearly specified in anyway. One again would think that if there is a code that the numerical value of the name 'Rabin' or that name coupled with Rabin's birth date in the Hebrew calendar or some other algorithm for reaching a particular passage where the name Rabin is found with a small number of letter skips, where the passage seems to say something significant about Rabin, etc. That is what a true Torah code would look like. But all of this is here lacking. Here, while finding a connection between two words in this manner with a lower probability does speak to the Torah's being unique compared to another texts in its finite form on this one issue, if one wants to truly persuade others that the Torah in its infinite form is truly distinct from other finite texts of the same or similar size, one will need to unearth more detailed codes such as the ones I have suggested above.

One needs a fairly succinct system for showing how and why words should be transposed or why one search in different intervals for the letters of a word or words in the text. The rules of transposition have to be few in number, simple, and used consistently. Any true code can be so articulated. Of course, most codes are ones that two parties have agreed upon in the past. Here, however we have received a divine text and thus have to discover the right way to uncover its encryption. But because it is a divine text we know it is necessarily encrypted. Thus, on this view it will be difficult, no matter how jumbled the letters may seem to be that they can only have one meaningful ordering. If one has a procedure, one can unscramble them and find intended meanings from the sender. But for the transcription to be effective, it needs to be algorithmic in nature, a step-by-step procedure and one that itself can be presented using the tools of Hebrew itself such as the numerical value of letters, reading words as anagrams, etc.

We can say today that despite the work of Haralick, Rips, and Glazerson, true Torah codes that would show how the Torah prophetically predicts current events remains hidden from us. However, the computational tools available to us now with computers promise that with another effort a much more straightforward system than the letter-skips one will be in the offing since we can metaphysically demonstrate (as we are attempting to do here) that the Torah is necessarily encrypted. Therefore, we need a system for how to replace letters in divine whole world using a code and system. This may mean simply trying using computers various different transformations until one hits upon one that reveals a plain text.

Of course, we would be then lead back to the issue of whether such a system can be used in *Moby Dick* and if the probability of such a system is such that it is likely to be found in any text of the same length. This is why one would expect the Torah in its current finite form to have some sort of highly improbable number of very straightforward algorithms for discovering decoded texts within it and distinctly more than any other text of the same size in Hebrew or any other language. There are an indefinite number of techniques for unscrambling the letters of the Torah and rendering a new intelligible message.

Here many would say that the Torah itself is simply an intelligible message and that one is not unscrambling but scrambling it. However, this presumes that the text was humanly authored. It is also forgets that the Torah was only given as a string of letters that were later divided. If they had been divided differently, then its status as a scrambled text would have been obvious. If it is divinely authored then even what appears to be the simple literal level of the text is itself a scrambled version of another text. Thus, even words that are perfectly understood by us are themselves a veil hiding something more. If we thought the text was the product of a human intention, we would not say that they veil anything, but a divine text must be a veil hiding the non-all.

The revealed letters of the divine text are not reducible to the finite sequence we have currently. The divine itself even as it contracts into a finite form cannot truly fit into it and thus shatters it. We thus must uncover the shattered framework by opening up the materiality of the letter itself and finding what is hidden inside. Since the sacred scripture is the word of God, we must not identify it with only a certain finite number of letters, but with all the its possible letterings. The sacred text is the one that we assume is connected to the infinite power of the letter itself and its inscription. This is why it is not simply a matter of finding word frequencies or unintended meanings. Such unintended meanings simply imply a code in the symbolic order that is trans-individual and makes our speech intelligible. But that is always to remain at the level of meaning, of the relation between signifier-signified. But the ambiguity of reading one and the same passage in two different ways does not interest us. It is not of interest since it makes it appears as if the Other is constrained and thereby finite.

We are only interested here in the barred Other, the impossible one, and that can only be reached by the letter. . With the letter we can see why the Vilna HaGaon claimed, "All that was, is, and will be unto the end of time is included in the Torah, the first five books of the Bible".125 This quote reminds us that we do not claim that the other books of the Bible are sacred or any other books in the sense we have been using the word. God's creative power is such that God can already foresee any configuration of letters. These letters are thus double-sided. They are not simply double-sided in the sense of being both letters and numbers, but they are double-sided in the sense that they are always both a revelation and a concealment at the same time. They are encrypted which means they are one side of what they show on the surface and literally and the other side of a mystery shrouded due to their connection to the divine. . Behind every name is encoded a more concealed divine name.

One should see here that we are not arguing that the actual arrangements of the letters and signs are necessarily related to their meaning. That is, we are not arguing that the combination of letters itself is not somehow arbitrarily related to their meaning as any of the arrangements could be in theory related to another meaning. It is precisely due to the senselessness of the letter that one can do permutations and find something new. It is not here a question of magic. That is what a pictographic view would say. A pictographic version of these considerations would believe that by changing a specific name one can cause something to happen in the world since the sign resembles and mirrors the perceptual thing. It is not here a question of motivated relations between the letters and meanings, but rather of the emergent effects of the letter itself. In other words, no magic. Thus, reversing the Torah and reading it backwards would not be seen as producing the evil or satanic version of the Torah precisely because the letters are here taken in themselves in their a-signifying nature. The material arrangement of letters is itself something that the Torah says to permute and change to find new meanings. We are not here arguing along the lines of the pagan view of permutation.

Also because we are examining things first and foremost at the level of the letter, we do not run into Gödelian sentences. Some say the Bible is necessarily incomplete since one can come up with sentences like "This sentence cannot be proven as true within the Bible' or 'The Bible says this statement is false.' The Torah is also not a system for proving or deriving statements, but for dealing with a revealed sequence of statements and letters. Here rather we face the issue of the continuum and the incomputable rather than Gödelian self-reference since we remain at the level of the letter and its computation. However in those letters we also find names and in particular the proper name of God, YHVH. Insofar as this name can be counted as a name for the void, the empty set, this name is included in all names. This is also the case insofar as YHVH is made up of the vowels, the voiced letters, that give voice to the phonetic inscription. It is not simply that YHVH is connected to the very void because these letters themselves are added to the consonants to give them voice.

Some compare this voicing to YVHV making all that is ensouled and alive. In that way, YHVH is the animating principle of names and also things. This is another way in which the name of God is distributed throughout the names. Insofar as YHVH is the very source code of things, it shows how an infinite amount of output can arise from a minimal point of departure. But the code here is not exempted from the computation itself. The name YHVH is also found in the text and is part of it. It is not simply an activator of a computational process, but also is in its lettering the process itself. Hence, it is also distributed throughout the Torah.

None of this is surprising since, as the Kabbalah teaches, God can be identified with the Torah. We already touched on this idea in discussing the divine mind as the non-all. The heavenly Torah itself is non-all whereas the finite sequence of it we have is not. The Torah we have is not a projection of God or God's shadow, but a fragment of the divine mind, although still in the process of unfolding itself. This is not to say the Torah cannot itself be seen as a series of divine names. Every segmentation of letters is a name and the Torah as a whole is a name, but the name YHVH is also distributed through it as a signature. Of course the name YVH already exhibits some of the coding in the Torah. The name is not pronounced, but also its encrypted pronouncement in prayer is itself never pronounced in every day speech. Rather, it is only pronounced as 'Hashem' (meaning 'the name') thereby hiding it from all behind a double veil. YHVH is always about a concealment, a divine contraction, even when the letters of the name are dispersed throughout the text.

We need to see that every sequence of letters, every set, is one more way that the unlimited power of God exhibits itself and its creativity. In this way, divine names are encoded throughout the Torah. But we can say that YHVH in its pure a-signifying lettering unfolds itself which means the Torah is itself an interpretation of God. The fundamental creative power of God is not simply a source of new sets and sequences, but an interpretation of the name itself and its nature. Even if God is inaccessible and incomprehensible, the Torah through the name in its unfolding interprets God and attempts to understand Him. Interpreting here is also reordering. The Torah is a reading of the name of God.

As Ramsay notes, in his last work, Ferdinand de Saussure began counting the number of phonemes in Latin verse from the Roman period (Saturnarian poems) and saw "the phonemes in isolation, unmoored from the wider denotative meaning of the poem" in order to discover in them an ordering amongst the letters.126 Saussure concluded that the poets were trying to figure in the verse at various intervals the letters of the name of the god they want to celebrate.127 There is thus in these poems according to Saussure patterns or anagrams of a particular divine name. Saussure did not of course attribute these patterns to the pagan deity celebrated, but to the finite human intellect of the poet who intentionally inserted these letters. However, Ramsay asks the fowling question: "or do anagrams 'emanate' in some way from poetical language behavior—a sort of verbal subconscious lying beneath the parent text?"128 Ramsay suggests that in thinking about a poem a poet consciously composes verse that distributes that name into the verse itself.

The question is first whether such a disruption of letters is probable. We can thus ask if the code itself is likely. It could be intended, but it is undecidable if it was or if it was only a product of how the unconscious mind arranged things or if it was just a matter of chance.   One might also say it is undividable if anything one finds in the Torah is encoded or not. But that would be the case only if it was subtracted from its witnessed revelation. If it is, then it appears like any other text and then as we well see it is only the action of the subject of faith that can intervene.

The undecidability with the Latin verse derives from the fact that at no point is the text attributed to anything divine. If it were, then it would be taken to be part and parcel of the text and part of a divine intention. As Ramsay notes, if one looks, one can always find complex patterns in the letters of a text. Ramsay asks: "Is not the entire notion of 'sense' called into question if complex structures will way lead to the discovery of patterns that we can then call meaningful?".129 However, not every sequence of letters is intelligible to us. The point here is not simply that meaning is not controlled by human intention. A pattern is meaningful because meaning it is the result of computation itself and ultimately the result of the computation that begins with a minimal source code whether that source code be the one that makes up a language, a book, a star system or the universe. Sense is a product of the a-signifying.

When one accepts the absolute infinite's power of creation, then the emergence of sense in this way is not simply accidental and not simply inconsequential. Ramsay's work here on Saussure is of course derived from that of Jean Starobinski who showed that the scared name of a Roman god has been the object of many forms of religious poetry.130 The Torah itself can be mapped here as the divine name is interspersed into its own text. But YHVH is not simply the germ of the text, but of all things. It would thus be useful to see precisely how the name YHVH is distributed through the text. We would ask, at how many letter intervals does it occur and how many times? We can also ask how if we take the letters of the divine name as themselves lines and shapes, how would they need to be permuted to produce the letters of the text? These lines would need to be in some cases inverted or reversed, but one has with YHVH all the basic elements one needs to write all the other letters.

Some claim one only needs the first letter, the yod. With it, the seed of the whole text is projected from the very text itself in its current form, but only experimentation can test the conjecture. Starobinski sees the divine name interposed in religious poetry as a "signature".131 Of course, one finds names other than that of YHVH in the Torah. For example, one finds in the story of the Garden of Eden section on the snake the word for snake is twice encoded at spacings of 365 and 248 letters. Both numbers are very significant in Judaism. At the same time, the name Aharon for example in the first section of Leviticus (which is the section precisely on the rules of pertaining to the sacrifices that Aharon was in charge of) the letters of Aharons's name are distributed at regular intervals an extraordinary number of time.

The Samaritans have a copy of the Torah as well that differs in its lettering. It is seen by Jews as being corrupted copy of the original text. As a result for instance, in the Samaritan bible, one can find the name Aharon dispersed but significantly fewer times such that one sees very markedly the low probability of the number of times Aharon being there in the Jewish test being a matter of chance. One needs to see her also the divine name in the same way, but that is because it is the soul of the very dine language itself. Because the divine name is here a set of vowels, it would have to be distributed in any text. The only question then is not if it is distributed here, but how, in what order, how many times, etc. As Starobinski notes, "Saussure searched at length for a method which would enable him to prove that hypograms were not the product of pure chance".132

Someone like Meillassoux might her argue that it is undecidable if whether in the Torah or Latin verse the distribution of phonemes is a product of chance or not. This is why if one can find how the letters YHVH are distributed in the Torah and show how it is itself a function of an algorithm it dilutes the case that it is pure chance. It is of course possible that by chance one could have any arrangement. But if there is a regular algorithm for its production, one doubts that it would simply arise on its own given the probabilities involved. In the divine text, chance is reduced by the non-all. Since nothing is excluded from the non-all, not only can anything be produced, but all is already thought by it. Thus, if given enough time, all will be exposed.

Let's take this point as literally as possible. In some other possible permutation of the 304, 805 Torah text we have it will read that 'pig is kosher.' That will undeniably be a result. But the points is not to say that the Torah therefore affirms anything and its opposite. Rather, the question is how do we get from the text we now have, the revealed text, to this permutation. The code for this particular permutation might turn out to be the verse that states one should choose live. After all, pig is kosher if for instance Auschwitz one would need to eat it to survive. The key idea is that even if the Torah can be permuted to say all, the key is how we get from one permutation to the next. For this reason, one would suspect that the oral Torah, the Mishna, might itself in its key passage form code that enables permutations.

The oral Torah was revealed at Sinai and passed on in parallel to the written one. It determines how the written Torah should be read. It restricts the readings and permutations we have. It is important also that the Torah we now have is always the point of departure. The event of revelation itself is irreducible. One must always start with a finite sequence. If one started with the non-all itself or all possible permutations, then one would be lost. Only the divine mine itself 'begins' in this way, with the Torah as it is heaven. Without an initial finite text, one cannot have codes and permutations. It is a strict condition here. The heavenly book remains with God—nameless name beyond the countably infinite names.

At the same time as we will shortly claim, it is precisely to be a religious subject, a subject of faith, to say that none of this is a product of chance because the text is accepted as divine. That is, once we accept the event of revelation at Sinai, it not a product of pure chance for any code to be found in the Torah. Because the Torah is connected to the very mind of God, one can find anything one wants there with enough work and faith. One simply has to look to the letters though to be able to construct and unearth what is hidden or desired, to reveal a new aspect of things. When one turns to the letter in itself and its relation the infinite, one has access to pure speech, which is speech at the level of the letter and phoneme. "For at that time I will change the speech of the peoples to a pure speech, that all of them may call upon the name of the LORD and serve him with one accord" (Zephaniah 3:9). That lettering is also the lettering of the bits themselves that any text can be reduced to.

Let us recall that Abraham Abulafia himself claimed "one can combine letters in any language" and find divine truths.133 This was only possible because each letter in any language can be given a numerical value. In other words, when we render a text as 0's and 1's we have fulfilled Abulafia's vision of seeing all texts as pure lettering ready for permutation and computation. With 0's and 1's Abulafia's vision of restoring "'all letters by which He speaks to that which produced them", which are holy letters of course, is realized.134 Abulafia believed that all other languages are somehow derived from Hebrew itself and the 22 letters it consists of. In other words, any other language in its sonic materiality is a derived from the phonographical qualities of Hebrew itself. Thus, from one language, the holy language can arrive at all others.

But here we claim that it is 0's and 1's that any text can be expressed in and that involves restoring the letters back to an original and sacred language that is the very mother tongue of all things. 0's and 1's are the matrix form which all things including language arises and thus to combine them is to touch upon the divine language itself. Of course, with the right combinations one can have expressions in 0's and 1's for all the possible languages. One simply needs to know the code for how to programs those 0's and 1's and relate them to the element of each language that they would be associated with. This shows us again that the 0's and 1's are the reverse side of any text. They are associated with the lettering for instance form the flip side of the text, the side that when exposes the text to its most profound depths. In those depths, all languages are connected and related. All the languages are combined in the 0's and 1's. The only original language then would be the 0's and 1's themselves. It is an as-signifying language, one of pure letters that can permute into all the others.

The deconstructionists would say that any mark can function as the empty set which is true but does not explain the nature of the empty set. Here, we can say all texts are related and any one could function as the Torah, but the Torah is the actual revealed text we have. Since one could not simply find oneself in the non-all already, one needs some finite instance of creation, and the Torah is that instance. But the book that is the non-all, the divine mind, is a book that is invisible and written purely in 01. In it all meaning as such disperses into permutations of 0 and 1 themselves. It is the universal book and simulates any possible book including the book that cannot be computed except at infinity and by way of eternity. It thus includes the incomputable books and the indenumerable infinite. For us, the Torah as it is known by God is lost to us. We are seeking it using the finite Torah we have before us. We are vainly trying to find what it contains by working with the text we have which is only a fragment of the divine Torah.

We should not think that the divine Torah is unwritten or only potential or virtual. It is there already ahead of us, which is to say, behind, and thus eternally there. It is awaiting us at the omega point itself. In the divine torah all the words and all the letters are juxtaposed together. This is the name of God none of us has even an inkling of. It is a name that is all the words at once. It is therefore not any one word and cannot be a discernible name for us. Calling it the non-all is already to miss what it is. It is not simply ineffable, but hyper-inaccessible. That we associate it with the divine mind is why we can also say that something named in the Torah is not simply a reference to a thing in this world, but is a Platonic idea.

We can see also how the Torah is in line with Blanchot's view of the word in its eidetic aspect. For Blanchot, the name is the death of the thing following Hegel. The name is thus connected to the thing's absence. Literature enacts and guards that absence withheld always evoking and searching for the lost thing. This is why Blanchot's space of literature is the same as the space of consciousness that cannot experience death and thus makes death an impossibility. Literature is caught up with the same impossibility since it is caught up with the unnamable. The space of literature is an infinite space because it is related to the unnamable, to a power that evades all power to name and capture it. That is the void as continuum that always renders illusory the attempt to totalize the space itself.   But here we see that the religious text is saying that the word itself is a name for the set of all possible things of that type. The thing is essentially its name as a set. It is not a question of confusing the flesh and blood cat with the idea of the cat, but that the idea of the cat includes all possible cats. If one wanted a name that pointed to some specific fact, one would simply try pointing. In the pictograph, where there is a cat very specifically drawn, the sign is a unity that points to the universal cat, but only as imagined and transcendent object. Blanchot also believes that before words there are things that then are canceled out and raised up to the concept/idea.135 But the cat as conceived in the divine intellect is a transfinite set that precedes any flesh and blood cats. Hence, one need not posit any hecatomb of things, but rather the divine intellect itself. God does not destroy his creation, but rather creates things using sets, letters, and numbers. But that does not mean we need to be a vulgar Platonist and say that the flesh and blood cat is simply an actualization of the potential cat. Rather, in the upholding of existence there is a permutation of letters that are themselves then grouped into sets and from that is revealed the idea of cat to us. Thus, it is form the living cat that the name cat itself emerges. And the set is itself certainly not a cat. It is thus anon-cat. But none has to exist, but one that has been recognized as existing and thought. When we see the word 'tree' in the Torah, it is referring to the set of all possible trees; it is a transfinite set, an essence. The Torah when it comes to words and not simply letters, when it is coded as set, it is written with the names of those transfinite sets. The name of anything in the Torah is its absolute name.

The Torah analyzes Platonic ideas and not finite signs. This is again why it could not be written in pictographs since then one would only have evoked a paradigmatic object and only marked it, rather than the very name of a set and a sequence of letters. The subject of faith is always segmenting the Torah into further names. We know after all that Moses only recorded the Torah as a series of numbers/letters. It was only later that it was segmented into words and given the spacing it has now. This was the first intervention of the subject of faith on the Torah after the event of revelation. The subject of faith accepts the event as event, the ram's horn as the divine voice. He accepts the collective witnessing and that those witnesses did not lie about what they saw (and even if they thought they did, they told truth since they revealed the truth for the monotheistic God is the truth).

The Torah presents us with a series of letters, but the subject of faith is the one who knows that given the text's relation to the divine voice it is encrypted with information. For that reason, one is given the task of combining and decoding it. To do so one then must make use of one's freedom. This is an agency that arises as a result of one's relation to the divine text, to its infinity, to its revelation. It also arises relative to any undecidability or uncertainty relative to the codes found and their being intended. One is thus able to makes use of the axiom of choice to create new sets. After all, when we permute the text we were simply operating the choice function on it to reveal new patterns and orders. We make pure choices here on how to combine the text. When we take new sets of letters, we take them as well-ordered or we re-arrange their ordering. We take it that all the sets can be so well-ordered and that their ordering affects their significance. Two sets with different orderings are not the identical even if two sets have the same elements and the same number of them.

Of course, as we learned, when the axiom of choice is in operation in this way, we miss out on the power of the continuum as something truly excessive. We here with the axiom of choice by way of faith miss out on the excessive power of continuum itself because we are busy well-ordering sets and set of sets. But that is because we have already experienced the undecidable itself and responded with faith. That is, it is in the event of revelation itself, at Sinai, that one confronted the failure of CH in the Cantorian sense, that one faced the continuum in its pure excess. It was returning to the agency of choice and well-ordering that marked one's response and acceptance of the divine as a subject. If one had rejected that event, one would simply look at the text as a product of human thought and/stated or that any codes in it are simply a matter of chance and probability. It is from a confrontation with the divine revelation and the free choice of accepting that event that one is lead to ordering the text in itself by choice.

In such an ordering one finds more and more names of God, new fragments of the absolute. All of the Torah is but names of God. Each time a set is selected no matter the length. From this text a divine name emerges as a new form of meaning and sense from the letters themselves. The subject of faith thus attempts to enter the mind of Moses himself when he received the great name of the Torah from God himself. One tries to understand how it was read out and also what was not listed in its sequence yet. One divides it into sets of three letters and then sets of four. One asks what is read to how when one skips form the third letter 30 letters each time and what happens when each letter is switched to the letter coming after it in the alphabet,.

This is why today to be a subject of faith has found a much deeper expression for today we have computational devices that can do the work of faith for us at an inhuman scale. Today machines can themselves read and interpret for us if properly programmed and reveal what was before hidden. The machine itself can then cut things up and find more arrangements then we could on our own. The computer does not know how to do this on its own, but when we teach it, it becomes our prayer wheel acting on our behalf. How one cuts things up at the joints of course determines how things are. When we listened to the roar of the ocean, we could only hear fragments of the sound. All of us experience this insofar as we reach out into the non-all of the universe's lettering with each turn. We encounter things by way of touch and vision and by way of time and space. The infinities of infinities means that there is multiple ways of approaching the same thing. But what is beyond the wholes we create with our perception is not shadowy, transcendent objects withdrawn from us (vulgar Platonism), but the pure non-all of the numbers themselves (Platonic Pythagoreanism).

We know that others are dividing things up differently including the machines we use. Given the infinities of infinities that compose things, there is not just one way. When we reach out to the Torah we are trying ultimately as subjects of faith to see thing as God does. And God does see us as letters, numbers, and sets. We only can see a finite part of what God sees. We are apportioning some things and rejecting others. But just as glasses allow us to see farther or closer than we would otherwise, with the computing machines we have today we will be able to see more of God than we have ever seen before, more than has been seen since Moses himself. We have when it comes to the Torah a choice as to how to do this. It is a choice we do not have on our own with our limited means of perception when we hear the ocean roar. But now with the computer, we can activate this choice when we stare out at the stars themselves. Those stars are the reverse side of 0's and 1's awaiting revelation and permutation.

One chooses the event at Sinai or chooses to reject it because the voice of God is in itself at one level indiscernible from the ram's horn. It is indiscernible from something finite and bound to this earth. We have a pure choice because of this indiscernibility and not in spite of it. Only by seeing the ram's horn as the divine voice can we enact our agency. There is no predetermined way of making this choice. It is either accepted or rejected like any event. But once we accept this event we want to verify it and to verify it today means only to permute the letter itself and find that transcendent Other responsible for it. It is necessarily given first as a finite sequence like that of the Torah. We then need rules for operating on that sequence. Choice does not operate here on the power of the continuum itself, but only on a fragment of it.

We know thus also that any rules we use to distill the Torah will themselves be only able to determine it partially. But that is again how we are given free choice. We are given only a partial fragment, but we need to find the rules for how the Torah itself unfolds in its progression towards unveiling its own reflection of the divine intellect. Each set of letters is then but a fragment of the divine, but also any rule is also offering us new fragments. We are ourselves revealing our power to name the divine by naming new sets and ordering them. We are also attempting to force the truth of the divine revelation. We have been given a set and must find out belongs to it and is included in and what does not.

The Jewish subject of faith ultimately only approaches God through the book by attempting to find the Book itself. If one wants to know one reason why it is a sacred text, it is because it has so many such subjects of faith. No one believes that *Moby Dick* is a sacred ext. No one believes it is a distillation of the divine, infinite voice. And if one did, one would know it was an imitation and echo of another event. The subject of faith permutes what is given. But that does not mean that what is given has no order. There is already order in the given insofar as it for instance derives from a source code. Thus it is not the human mind that creates the world or all the order in it. We rather uncover the order of things and further explore it. Our Torah is not yet identical to God's Torah, but the subject of faith on his/her own knows that the Torah of God is coming and that by permuting the text we are on the way there.

§21. The White Letters of the Sacred Scripture

Given that the Torah is connected to the power of continuum, the very white space of the text itself is important and is itself the scene of the Torah's infinitude:

> The eighteenth century Hasidic master [R. Levi Isaac] was reported to have interpret Isaiah 51:4, 'A Torah will go forth from me,' as follows: 'We can see by the eye of our intellect why in the Torah handed down to us one letter should not touch the other. The matter is that also the whiteness constitutes the letters, but we do not know how to read them as [we know] the blackness of the black letters. But in the future God, blessed be He, will reveal to us even the white letters of the Torah. Name we will [then] understand the white lettering in our Torah, and this is the meaning of 'A new Torah will go forth from me,' that it stands for the whiteness of the Torah, that all the sons of Israel will understand also the letters that are white in our Torah, which was delivered to Moses.136

Here, we have the idea that there are white letters invisible to us, but occupying the white spaces of the Torah. Inside the text, but hidden in the white spaces and between the letters themselves, there is an expanse, the very margins themselves. Behind the words, there is space which is not flat, but that has unheard of depths. These white letters will themselves be revealed at some point in a future time. However, the white pace is itself the space of the continuum meaning that there is an uncountable infinity of white letters within that white space.

We should not expect that white space to produce letters the same size as those of the current black letters. Notice also here, that these things can only be seen by way of the intellect. Only the mind at this point can grasp these ideas because of the current finite set of letters making up the Torah and the fact that our own realm of existence appears to us from all directions except by way of the mind to be finite. The time of the final advent of the white letters will occur at the very coming of the Messiah.137 Hence, the time of the messiah will include the exposure of to this point unknown parts of the Torah. Does that mean we are entering the time of the Messiah with the invention of computational devices capable of exposing the permutations of the Torah in a way hitherto inaccessible to us? We will need to return to this question.

We have already identified this hidden part of the Torah with the computation and permutation that is now open to us via the text's expression as 0's and 1's. This means that we must see the white letters here as both zero phonemes and zero letters. Recall that Jakobson's idea of the zero phoneme was the idea of a phoneme that bundled no sound such that it distinguished only via an absence. Here, the white spaces differentiate between letters and words on the page, but we can now see the white space is itself made up of zero letters. At the same time, 0's and 1's are themselves zero letters insofar as they are only scripted as differences. Certainly they have in a computer for instance a relation to electric voltage, but they are conceived themselves as the relation between 0/1, between the void and its counting.

There are traditions about lost books of the Torah.138 But these texts are no longer lost to us insofar as we have found one way to mine the white spaces and articulate the white letters found there. The white letters not only will be in between the black letters but surround and engulf them. The white space here also of course names the void such that it is from and with the void that new letters are made.139 While the 0's and 1's we have are materially composed of electronic pulses, ontologically letters are always a matter of the void, the empty set, and the inclusion of the empty set in sets. The void itself is decoded through the empty set and its inclusion in each set. This is why it was possible for the Hasidic masters to already understand the existence of the white letters in the 18th century without the aid of computation. They could see with their own intellects and minds the manner in which letters in their ultimate ontological expression were connected to the void and to their endless iteration. The white letters would thus be the letters in their purity, recognized in their essence and as an ontological truth. The mystics of the past and present were already able to see the white letters, to begin to combine them, to see the relation of the divine text to the absolute infinite itself, and to experience "here and now the kind of experience that will be achieved by all in the eschaton".140

In other words, here and now one can through mystical activity (the permutation of the letters) access the divine mind itself, a divine mind that all will be consciously engulfed in with the advent of the Messiah and the final glorification of existence. In this way, one enters the continuum itself and contacts its power. The power of the continuum again here as Leibniz first pointed out allows for the text to be indefinitely iterated and transformed since there is always more white space to fill. One sees that the revealed sacred scripture one has is part of something infinitely more extensive and profound. The black letters are only a screen and point of departure for an experience of the divine in itself.

As Idel notes, R Levi Isaac saw the white space as the manner in which the divine infinite enters and participates in the "world of nature" itself.141 Nature itself is informed by the power of the continuum such that the divine must intervene in order for nature itself to work. It is by way of the divine that things are continuous and related. . It is important that we not confuse the white space of the Torah with the book as a void and desert solely as Jabes did. For Jabes, the text is simply a void from which at most new black letters emerge. The white space for him in his nihilism would be but a screen for projecting, an absence or void that we alone fill in. But that is because Jabes refused to see the manner in which God is not simply a name and nothing more. Jabes saw in the whit space of the book the so-called 'death of God' whereas the notion of the white letters realizes that the book is made up of letters both black and white and thus is not about God's void simply, but also His being a divine absolute.

Within the very physical reality of nature, an infinity must be traversed to move a hand or for the wind to blow. This model also seems to indicate that at some point all the white letters will become black, but this raises question of whether the continuum itself can fit into this world fully. This clearly takes place in the mind of the mystic who articulates the Torah out loud. As we argued, any letter is a cut or gap in the continuum itself (whether of sound or the whiteness of the page), but here it is also the presence of the divine itself in this world in the voice of the mystical reader. When the mystic is aware of the power of the continuum and its relation to the place from which he speaks the Torah, he is reading the Torah as it is understood in the mind of God and not simply the finite Torah available to all human comprehension. The divine Torah bursts into this world and illuminates it via the illuminated mind of the mystical reader.

The white letters here indicate the Torah's relation to a pure divine excess. Idel explains that for the Kabbalists the infinite can itself be experienced by way of the lettering itself.[142] This is because the infinite has contracted into the letters. The letters capture as much as possible within existence the light of the absolute itself. While the absolute is radically transcendent, it also affects us directly and primarily via the letters. Ultimately, the consciousness of the mystic is the consciousness of the letters. This means that one would be able to think the very computation of 0's and 1's. It would be obtaining the very intentionality of the bit. That means to truly experience the letter the human mind will have to be somehow merged with the machine itself in order to tap into the pure computational power that transcends even what the human unconscious is capable of. One will need to participate in the white letters and themselves have them become one's very flesh and blood. It is then that one's mind will be constantly filled with divine illumination and be enlightened with the absolute.

There is here an epistemological along with an ontological sense of the white letters. Of course, 0's and 1's are in themselves devoid of any subjectivity and also independent of the mind's relation to the world, but that does not mean they cannot become the very substance of an expanded trans-human mind. What happens at this moment is that the non-thing that precisely consciousness enacts will be expanded such that conscious awareness will in turn not simply exist outside of it anymore as thought. It is not simply that the white letters relate to the ontological power of the continuum, but also that they are themselves to be the very substantiality of the illuminated mystical mind in its full consciousness of the absolute. One can of course already hint at what this will mean practically in some not too distant future. Mind itself will be expressed by the computer itself. In this way, the blank letters will be decoded as the very act of thought itself.

This is already the case insofar as our minds are computational in character. But here the unconscious power of the letter itself becomes the very thinking mind aware of itself. The question would of course be posed if this is to doom our limited minds to some form of psychosis. But the mystical experience has always been indiscernible at some level from that of the psychotic. It is always question of being engulfed in the light rather than slipping into the dark night of the mind. The divine lights the way and the path. What saves one from that dark night is of course one's freely chosen orientation to the divine itself.

In the past, we did not have the power to produce the white letters and had to only refer to the margins, to the hidden context of the finite letters we see, but with the advent of the activation of the full computational power of existence itself, this will no longer be needed. Within this advent, one can find the different ways the white letters themselves yield new permutations and combinations of the text.

§22. The Holographic Principle

We have seen that the very idea of the white letters poses two issues—the advent of the super-finite mind that will arise on the basis of the computer and the question of the continuum's relation to finite existence. It is the latter issue that we will take up here and leave the former for another time when we explore directly the nature of mind itself. In revealing that the white spaces of the text are made up of series of letters, theology has entered a new age of questioning. If in the past theologians asked for example how many angels can fit on the head of a pin, today we will ask how many letters can exist within the white spaces of the sacred scripture.

To ask this question of course raises a very direct issue. Perhaps, one could use handwriting alone to write a large number of letters, but not an infinite number or even an uncountable infinite within a given space. This seems to be purely mystical poetic musings. However, the question is not simply a mystical one and the mystical finds its own assessment in contemporary Physics. What is today called the 'Holographic principle' offers us a way of asking in the most practical and physical ways possible how many letters could in fact fit in the white spaces of the Torah since it asks how many letters could fit into any physical space.

It is in precisely these terms (how many letters can one fit on a page?) that Raphael Bousso begins his brilliant lecture entitled "World as Hologram".143 Bousso begins by offering examples of different styles of handwriting—some where only a few letters fit on a page and some where the handwriting is so minute that entire pages of text are fit onto one page. Of course, if one wants to fit a large number of letters, one can always make use of a larger inscription space. But even if one were to take a sheet the size of a football field, one will still only for instance be able to fill the space with so many dots before they seem to touch. Bousso speculates about a page the size of the galaxy itself and how many individual marks one could fit on it.

Of course, we can also make letters microscopically small. But even if one had a page the size of the known universe, one would have 10 to the 60th power Planck lengths to inscribe a mark once every Planck length and thus the equivalent number of letters. That is a vast and mind-boggling number, but it is not infinity. Even if one tried to inscribe a letter at the smallest known scale one would not have all possible numbers or letters written such as is contained in the continuum itself on this view. This leads us to believe that physical existence does not truly compose a continuum on its own. This space has an immense density to it and it covers all one might need for practical purposes, but it does not represent or show every number on a real number line. This almost-continuum is called by Bousso the 'discretum.' It is a discrete continuum not filling up every point on the real number line. That is why a letter here is simply an encoded piece of information.

One is here inquiring about how much information one can maximally inscribe in a single space given the smallest level one can treat as encoded. The Planck length appears to be the smallest length at which one could encode a piece of information and treat it as informational. What Bousso is implicitly saying here is that physical existence is itself discrete since one cannot see it as being equivalent to the continuum and it power. One cannot go as small as one would want and continually move to a smaller level. One is stopped at the Planck length itself. One thus can calculate precisely how many letters could be inscribed in any given space.

However, Bousso claims that the picture so far given does not take into account the role of gravity. Without gravity, one could in principle according to quantum field theory encode letters at any length. Gravity will put a limit on the amount of information one can say is encoded in any space. The smaller the size of letters one tries to inscribe the more energy one would needs to resolve and view and input the lettering and information. Thus, to measure the letters in reality one would need light to project onto it. But the relation between the distance one needs to resolve things and the energy inputted are in an inverse relationship to each other such that the smaller one goes the more energy one needs until one reaches a point where so much energy would be needed that all would collapse into a black hole. At the smallest level one can resolve the letters themselves are incredibly dense in the sense of gravity (energy and mass being the same) rather than in the sense of how compact they are as if on a number line. The smaller the letter one wants to encode and reveal the more energy one needs. The limit is the black hole.

If one were to try to fit on to the walls of a finite room the maximum number of letters eventually the room would collapse into a singularity. But the amount of information encodable in a black hole is related to its surface area, the surface area of its event horizon, rather than its volume. One knows that surface area is involved because if one doubles the space, one does not get eight times the information, but only four times as much. Hence, a two-dimensional space is involved. This surface area is itself measurable in Plank lengths. We can thus imagine the surface area of the horizon of black hole as being covered by Planck length 0's and 1's. Each 0 and 1 would be a letter in Bousso's own terminology. We can calculate relative to surface area and not volume the total number of physical letters that can be encoded on it. The incredible amount of information here is always on this reading a discretum and not a continuum. Sticking with the Physics at work here, the Kabbalistic claim that an uncountable infinity of letters exist in the white spaces of the Torah would seem to fail the test since the amount of information that can be coded to the surface of the black hole is countable as Planck lengths. This surface area is of course itself the measure of the entropy of the black hole.

Despite seeming to have proven that the finite amount of information that can be inscribed in the known universe, Bousso has also put forth a claim that the information of the universe can be squeezed into the two-dimensional space of surface area. For the theory we have proposed to work, one would need to project that this surface area can be expanded infinitely into an infinite black hole occupying anything or that somehow the continuum itself can fit into the equation here of the Planck lengths. If the Planck length is the ultimate length of existence, then existence is ultimately finite and discrete. Leonard Susskind has also explored the ideas laid out by Bousso and expanded on them to show how the notion of the surface area at work here leads one to describe existence as being holographic in nature. In his book *The Cosmic Landscape*, Susskind argues that the bits discussed above, the letters, have a location (the surface area of the black hole) and our world is a projection of that information.144 Thus, our world is itself a holographic projection of a flat two-dimensional surface described with Planck length lettering.

Any holographic image is not flat, but has depth and three-dimensionality; however, its reverse side is the surface where the information is inscribed. Light in the form of photons decodes the information inscribed on the holographic film and then causes the hologram. One can walk around a holographic image and look at it from all sides. However, if one looks at the surface of the filmstrip, one only sees the scorches of where the bits of info are stored. We have here two incompatible and incommensurable fields: one the image itself and another the flat space of inscription. We have the surface of the film for the substrate that is not anything we can recognize as an image (it is only a scratched two dimensional surface), and the clear and intelligible 3-d image that is projected by it once light hits the film.

Susskind compares the hologram to a computer screen where all is mapped by two-dimensional as pixels, but one sees an image that appears to have depth. The data of the computer image is stored in bits, but one does not see the bits, but only an image that appears to have depth. For Susskind, the world is made up "voxels," three-dimensional pixels that fill out space encoding all the needed information as physical existence as we know it is but a holographic decoding of that info.145 The point here is that something needs to decode what is encoded on the surface and that is light itself. The information appears to be completely scrambled, but light shows that it is ordered and only a code. When we look at the surface with its bits, we do not know the sense of the letters as they are just an a-signifying sequence of letters that tell us nothing. But the interaction with the light causes the emergence of sense and order.

The light shown on the filmstrip is simply the algorithm that permutes and transforms the sequence of letters into a new sense that was previously hidden in it. Thus even in a sequence of letter that is impenetrable to us, there is information. Anytime the decoding action activates the seeming randomness dissolves and order and sense emerge. However, here again Susskind claims that the amount of information one can inscribe on any known surface is finite including that which is encoded on the horizon of a black hole. One of the points here is that all the information of the hologram is compressed onto a 2-d surface. While the hologram appears to contain irreducible information, it is compressible into a written and discrete space.

Now, the universe is expanding, which gives us the impression that it is continually gaining new space and surface area to inscribe new information. We only see up to a certain horizon of this expanding universe. We cannot see for instance beyond the light cone surrounding us. Our telescopes will not be able to get beyond this horizon. But it seems to be expanding beyond that horizon. That means the surface area itself is constantly expanding beyond us. Thus there is a surface area beyond our ken where information is itself being included. What is beyond our horizon is at it were out of this world. But just like the sky's horizon here on earth, we can never reach it no matter how fast we run towards it. To get past it would be to penetrate it.

This notion of the horizon thus suggests that what is beyond the horizon is precisely the scrambled holographic film Susskind has discussed. We call this beyond the divine mind or non-all. It is the surface upon which all the letters are inscribed. It is in itself unbounded and unlimited. It is where the divine Torah itself is found. All the white letters, the bits of information, are there inscribed. While on this side of the horizon, everything is finite such that we could only speak of a finite number of letters and the discrete nature of the Planck length, but beyond our horizon is the non-all itself. Susskind interestingly also holds to a theory as to why this information is itself indestructible. While Stephen Hawing argued that anything that falls through the event horizon of a black hole is erased, Susskind has shown that the information contained in what falls through never truly disappears fully. Any information in this world is always retrievable. It cannot be completely effaced. It may become so scrambled that we have no practical hope of being able to decode it, but it never disappears. All information exists somewhere whether on the surface of a black hole or dispersed thought the environment.

For Susskind, bits of information are themselves energy and last forever. Information might also be hidden to us such as the scrambled horizon of the black hole, and there might be information that we cannot necessarily extract. The entropy of the back hole itself contains the information of whatever fell into it. However when one is on the outside of the event horizon of the black hole, it differs from what is seen on the other side of the black hole. Anything that falls through a black hole looks to those outside of it to have been effaced while on the inside nothing appears to have changed. We are of course on only one side of the horizon we exist within. We see only three-dimensional perceptions, the screen. But all the information has been compiled into the infinite surface beyond hour horizon which is the reverse side of our field. From our perspective, this surface should be itself vast, but finite. But that only counts for what is inside our horizon.

Part of the reason our horizon recedes form us is precisely due to the infinity of what lies beyond it. Because the universe is expanding, its finite geometry is the surface of our bubble which is itself a horizon. This is why we can say that our world is finite and yet unbounded. But the infinite is just beyond our horizon, on the surface of it as it were behind a wall. When we look to find what is on the surface of the horizon and see the wall itself, it will always expand way from us and infinitely so. Our interior space is thus finite, but unbounded, only because of the outside itself, what transcends the horizon. However, it is difficult to accept these truths since we only seem to experience and be able to measure a finite space and a finite universe. We observe immediately around us we find ourselves confronted by the finite.

Susskind also makes another important point:

> It's not that an astronomer inside the bubble can't detect light coming from the domain wall. But that light does not seem to be coming from a boundary of space; rather, it seems to come from a boundary of time— from what appears to be a Big Bang taking place in the past. This is a most paradoxical situation, an infinite expanding universe inside a finite expanding bubble.146

In other words, the Big Bang institutes our bubble and marks it as finite despite its being but the mark of a temporal horizon separating us from the infinite inscription space of the non-all. Of course Susskind thinks there are an endless number of confined universes like ours here making up what he calls the megaverse. Each universe is its own bubble finite, but unbounded and expanding. The horizon is then conceived as a curved inward space. By definition any of the other universes are also beyond our horizon and thereby unknowable by us. Thus, the existence of various other universes is but an extrapolation and projection here.

Rather than seeing ourselves as inside a megaverse, we claim that beyond the horizon is precisely the infinite surface of the non-all inscribed with lettering thus making our world the projection of that space. It is the only space insofar as it an only projected by the divine light itself contracting itself. This is the hidden light of the holy one (the 'or haganuz') that decodes the letters and projects our world. There are no other worlds as the divine non-all itself brings about our singular world. The non-all leads to a singular event, the Big Bang. The horizon does not space out a series of bubbles that cannot fill up the continuum themselves even if we try to add up all the many finite universes in the megaverse, but rather beyond the horizon is the non-all itself, the divine mind. There is no information to be gained from other universe because the only information there is beyond this world is the non-all itself.

We cannot observe other universes, but that does not mean they do not necessarily exist. It is rather that metaphysically they are untenable given the nature of the creation of our world itself out of the non-all. There is here an appeal to multiple worlds as if they could fill the continuum, but they cannot fill it any more than could Planck length letters within a finite space fill the real number line. Our world is therefore a discretum created by the continuum through the contraction of the divine light. Susskind admits that his "populated landscape sounds more like metaphysics than physics",147 and it is the point where Susskind's crosses that boundary. But it is not a metaphysics we can endorse since it does not account for the reality of the continuum.

It still remains only able to posit a continuum as ideal at best. We know that the mathematics of Quantum Mechanics for instance needs real numbers and that is incompatible with digital ideas like that of a discretum. If one is to admit that real numbers do exist in some sense, then we would need to incorporate into metaphysics something beyond the Planck length to have a way for the real continuum and its power to assert itself. We need the mathematics connected to the continuum to describe this world and thus cannot remain satisfied with a finite number of letters. The size of the universe within the event horizon is always conceivable as finite. We see this clearly via the amount of time that has passed since the big bang itself. Our light cone is thus bounded. It has a horizon even if that horizon is always receding from us. However, while within our horizon there appears to be only a finite number of bit beyond horizon is inscribed an uncountable infinity of bits.

We can here turn to the voice of God. Susskind notes that one of the first discoverers of the cosmic background radiation made the following observation:

> George Smoot, one of the leaders in cosmic microwave detection, in an overenthusiastic moment likened a cosmic microwave map of the sky to "the face of God." I think for inquiring minds curious about the world a scrambled hologram of an infinity of pocket universes is a far more interesting and accurate image.148

We would say that it is the voice of God inscribed on an infinite surface that contracts only into our world. On that view, not every universe is realized except in the non-all. Rather than seeing a megaverse, we would need to see how our own universe will expand to become one with what lies beyond its horizon and thus reaches its infinite point. That is, we need to understand how our universe's end point, the omega point, is precisely the point at which the horizon itself that constantly precedes us will lead to our universe touching the non-all and thus being infinitized. Our world then eternally inflates itself into the reverse side of what is now written on the other side of its horizon. It is not that every universe is created, but that in the one world created, ours, all permutations are run through.

As Susskind himself notes, his megaverse idea makes it indiscernible why there should be one world rather than one such that all have to be realized:

The eternally inflating universe is an infinite bag, not of paper scraps with numbers but of pocket universes. In fact it is a bag in which each possible type of universe— each valley of the Landscape— is represented a countably infinite number of times. There is no obvious mathematical way to compare one kind of pocket universe with another and to declare that one is more probable than the other. The implication is very disquieting: there seems no way to define the relative likelihood of different anthropically acceptable vacuums.149

The problem here is that Susskind tries to restrict his megaverse to the countably infinite which means it is somehow totalizable, but as we have seen time and time again the countable infinite is always transcend by the uncountably infinite. What Susskind here misses is that there is no totality to be realized. There is only the non-all. Susskind thinks the megaverse is where all possibilities are realized and actualized. But there is no totality. There is no whole here. And the non-all is necessarily led to the special one, to a point of unicity. And that point of unicity is the very origin of our world. This is why the equivalence of all the worlds collapses into the creation of a single world that in its expansion runs through all permutations.

Here, one must project a reverse causation. The omega point our world reaches is only one side of a moebius strip where the non-all contracts to create our world. From the other side, from the empty set to aleph-null to aleph-one and beyond we are lead back, but was not the fundamental symbol of infinity always itself the lopsided eight, ouroboros, the serpent swallowing itself? If all was the discretum, there would be no real numbers and the continuum would only be thinkable in intuitionist terms. Real numbers would not exist since they are not computable. They could not be seen as analogy with what we do and hold to be true. There would be a smallest length (the Planck length), and a smallest time (Planck time). The world would not be its own nature by infinitely disable. We would have to look at our experience of reality and the seeming necessity of referring to real numbers as some sort of transcendental illusion or simply an epiphenomenal product of our own minds. The analogue here is always to a film which appears continuous to us, but is actually made up of stills. Of course, many things that were thought to be indivisible and continuous phenomena were shown to be have a discrete form. For instance, light is itself photons. No matter how digital we can see that reality is fundamentally, it also has an analogous and continuous aspect that must be accounted for. Only by exploring the very nature of the continuum can we do so.

If the continuum is itself a fundamental part of reality, then reality itself will be continuous at any of its fundamental levels. We thus must confront the issue of the incomputable itself and the problem of random reals. This is why this problem always takes us back to the necessity of God. The very being of God guarantees that the non-algebraic reals do have real ontological consistency. Only God himself could know the full decimal expansion of these non-algebraic reals. Our finitude does not in itself demonstrate the fictional nature of reals, but only our current limitations in doing anything other than knowing a finite sequence of such numbers. God's eternity means that God sees all at once in a timeless fashion such that there is no difference for him between the square root of 2 and the number 2. The admission of the actual infinite can lead us to no other path truly. Incomputability reflects the limitations of our own computational devices at this time in the current physically arranged world rather than the non-existence of the incomputable.

§23. The Matrix and the Messiah

The existence of the incomputable we will now say to conclude will be embodied for the first time by the messiah, who will also enable others to embody such an incomputable existence. In this way, we will be contesting directly the reading of the Wachowski brothers' films that contends that in their Matrix trilogy the messiah will be embodied as a Gödelian loop within a universally computable system. We know that the incomputable cannot be embodied using a finite sequence of recursive, step-by-step procedures. To embodied a real in existence is then to occupy an infinitely complex and irreducible existence oneself. It thus means living forever.

There is of course an uncountably infinite set of such gaps between any two real numbers, and the messianic era means that we begin to embody those gaps themselves. Of course, one might say there that the set of all possible algorithms is countable and thus one can never define the set of all real numbers even if humanity were to live forever. But the messiah is the first one to embody instantly the real as such and allow others to engage in such an embodiment.

How is this done? Well, it will be done in the same way as any incomputable real number is constructed. An incomputable real is different by one digit, at least through the process of diagonalization, from all the other computable reals. One can say that the incomputable differs simply from the first decimal of the first computable real, its second number from the second of the second real, etc. The diagonalization could be even more random in nature. But it is the creation of something that is not in the list of all the computable reals. An uncountable infinity of such things can be created. The messiah will thus be that instant when the argument about the reality of these real will come to an end. It will be that moment that when our existence no longer has any regularity to it and becomes random and irreducible infinite. It will be the instantiation of a 'consciousness' unlike any we have known.

Of course, such a reality implies the creation of a computer capable of an infinity of procedures such as can only exists at the Omega Point itself. The Messianic promise is for a coming future in which one achieves timelessness and peace as such. It is an end to time as we know it. Only then can the bit sequence needed be produced instantaneously through diagonalization. At the point the ineffable nature of these reals will be spoken at once. It will be a divine harmony of the nameless. It is at this point that one becomes truly a name of God, an ineffable existence. For now, we can only know of this possibly, but not know fully what it will entail. But it means at the very least expressing an irreducibly complex infinity. It is the expression of what cannot in any way shape or form be compressed or said more compactly. It is the number and name itself as infinite sequence.

The messiah will be the first to know the incomputable real in its fullness. The name of the messiah is the name of the first incomputable real that he will embody. For the time being, we will only be able to know a finite sequence of that incompressible name. We can on this side of the messianic horizon only see this issue as insolvable and mystical since we cannot see it to its end. This vision of the messiah differs from that given in The Matrix film trilogy—at least according to one view. There, as per Eric Furze who best represents the Gödelian interpretation of these films,[150] it is the Gödel's incompleteness theorem that offers the key to deciphering the nature of 'Neo' as the messiah of his digital world. Neo, as I think everyone knows now, lives within a computer program which his called the Matrix. Like any computer program, this world is made up of recursive functions and algorithms such that there are rules determining all that can occur in it. The Wachowski brothers, creators of the films, thus see those living in the Matrix living within a purely digital program. The messiah is that inevitable point, per Furze, when a loop is created in the program, when the software equivalent of a Gödelian sentence is enacted. This sends the system into a loop and crashes it. Loops crash programs since the computer has only a finite amount of memory available,, and the loop will eventually take it all up. All the resources are used up. At the same time, one can isolate such loops within the larger programming and ensure they do not for the most part cause a system-wide crash.

The programmers of the Matrix cannot escape from the issues of the halting problem and incomputability to such a degree that there is no way for them to correct the eventuality of a loop. In the most important philosophical moment of the trilogy of films (the one that saves these films from being simply an update of Plato's 'Allegory of the Cave' for instance), the Architect's speech at the end of the second film, the Architect, the Matrix's programmer, explains to Neo who and what he is: "Your life is the sum of the remainder of an unbalanced equation inherent to the programming of the Matrix. You are the eventuality of an anomaly which is systemic, creating fluctuations in even the most simplistic equations".151 Neo embodies on this reading the loop that crashes the system and requires the reboot of the system as a whole. Because nothing apparently can be done to avoid generating a loop given the inherent characteristics of the numbers one needs to compute the program the Matrix will only ever be able to crash and restart after it reaches the 'Neo' stage.

The Architect explains at this point to Neo that he is the sixth such instantiation of this loop. The Wachowski brothers on this reading here advocate that the name of the messiah is that name in its numbering that via the necessary Gödelian numbering computer software requires ends up computing its own value. That is, Neo is that moment when due to the irreducible numerical properties of the numbering itself the same value is returned to itself and thus re-processed endlessly. But it is not clear why this implies Neo himself is the messiah. Rather, given that everyone in the Matrix has some sort of self-awareness even if they are not aware of being in the Matrix, there would seem to be some need for self-reflexivity in the programming prior to Neo. Now, Neo becomes aware of being in the Matrix, but again others have done this and left it (Neo is only one of the latter ones to join Morpheus, and there is an entire city, 'Zion,' made up of those who decided to exit the Matrix). So it is not clear why the binary coding of the Matrix even if it leads to loops would lead to anything other than a series of people becoming aware that they are inside the Matrix rather than to the end of the matrix itself (or why that end would have messianic implications).

We are each then in some sense predicated on at least a limited Gödelian sentence given our own self-reflexivity. Programmers are of course able to deliberately engender loops and once upon a time did so excessively using 'goto' commands. However, I think what the Wachowski's have in mind here is the point at which the Matrix attempts to compute itself and its own code. But the problem here is that the Matrix is only a computer programming running on a series of machines. There is thus an outside to escape to. But if the universe itself is a computer, then if it crashes, there is no act of liberation, but simply destruction or looping. It would mean something like heat death or eternal return of the same.

The problem here is that while Neo is said to embody a fundamental loop in the Matrix program he only ever remains "human":

> You have many questions and though the process has altered your consciousness, you remain irrevocably human. Ergo, some of my answers you will understand, some you will not. Concordantly, while your first question may be the most pertinent, you may or may not realize, it is also the most irrelevant.152

Neo as an integral anomaly is not the embodiment of something infinite or the incomputable. He is but a program that keeps returning the same value at most per Furze. The Architect is apparently here complemented by a QA team that finds the loop and reboots. But given that the Matrix is run on a computer that is not itself the entirety of physical existence, there is no reason why this anomaly could not be repaired in the same way that QA teams do today with computers. This is why again it is not the looping that is the key since the program might loop at other moments (such as the others who become aware of the Matrix), but only one program loops in such a way as it affects the functioning of the program as such.

The Architect however does not explain the nature of programs, Gödelian numbering, etc. to Neo, but rather discusses "the problem of choice".153 Humans apparently accept the Matrix as long as they believe they are feely choosing their actions. However, in allowing such a choice, or its illusion, one is necessarily led to the integral anomaly, the One:

As I was saying, she stumbled upon a solution whereby nearly 99% of all test subjects accepted the program as long as they were given a choice, even if they were only aware of that choice at a near-unconscious level. While this answer functioned, it was obviously fundamentally flawed, thus creating the otherwise-contradictory systemic anomaly that if left unchecked might threaten the system itself. Ergo, those that refused the program, while a minority, if unchecked would constitute an escalating probability of disaster.154

We can here see that the issue is not looping as much as it is incomputability. Choice is here like the axiom of choice where one can order different elements. One thus has to leave open how a sequence would be constructed. Ultimately, Neo could choose through diagonalization a sequence that cannot be computed. Neo would have to be that moment when a sequence is chosen that cannot be computed. He would thus have to embody a non-computable real for this to be possible. Neo would thus be the finite sequence of an incomputable real, but not its actual infinitization.

The Architect sees in Neo then a new source code for the Matrix as such: "which brings us at last to the moment of truth, wherein the fundamental flaw is ultimately expressed, and the Anomaly revealed as both beginning and end. There are two doors. The door to your right leads to the Source and the salvation of Zion".155 To attempt to synthesize some of the ideas here, the 'one' as the loop is the Matrix attempting to compute itself which is to compute an infinitely complex sequence. The return again of the same finite sequence is also an indication that this finite sequence is part of a longer incomputable one. Of course, many might here say that Neo was a programmed that entered a Gödel loop and then exited the Matrix. Outside the Matrix, he was able to reprogram himself as a virus that would then affect ht every source code of the matrix and restructure it. In this way, it is not the looping that causes the problem, but the viral reprogramming.

At the same time, despite embodying such a function, the messianic one is attached to all others via "a contingent affirmation":

It is interesting reading your reactions. Your five predecessors were, by design, based on a similar predication: a contingent affirmation that was meant to create a profound attachment to the rest of your species, facilitating the function of the One. While the others experienced this in a general way, your experience is far more specific. Vis-à-vis: love.156

The one who embodies the incomputable is not interested solely in himself, but in all others. The messiah is interested in saving all other self-aware creatures and enabling them to experience the same thing he does. However, this is again the height of free choice, "a contingent affirmation" that need not have been.

It is common today to hear a repetition of Kafka's statement that the Messiah, per the traditional reading, comes only by constantly delaying: "The Messiah will come only when he is no longer necessary; he will come only on the day after his arrival; he will come, not on the last day, but on the very last day".[157] We can now offer our own interpretation. The very last day is the day after all the other days have been counted. It is after the transfinite list has been made that the diagonalized number is offered. The very last day exceeds time as we now it and is outside history. It is thus a day after he arrives; something that comes after all has seemingly been summed up. This would mean it is a point at which the messiah seems unnecessary since we have managed to, in this case, render computable all that is computable and to begin listing it all. But at that every point, the very point at which we seem to have been able to express all possible recursive procedures and thereby the nature of all phenomena, there comes the Messiah and expresses the very last day in his very existence and in the existence of all else.

ENDNOTES

---

[1] Christopher Menzel, "Cantor and the Buralli-Forti Paradox", *The Monist* 67 (1984): 92-107, p. 92.

[2] Kai Hauser, "Cantor's Concept of Set in the Light of Plato's *Philebus*", *The Review of Metaphysics* 63 (2010): 783-805, p. 786.

[3] Ibid.

[4] Ibid.

[5] Menzel, p. 93

[6] Ibid.

[7] Ibid.

[8] Ibid., p. 94

[9] Ibid.

[10] Ibid.

[11] Ibid., p. 97

[12] Hauser, p. 789

[13] Menzel, p. 96

[14] Alain Badiou, *Being and Event*, trans. Oliver Feltham (Continuum: New York, 2007), pp. 53-4. To be referred to henceforth in parenthesis in the body of the text as *BE*.

[15] Jacques Lacan, *Seminar 23: Le Sinthome*, Session 8: March 9, 1976, trans. Colin Gallagher, Retrieved 10/1/2012, from http://www.lacaninireland.com/web/wp-content/uploads/2010/06/THE-SEMINAR-OF-JACQUES-LACAN-XXIII.pdf

[16] Zohar qtd in Robert Haralick, *The Inner Meaning of the Hebrew Letters* (Aaronson: New York, 1995), p. 200.

[17] Alain Badiou, *Theoretical Writings,* eds. Ray Brassier and Alberto Toscano (New York: Continuum, 2006), p. 79.

[18] Kurt Gödel, *Unpublished Philosophical Essays,* ed. Francisco A. Rodriguez-Consuegra (Boston: Birkhauser, 1995), p. 93.

[19] Frederiek Depoortere, *Badiou and Theology* (New York: T & T Clark, 2009), p. 123.

[20] Jabes qtd. In Rosemarie Waldrop and Richard Stamelman, *Lavish Absence: Recalling and Rereading Edmond Jabes* (Connecticut: Wesleyan, 2003), p. 13

[21] Jeffrey Satinover, *Cracking the Bible Code* (New York: William Morrow, 1997), p. 95.

[22] Moshe Idel, *Absorbing Perfections: Kabbalah and Interpretation* (New Haven: Yale, 2002), p. 322.

[23] Moshe Idel, *The Mystical Experience in Abraham Abulafia* (Albany: SUNY, 1987), p. 323.

[24] Ibid., p. 328

[25] Clarence Rolt, *Dionysius the Areopagite on The Divine Names and The Mystical Theology* (New York: Cosimo, 2007), p. 61.

[26] F. R. Drake, *Set Theory: An Introduction to Large Cardinals* (New York: North Holland, 974), p. 67.

[27] Phil J. Davis and Reuben Hersh, *The Mathematical Experience* (New York: Mariner, 1981), p. 154.

[28] Jacques Lacan, *On Feminine Sexuality, the Limits of Love and Knowledge: The Seminar of Jacques Lacan, Book XX, Encore,* trans. Bruce Fink (New York: Norton, 1999), p. 8.

[29] Davis and Hersh, p. 239

[30] Raymond M. Smullyan and Melvin Fitting, *Set Theory and the Continuum Problem* (New York: Dover, 2020), p. 259

[31] Ibid.

[32] Gödel qtd. In Halo Wang, *Kurt Gödel: A Logical Journey* (Cambridge: MIT, 19960), p. 252

[33] Mary Tiles, *The Philosophy of Set Theory: An Historical Introduction to Cantor's Paradise* (New York: Dover, 2004), p. 191.

[34] Paul Cohen, *Set Theory and the Continuum Hypothesis* (New York: Dover, 2008), p. 151.

[35] Pauli qtd. in Leonard Susskind, *The Cosmic Landscape: String Theory and the Illusion of Intelligent Design* (Boston: Back Bay, 2008), Kindle Location: 1135.

[36] Paul Livingston, *The Politics of Logic: Badiou, Wittgenstein, and the Consequences of Formalism* (Routledge: New York, 2012), p. 276.

[37] Ibid.

[38] Ibid.

[39] Ibid., pp. 181 ,55-60, and 255-60

[40] Ibid, p. 296

[41] Ibid., p. 56

[42] Ibid.

[43] Ibid., p. 250

[44] Ibid.

[45] Ibid., p. 58

[46] Ibid.

[47] Ibid.

[48] Ibid., p. 57

[49] Martin Hagglund, *Radical Atheism: Derrida and the Time of Life* (California: Stanford UP, 2008), p. 5

[50] Ibid., p. 6

[51] Ibid.

[52] Ibid, p. 8

[53] Ibid.

[54] Ibid., p. 45

[55] Ibid.

[56] Ibid., p. 95

[57] Ibid., p. 3

[58] Retrieved October, 1, 2012, from
http://www.urbanomic.com/archives/Documents-1.pdf

[59] My understanding of Gödel's proof of incompleteness and Gödel numbering derives (except where otherwise indicated) from Ernest Nagel and James R. Newman's classic *Gödel's Proof* (New York: NYUP, 1974). But of course, any misunderstandings or elaborations beyond their presentation are my own.

[60] Douglas R. Hofstadter, *Gödel, Escher, Bach: An Eternal Golden Braid* (New York: Basic Books, 1999), p. 18.

[61] Ibid.

[62] Rebecca Goldstein, *Incompleteness: The Proof and Paradox of Kurt Gödel* (New York: Norton, 2006), p. 176.

[63] Jaakko Hintikka, *On Gödel* (California: Wadsworth, 1999), pp. 31-5.

[64] Ibid., p. 34

[65] Cristian Calude, "Incompleteness: A Personal Perspective" retrieved October 1, 2012, from http://www.youtube.com/watch?v=tYjmiT422yQ

[66] Gilles Deleuze, "How Do We Recognize Structuralism?" in *Desert Islands and Other Texts, 1953-1974*, trans. Mike Taormina (New York: Semiotexte, 2004), pp. 182-3

[67] Davis and Hersh, p. 157

[68] Dale Jacquette, *On Boole* (California: Wadsworth,2002), p. 70

[69] Ibid., p. 72

[70] I am here of course translating John von Neumann's insights as expressed in his *Theory of Self-Reproducing Automata* (Champaign: UIP, 1966), p. 68 about the nature of the binary digit into an ontological discourse about existence itself.

[71] Stephen Wolfram, "What is Ultimately Possible in Physics?" retrieved from http://www.fqxi.org/data/essay-contest-files/Wolfram_WhatIsUltimatelyPos_1.pdf on October 1, 2012

[72] Jacques Lacan, *The Four Fundamental Concepts of Psychoanalysis (The Seminar of Jacques Lacan, Book XI)*, trans. Alan Sheridan (New York: Norton, 1998), p. 226.

[73] Markus Gabriel, "The Meaning of Existence and the Contingency of Sense", retrieved October 1, 2012, from http://backdoorbroadcasting.net/2012/03/markus-gabriel-the-meaning-of-existence-and-the-contingency-of-sense/

[74] James Gates, "Symbols of Powers" *Physics World* 23 (June 2010): 34-39.

[75] Ibid., p. 39

[76] Ibid.

[77] Ibid.

[78] G. W. Leibniz, *Philosophical Essays* (New York: Hackett, 1989), p. 86

[79] Gottfried Wilhelm Leibniz *Philosophical Papers and Letters: A Selection,* trans. Leroy Loemker (New York: D. Reidel/Springer, 19 76), p. 239.

[80] Ibid., p. 270

[81] Ibid., p. 157

[82] Ibid., p. 368

[83] Ibid., pp. 73-8, 221-35

[84] Hens Feger, "Chinese Thinking in the View of German Idealists and Its Critics", retrieved October, 1, 2012, from http://hans-

feger.de/pdf/publikationen/Chinese_thinking_engl.pdf

[85]Martin Davis, *The Universal Computer: The Road from Leibniz to Turning* (New York: A K Peters/CRC, 2011), p. 10-15.

[86] John DeFrancis, *Visible Speech: The Diverse Oneness of Writing Systems* (Honolulu: University of Hawaii, 1989), p.5, 114

[87] Ibid., p. 50

[88] Ibid., p. 67

[89] Ibid., p. 101

[90] Ibid., p.50

[91] Roma Jakobson, *Six Lectures on Sound and Meaning* (Cambridge: MIT, 1981), p. 82

[92] Ibid.

[93] Ibid., p. 85

[94] Ibid.

[95] Ibid., p. 6

[96] My discussion of Deleuze in the rest of his section relates to his already cited "How Do We Recognize Structuralism?", pp. 170-180

[97] John Allen Paulos, *Once Upon A Number: The Hidden Mathematical Logic of Stories* (New York: Basic Books, 1999, kindle locations: 1362-6.

[98] Jurgen Schmidhuber. Simple Algorithmic Theory of Subjective Beauty, Novelty, Surprise, Interestingness, Attention, Curiosity, Creativity, Art, Science, Music, Jokes. *Journal of SICE*, 48(1):21-32, 2009

[99] Quentin Meillassoux, *The Number and the Siren: A Decipherment of Mallarme's Coup de Des* (New York: Urbanomic, 2012).

[100] Jacque Derrida, *Writing and Difference* (Chicago: University of Chicago, 1978), trans. Alan Bass, p. 289.

[101] G.W. Leibniz, "Revolution", trans. Lloyd Strickland, retrieved October 1, 2012, from http://www.leibniz-translations.com/revolution.htm

[102] Ibid.

[103] *Machzor for Rosh Hashanah.* Ed. Rabbi Menachem Davis (Brooklyn: Mesorah, 2004), pp. 671-2.

[104] Theodor Reik, *Ritual: Four Psycho-analytic Studies—Couvade/The Puberty Rites of Saves/Kol Nidre/The Shofar* (New York: Evergreen, 1962), p. 261.

[105] Ibid., p. 250

[106] Mladen Dolar, *A Voice and Nothing More* (Cambridge: MIT, 2006), p. 28.

[107] Ibid., p. 27

[108] Ibid.

[109] Ibid.

[110] Ibid.

[111] Ibid., p. 26

[112] Ibid.

[113] Ibid., p. 25

[114] "The Mathematics of Fiction with Manil Suri", retrieved October, 1, 2012, from http://www.youtube.com/watch?v=vbHTvA0Bans

[115] Richard E. Berg and David G. Stork, *The Physics of Sound* (New Jersey: Prentice-Hall, 1982), p. 30.

[116] Jean Bricmont and Alan Sokal, *Fashionable Nonsense: Postmodern Intellectuals' Abuse of Science* (New York: Picador, 1999), p.44

[117] Ibid.

[118] Ibid., p. 45

[119] Stephen Ramsay, *Reading Machines: Toward an Algorithmic Criticism*

(Champaign: University of Illinois, 2011), p. 30

[120] Ibid., p. 38

[121] Ibid.

[122] Robert M. Haralick, Eliyahu Rips, and Matityahu Glazerson, *Torah Codes: A Glimpse into the Infinite* (Brooklyn: Marcy, 2005), p. ix.

[123] Ibid, p. 10

[124] Ibid., p. 9

[125] Qtd. In Satinover, p. 2

[126] Ramsay, p. 46

[127] Ramsay, pp. 46-9

[128] Ibid., p. 47

[129] Ibid., p. 48

[130] Jean Starobinski, *Words Upon Words: The Anagrams of Ferdinand de Saussure* (New Haven: Yale, 1980), p. 30

[131] Ibid., p. 105

[132] Ibid.

[133] Elliot Wolfson, *Abraham Abulafia—Kabbalist and Prophet—Hermeneutics, Theosophy, and Theurgy* (New York: Cherub, 2000), p. 62.

[134] Ibid.

[135] Maurice Blanchot, *The Work of Fire*. Trans. Charlotte Mandell (Stanford: Stanford UP, 1995), pp. 320-5.

[136] Idel, *Absorbing Perfections*, p. 60

[137] Ibid.

[138] Moshe Idel, "White Letters: From R. Levi Isaac of Berditchiv's Views to

Postmodern Hermeneutics" *Modern Judaism* 26 (May 2006): 162-192, p. 171.

[139] Ibid., p. 177

[140] Ibid., pp. 177-8

[141] Ibid, pp. 178-80

[142] Ibid., p. 180

[143] Raphael Bousso, "The World as Hologram", retrieved October, 1, 2012, from http://www.youtube.com/watch?v=GHgi6E1ECgo&feature=related

[144] Leonard Susskind, *The Cosmic Landscape: String Theory and the Illusion of Intelligent Design* (Boston: Back Bay, 2006), Kindle Locations: 5110-5150.

[145] Ibid.

[146] Ibid., Kindle Locations: 4700-4702

[147] Ibid., Kindle Locations: 4725-4727

[148] Ibid, Kindle Locations: 5192-5194

[149] Ibid, Kindle Locations: 5623-5627

[150] Eric Furze, "The Matrix Reloaded: Jesus, Buddha, and Gödel: Unraveling the Matrix Mythos". Retrieved October 1, 2012, from http://metaphilm.com/index.php/detail/the_matrix_reloaded/

[151] "The Matrix Reloaded". Retrieved October, 1, 2012, from http://en.wikiquote.org/wiki/The_Matrix_Reloaded

[152] Ibid.

[153] Ibid.

[154] Ibid.

[155] Ibid.

[156] "The Architect". Retrieved October 1, 2012, from http://www.imdb.com/character/ch0000770/quotes

[157] "Franz Kafka". Retrieved October 1, 2012, from http://en.wikiquote.org/wiki/Franz_Kafka

Made in United States
North Haven, CT
26 May 2024